INTERNATIONAL LABOUR CONVENTIONS AND NATIONAL LAW

INTERNATIONAL LABOUR CONVENTIONS AND NATIONAL LAW:

The Effectiveness of the Automatic Incorporation of Treaties in National Legal Systems

VIRGINIA A. LEARY

Professor of International Law
Faculty of Law and Jurisprudence
State University of New York at Buffalo, U.S.A.

1982

Springer-Science+Business Media, B.V

Library of Congress Cataloging in Publication Data

Leary, Virginia A.
International labour conventions and national law.

Revision of thesis (doctoral)--Graduate Institute of International Studies at Geneva.
Bibliography: p.
Includes indexes.
1. Labor laws and legislation, International.
2. International and municipal law. 3. International Labour Office. I. Title.
K1705.4.L4 1982 341.7'63 81-22414
AACR2

ISBN 978-94-017-6720-0 ISBN 978-94-017-6804-7 (eBook)
DOI 10.1007/978-94-017-6804-7

To the memory of my
father, William H. Leary

Table of Contents

Acknowledgments

Many persons assisted me during the preparation of this book. It is impossible to mention them all, but some deserve particular acknowledgment of my gratitude. My major debt is owed to Professor Georges Abi-Saab of the Graduate Institute of International Studies at Geneva. Professor Abi-Saab provided invaluable guidance from the inception of the research to the conclusion of the writing of the doctoral thesis which, substantially revised and supplemented, has become this book. His high intellectual standards as well as his friendship and constant encouragement have all been greatly appreciated. I am also indebted to Professor Philippe Cahier of the Graduate Institute of International Studies at Geneva as well as to Professor Michel Virally of the Geneva Graduate Institute and the University of Paris II for their assistance. Professor Cahier read the final manuscript and suggested important improvements in the text. The Graduate Institute at Geneva provided an ideal intellectual environment for working on the book and I am grateful to the former director of the Institute, Jacques Freymond, and the present director, Christian Dominicé, for the opportunity to undertake the research and writing in such a favorable climate. All inadequacies in the book remain, of course, my own responsibility.

An intellectual debt is owed to Nicolas Valticos, Assistant Director General of the International Labour Office and Chief of the International Labour Standards Department of the ILO. Mr. Valticos is the author of a number of studies on the national application of labour conventions on which I relied extensively. He read the manuscript with great care and I am most grateful for his kind assistance.

The subject of this book was originally suggested to me by Mr. Klaus Samson of the International Labour Office. Mr. Samson not only suggested that the topic would be an important and interesting one but he also gave many hours of his valuable time to critique successive drafts. His extensive knowledge and his painstaking attention to detail have been invaluable aids. Ernest A. Landy, formerly Chief of the Application of Standards Branch of the ILO, also encouraged me to undertake the present work. His book on the effectiveness of the ILO supervisory system provided much of the information on which I relied in preparing Chapter 2. I am grateful to Theodoor van Boven, Hans Thoolen and Professor Antonio Cassese who discussed with me the portions of the manuscript relating to the Netherlands and Italy.

During the preparation of the book I was the recipient of two summer research fellowships granted by the Baldy Center for Law and Social Policy of the State University of New York at Buffalo and financial assistance from the Swiss Confederation. This assistance enabled me to carry my project to completion.

The successive versions of the manuscript were typed by Elizabeth R. Ryan, Patricia Taylor, Martha Howe and Sandra Maedl. Their patience and care are especially appreciated.

Abbreviations

A.F.D.I.	Annuaire français de droit international
Am. J. Comp. L.	American Journal of Comparative Law
Am. J. Int'l L.	American Journal of International Law
A.S.D.I.	Annuaire suisse de droit international
Brit. Y. B. Int'l L.	British Yearbook of International Law
Calif. L. Rev.	University of California (at Berkeley) Law Review (U.S.)
C.M.L. Rep.	Common Market Law Reports
I.C.J.	International Court of Justice
I.C.L.Q.	International and Comparative Law Quarterly
I.L.R.	International Labour Review
Mich. L. Rev.	Michigan Law Review (U.S.)
Minn. L. Rev.	Minnesota Law Review (U.S.)
Neb. L. Rev.	Nebraska Law Review (U.S.)
Neth. Int'l L. Rev.	Netherlands International Law Review
N.J.	Nederlanse Jurisprudentsie
P.C.I.J.	Permanent Court of International Justice
Proc., Am. Soc. Int'l L.	Proceedings of the American Society of International Law
R.B.D.I.	Revue belge de droit international
R.C.A.D.I.	Recueil des cours de l'Académie de droit international de La Haye
R.C.D.I.P.	Revue critique de droit international privé
R.G.D.I.P.	Revue générale de droit international public
R.I.T.	Revue internationale du travail
U.N.T.S.	United Nations Treaty Series
U.C.L.A. L. Rev.	University of California at Los Angeles Law Review (U.S.)
U. Pa. L. Rev.	University of Pennsylvania Law Review (U.S.)
Vand. L. Rev.	Vanderbilt Law Review (U.S.)
Z.a.ö.R.V.	Zeitschrift für ausländisches öffentliches Recht und Volkerrecht

Abbreviations of Titles of Publications of the International Labour Office

R.C.E.	Report of the Committee of Experts on the Application of Conventions and Recommendations (the number of the year precedes the R.C.E. citation and the page number follows)
R.P.	Record of Proceedings of the International Labour Conference (the number preceding the R.P. citation is that of the session; the page number and year follow the letter citation)
S.R.	Summary Reports on Ratified Conventions, submitted to the International Labour Conference (the number preceding the S.R. citation is that of the session; the page number and year follow the letter citation)

Introduction

The relationship between international law and national law, in the past, was largely an interesting theoretical problem, engaging legal scholars in a doctrinal debate; it has now become an important practical problem, primarily as a result of the increasing adoption of treaties whose scope is not inter-state relations but the relations of states with their own citizens. These treaties are concerned with "the common interests of humanity" and have a quasi-legislative character.[1] Their efficacy depends essentially on the incorporation of their provisions in national law. The purpose of the present work is to consider how effectively the provisions of international labour conventions, a type of quasi-legislative treaty, are incorporated in the national law of states using the system of automatic incorporation of treaties. Thus, while the narrower focus of the book is the automatic incorporation of labour conventions in national law, the broader focus is the relationship between international and national law.

It was not intended, however, to undertake a theoretical study of the relationship of international law and national law, but rather an examination of the practical problems and complexities which have arisen in the incorporation of labour conventions in national legal systems. This work is an empirical study which elucidates the classic problem of the relationship between international law and national law by focusing on the factual situation in an area where there is close interaction between the two systems.

The proliferation of multilateral treaties which lay down general norms concerning the internal economic and social policies of states is a contemporary phenomenon of the international legal system.[2] Although such treaties are couched in terms of obligations for the ratifying state, the ultimate intended beneficiaries are individuals within the state. In the absence of a supra-national legal system, the effective incorporation of the norms of these treaties in national law is of crucial importance if they are to accomplish their purpose.

The international community is attempting today through the use of the treaty—the one major instrument in its legal arsenal—to obligate states to improve the lot of their residents and to guarantee individual rights. Used from ancient times to regulate such inter-state or inter-communal matters as boundary lines and commercial exchange, the treaty is used today to regulate such internal matters as human rights, labour questions and economic policy. The reasons for this evolution are not difficult to perceive. It has become apparent that national resolutions of social and economic problems have significant repercussions in other countries. Hence, international regulation of such problems has become imperative. The use of the treaty for these purposes represents a radical transition in the purposes for which it has traditionally been employed. Can the treaty mechanism be effective in accomplishing these new purposes? The answer appears to be: Only if national legal systems effectively apply treaty norms.

States have adopted different methods of incorporating treaties in national law. Some states, such as the United Kingdom, the Commonwealth and the Scandinavian countries, employ the method of "legislative incorporation" (or "statutory transformation", as it is sometimes referred to). The norms of treaties become national law by this method only when enacted through the normal legislative process. A larger group of states have adopted the method of "automatic incorporation" whereby treaties become the "law of the land" immediately upon ratification (plus publication or proclamation in some countries). This method is employed by the United States and many European and Latin American countries.

This study examines the application of international labour conventions only in states which have adopted the system of automatic incorporation. It was decided to limit the study in this respect because automatic incorporation is widely considered to be a more effective and progressive method of ensuring the implementation of international conventional law at the national level than the system of legislative incorporation. Yet, the system of automatic incorporation raises a number of complex problems which do not exist under the system of legislative incorporation. A substantial number of states have adopted the technique of automatic incorporation since World War II. This study is thus particularly relevant to current constitutional trends.

International labour conventions were selected because they provide a wealth of primary source material for an examination of the methods, problems and obstacles of introducing treaty norms into municipal law. They are numerous and widely ratified and many have been in force for a considerable length of time. The extensive experience in the supervision of the implementation of these treaties by the International Labour Organization (ILO) has made it possible to obtain substantial information.[3] The same wealth of information is not available concerning the application of other similar types of treaties.

International labour conventions obligate ratifying states to make effective within their jurisdiction the standards laid down in the conventions. The conventions concern such matters as freedom to form trade unions, freedom from forced labour, non-discrimination in employment, social security and conditions of work.

In order to circumscribe the study within reasonable compass it was limited to an examination of the automatic incorporation of labour conventions within a selected number of states. Argentina, France, Mexico, the Netherlands, Switzerland and the United States were selected because they provide especially illuminating examples of problems of national implementation of labour conventions; they were not selected on the basis of geographic region or cultural diversity. Isolated examples from other countries, in particular, Colombia, Guatemala, Italy and Liberia, have also been included.

A comprehensive examination of the application of all types of treaties in each of the countries is not the aim of the study. The focus is rather on problems which have surfaced in the automatic incorporation of labour conventions only. The study has been organized, in general, on a "problem" not a "country" basis. Not all countries have had the same problems regarding incorporation nor to the same extent. Reference will not necessarily be made, therefore, to each country in the consideration of each point. Illustrative examples from the selected countries will be used as appropriate.

Only two of the countries included in the study—the United States and Liberia—are "common law" countries. The choice of constitutional system for the introduction of treaties into national law is not related to whether a country is a "common law" or "civil law" country. The two major "common law" countries—the United Kingdom and the United States—have adopted different systems regarding the introduction of treaty norms into national law. Although they are civil law countries, Argentina and Mexico have constitutional provisions similar to the "Supremacy Clause" of the U.S. Constitution which provides that duly ratified treaties shall become the "law of the land."

Problems relating to the incorporation of labour conventions are similar to those which are encountered in the incorporation of other comparable treaties. This study is particularly relevant in view of the recent entry into force of the two International Covenants on Human Rights.[4] Although labour conventions have some aspects not commonly characteristic of other treaties, these aspects do not invalidate conclusions regarding their implementation in municipal law. Important studies have been made on the domestic application of the European Convention on Human Rights.[5] The present work on domestic application of international labour conventions provides an additional examination of practical experience in the national implementation of quasi-legislative international agreements. Like the earlier studies of the European Convention it highlights many inadequacies of domestic constitutional systems in effectively implementing treaties in national law—in particular, the problem of "non-self-executing" treaty provisions which has occasioned an exceptional amount of doctrinal discussion.

National court decisions and reports of ILO supervisory organs have provided the basic research material on which this case study is based.[6] Governments have frequently reported to the ILO that conventions are effectively applied in their countries because under their constitutional system they are automatically incorporated in domestic law. The ILO supervisory bodies have examined these contentions in order to determine more precisely what limitations and problems exist in *effectively* applying treaties in automatic incorporation states. Their exploration of these limitations and problems provides the core of the study.

This examination of the automatic incorporation of labour conventions in national law touches on questions relating to public international law, the law of international organizations, and municipal constitutional law. It provides a striking example of the growing interaction between these various branches of law—an interaction which will inevitably become more widespread with the adoption of an increasing number of multilateral treaties concerning economic and social policies which are drafted and supervised by international organizations.

NOTES

1. For a perceptive treatment of the recent evolution of treaty law see Paul Reuter, *Introduction au droit des traités* (Paris: Armand Colin, 1972), chapter 1.

2. See Thomas Buergenthal, *Interaction of National Law and Modern International Agreements: Some Introductory Observations*, 18 Am. J. Comp. L. 233 (1970).

3. The present study of the national application of international labour conventions builds on the pioneering work of Nicolas Valticos. See references in bibliography.

4. See remarks by Louis Sohn in Stephen M. Schwebel, ed., *The Effectiveness of International Decisions* (Leyden: A. W. Sijthoff; Dobbs Ferry, New York: Oceana Publications Inc., 1971), p. 364: "... the U.N. has finally adopted the Covenants on Human Rights and the slow process of ratification has started. Once they become law ... many experiences of the ILO, and the European experience and others are going to become very relevant. It is really important to see the effectiveness of the various procedures that have been adopted by other organizations before embarking on the new U.N. venture."

5. Thomas Buergenthal, *The Effect of the European Convention on Human Rights on the Internal Law of Member States*, The British Institute of International and Comparative Law, International Law Series No. 5 (I.C.L.Q., Supplementary Publication No. 11 (1965)); Buergenthal, *The Domestic Status of the European Convention on Human Rights—A Second Look*, 7 Journal of the International Commission of Jurists, No. 1, 55 (1966); Philippe Comte, *The Application of the European Convention on Human Rights in Municipal Law*, 4 Journal of the International Commission of Jurists, No. 1, 95 (1962); Christian Dominicé, *La*

Convention européenne des droits de l'Homme devant le juge national, 28 A.S.D.I. 9 (1972); Andreas A. Khol, *The Influence of the Human Rights Convention on Austrian Law*, 18 Am. J. Comp. L. 237 (1970); A. H. Robertson, ed., *Human Rights in National and International Law* (Manchester: Manchester University Press, 1968).

6. The author also had access to unpublished information in files of the International Labour Office in Geneva.

CHAPTER 1

Labour Conventions and National Law

Lord McNair described the international labour convention as "one of the most striking innovations in the field of treaty-making which has occurred during the present century."[1] Since 1919, more than 150 labour conventions have been drafted and adopted by the annual Conference of the International Labour Organization. Although they concern different subject matter, these conventions (hereinafter referred to as "ILO conventions") share certain common features. A number of the innovative features of this large body of conventions result from the effort to regulate the internal law and practice of states through the device of the treaty.

Prior to the founding of the ILO, labour problems had traditionally been considered matters of domestic concern; the effective use of the treaty mechanism to achieve improved and more uniform labour standards necessitated new approaches to treaty-making. In order to ensure the ultimate adoption of appropriate labour standards by Member States, it was considered essential that employers and workers—in addition to government delegates—participate in the drafting of ILO conventions. Thus, employer and worker representatives participate on an equal basis with government delegates in the elaboration of international labour conventions. This feature has remained peculiar to the ILO and has not been adopted by other intergovernmental organizations. Other innovative features of ILO treaty-making (adopted because of the unique nature of labour conventions) are the omission of the practice of governmental signature to the text of drafted conventions, an understanding that no reservations may be made to the conventions and a requirement that Member States submit conventions to their legislative bodies.[2]

ILO conventions have not only been innovative but they have also been precursors of an ever-growing group of treaties, such as human rights treaties, which are intended to regulate national social and economic policy. Multilateral international agreements laying down general norms—so called "law-making" treaties—existed prior to international labour conventions but they largely concerned such inter-state matters as postal regulations, river and railroad communications and protection of the wounded in time of war. International labour conventions were virtually the first multilateral treaties primarily intended to improve the lot of individuals within states.

Child labour, excessively long hours of work and unhealthy working conditions were widely recognized in Europe and America in the late 19th and early 20th century as pernicious consequences of the Industrial Revolution which called for regulation. Social and industrial unrest led to demands for changes in working conditions. These demands led in turn to demands for international regulation, since it was feared that the adoption of national social legislation might place a state at competitive disadvantage if other states did not adopt similar legislation. The International Labour Organization was founded after World War I in response to the need for international regulation of labour problems. The primary work of the fledgling international organization was the adoption of conventions setting labour standards.[3]

1. The Norms of ILO Conventions

More than 130 ILO conventions are presently in force.[4] They cover a wide variety of subjects: conditions of employment, occupational health and safety, social security, employment of women and children, migrant workers, forced labour, freedom of association and employment policy. Rather than drawing up a limited number of conventions which cover a broad spectrum of social and labour matters the International Labour Conference has, with a few exceptions, drawn up separate conventions on specific subjects.[5]

A publication of the ILO has pointed out that

> the body of international labour standards has not been adopted according to a predetermined plan, but has resulted from a gradual accretion of instruments in response to priority needs as perceived by the Governing Body, when determining every year the questions to be brought before the Conference. However, over a period of more than half a century, the approach to standard setting has undergone considerable development. The instruments adopted in the early years of the ILO were aimed at meeting certain clearly defined but limited demands of workers, such as the 8-hour day and 48-hour week or measures for the protection of women and children. While conventions of this kind on particular aspects of working conditions continue to be adopted, a tendency has also developed over the years to deal comprehensively with certain areas of social policy. ... The widening scope of ILO standard setting is also reflected in the type and range of persons covered. The concern with the regulation of working conditions has been supplemented by a desire to protect fundamental liberties and to bring about a general improvement in the working and living conditions of certain population groups.[6]

The norms of ILO conventions vary greatly in specificity, precision and detail. Some international labour standards are expressed in precise, negative proscriptions such as "women, without distinction of age, shall not be employed during the night in any public or private industrial undertaking ..."[7] A number of conventions require ratifying states to "undertake" a certain course of action: "Each Member of the International Labour Organization which ratifies this Convention undertakes to suppress the use of forced or compulsory labor ..."[8] In recent years, the International Labour Conference has adopted a small group of conventions referred to as "promotional conventions",

> which by their very nature differ in form and purpose from most of the other instruments adopted by the International Labour Conference. Instead of laying down precise standards as regards the age of entry into employment, the prohibition of night work, social security and so on, these conventions set objectives of a more general character, such as equal remuneration for men and women workers, equality of opportunity and treatment in employment and occupation and active employment policy, etc. Objectives of this kind require programmes of action which can generally be achieved only by concerted and gradual measures over a period of time, involving therefore promotional methods appropriate to national conditions.[9]

An example of such a provision is Article 1 of ILO Convention No. 122 concerning Employment Policy: "... each Member shall declare and pursue, as major goal, an active policy designed to promote full, productive and freely chosen employment."

The majority of conventions, however, are

> drafted in such a way as to afford the maximum amount of flexibility consonant with the assumption by a State of a real measure of obligation. Consequently, the convention is often short in form and restricted to the formulation of a few broad obligations. It is not encumbered by unnecessary details which might only serve to impede ratification and may be dealt with more appropriately in the form of a recommendation. The normal convention is composed of a brief preamble, a few general obligations, a number of exceptions, implementing provisions which allow wide discretion to the national authority and the final clauses concerning ratification, denunciation, duration and revision.[10]

International labour standards are intended to regulate labour and social conditions in countries with widely varying climatic conditions as well as economic and social development. This aim has had an important influence on the drafting of the provisions of ILO conventions. A number of "flexibility devices" have been included in conventions for this purpose.

It has been pointed out that "vague and accommodating terms are liberally deployed throughout successive conventions, as may be instanced by the abundant recourse to such adjectives as 'reasonable', 'appropriate', 'adequate', 'effective', 'fair', 'practicable', 'necessary', 'sufficient', 'suitable' and 'proper' ..."[11]

Some conventions which contain precise rules or proscriptions also contain exemption clauses which permit exceptions from the rules or proscriptions in particular circumstances. Others permit wide latitude on the part of the "competent national authority" in applying and interpreting the rules of the convention. Some conventions permit a ratifying state to exclude certain parts of a convention when accepting the convention.

Occasionally, states which have ratified or are considering ratifying a convention raise questions concerning the interpretation of a provision of the convention. Article 37 of the ILO Constitution provides:

> Any question or dispute relating to the interpretation of this Constitution or of any subsequent convention concluded by the members in pursuance of the provisions of the Constitution shall be referred for decision to the International Court of Justice.

Only one case involving the interpretation of an international labour convention has been referred to the International Court.[12] A procedure has, however developed whereby the International Labour Office upon a request from a state will provide an interpretation of an ILO convention based on the language, the preparatory work and subsequent practice.[13] This interpretation is transmitted to the state with a reservation "that the Constitution of the International Labour Organization confers no special competence upon the International Labour Office to give an authentic interpretation of the provisions of conventions adopted by the International Labour Conference." The interpretation is communicated to the Governing Body of the ILO and published in the ILO Official Bulletin.

2. Obligations of States Ratifying ILO Conventions

ILO conventions do not come into force until at least two ratifications have been registered. In referring to the quasi-legislative character of treaties such as ILO conventions, Reuter points out that there is no intrinsic reason why such conventions should not come into force on the basis of even one ratification:

> It seems at first sight that in order for a treaty to make sense it must have at least two parties. While maintaining this principle in general, it should be recognized that there could be exceptions ... Suppose there is a treaty which contains rules which concern exclusively the rights of persons (human rights, labour questions); there is no technical obstacle to a decision that it should come into force as soon as one State has become bound by it; and this is true even if the treaty provides for an international supervisory system, as in the case of the ILO; in fact, as soon as even one State has become a party, the system of the Convention makes sense. As far as the ILO is concerned it is more because of legal caution than substantive reasons that the number of *two* States parties has always been required for the entry into force of international labour conventions. This shows how much modern conventions resemble legislation.[14]

States which ratify ILO conventions are required both by international law and by the provisions of the ILO Constitution to bring their internal law and practice into conformity with the conventions. Since ILO conventions are international treaties, the obligation under international law to apply them would normally arise immediately upon ratification, assuming the treaties were in force. ILO conventions, however, contain a provision that they come into force for any Member State twelve months after the date on which its ratification has been registered—which provides time for the necessary legislation or regulations to be adopted.

In addition to the general obligation under international law to conform its laws and practice with ratified treaties the Member States of the ILO are required by the ILO Constitution to "take such action as may be necessary to make effective the provisions of such Conventions."[15] The ILO supervisory organs do not require that the provisions of the convention must be incorporated into national law in order to "make effective" ILO conventions internally if they are assured that the convention is effectively applied in practice.[16] Article 19(8) of the ILO Constitution provides that "in no case shall ... the ratification of any Convention by any Member be deemed to affect any law, award, custom or agreement which ensures more favourable conditions to the workers concerned than those provided for in the Convention ..."

International labour conventions are integrally linked with the International Labour Organization. It has been suggested that they are primarily commitments of states to the ILO rather than mutual commitments among states.[17] The conventions may be ratified only by Member States of the ILO, although a state which has withdrawn from the ILO remains bound by the obligations of conventions it has ratified. International labour conventions contain provisions permitting denunciation of the convention by a ratifying state at certain regular intervals.

In addition to the obligations imposed by the terms of each convention the ILO Constitution imposes a further obligation on states which have ratified conventions. Article 22 of the Constitution provides:

> Each of the Members agrees to make an annual report to the International Labour Office on the measures which it has taken to give effect to the provisions of Conventions to which it is a party. These reports shall be made in such form and shall contain such particulars as the Governing Body may request.

An effective system of regular supervision of the application of ILO conventions has been developed from this constitutional provision. The ILO Constitution also provides for complaints by other states and industrial organizations relating to failure of states to comply with the obligations of conventions they have ratified. This system for the supervision of ILO conventions is considered in chapter 2.

3. International Legislation? Model National Laws? Treaties?

The aim of ILO conventions—the incorporation of labour standards in national law and practice—and the innovations necessitated by this aim created confusion in the early history of the ILO concerning the legal nature of the conventions. Were they truly treaties? or international legislation? or simply draft laws to be adopted by states?

Scelle considered ILO conventions as a type of international legislation which, in order to acquire binding effect, required an *acte-condition.*[18] As recently as 1968, Clive Parry maintained that ILO conventions were not treaties: "... international labour conventions so-called are not in fact treaties but rather *projets* of municipal legislation ...".[19] The contentions of Scelle and Parry are not generally supported but they emphasize the distinctive features of ILO conventions. In 1930 Scelle observed:

> The International Labour Conference is truly an international legislative body. ... [T]he text which results from the deliberations of the Conference ... is the expression of the international legal rule which the Conference has the competence to discover and formulate. But because of insufficient international social organization, this legislation remains optional until its acceptance by states through ratification ... It is because of verbal tradition ... that we persist in speaking here of conventions or projects of conventions. Perhaps it is also because of diplomatic prudence, in order not to invoke before suspicious governments the phantom of supra-national legislative power, which they fear particularly, but which obstinately reappears because in fact it is not a phantom but a living reality.[20]

When the ILO Constitution was originally drafted the British proposed that each Member State commit itself to ratify a convention within a year of its adoption unless the national legislature refused. This proposal was not accepted. Instead, a provision was inserted in the Constitution that within a period of one year to eighteen months from the closing of a session of the Conference, Member States must submit conventions and recommendations adopted at the Conference "to the competent authorities within whose competence the matter lies for the enactment of legislation or other action ..."[21] The purpose of this provision was to stimulate ratification and the adoption of legislation applying the convention. Other proposals to give true legislative power to the ILO were also rejected at the time of the drafting of the Constitution.[22] As a result, ILO conventions, as other treaties, must be explicitly accepted by a state before they become binding on that state. They are, therefore, not true legislative acts.[23]

The contention that ILO conventions are merely model laws for incorporation into national legislation is incorrect. Except for an initial period in the early days of the ILO, referred to above, governments have recognized that ILO conventions involve international obligations. While there may be differing interpretations concerning the effective application of the conventions there is not presently any serious disagreement as to whether the conventions, once ratified, create international legal obligations. Representations and complaint procedures under Articles 24 and 26 of the ILO Constitution have been initiated concerning obligations arising under certain conventions.[24] While the conventions are sometimes drafted in a form suitable for verbatim incorporation in municipal law, this is by no means always the case. When it is intended to prepare ILO instruments as "model codes" the recommendation rather than the convention seems to be preferred.[25] ILO supervisory organs have not considered it necessary that verbatim provisions of ILO conventions be incorporated into municipal law in order to guarantee application.[26]

Finally, the thesis that ILO conventions are only model laws for incorporation in municipal legislation does not find general support among international law publicists. McNair, Rousseau, Reuter, O'Connell and Briggs, inter alia, have pointed out the unusual features of ILO conventions but have presupposed that these instruments were binding international agreements.[27] The government delegates at the Vienna Conference on the Law of Treaties assumed that ILO conventions were within the scope of the then proposed Convention on the Law of Treaties as is evident from the discussion concerning the adoption of Article 5 of the Convention, reserving the possibility of special rules for treaties adopted within an international organization.[28] The controversy over the legal nature of ILO conventions is thus settled. It is clear today that they are international treaties whose ratification creates binding international obligations.

4. Ratification of Labour Conventions

Some of the countries considered in this case study have ratified many ILO conventions and others have ratified only a few. France had ratified 102 ILO conventions as of 1 June, 1980 and is among the countries with the highest number of ratifications of such conventions. The United States had ratified only seven as of the same date and was among the countries with the fewest ratifications. Yet, interesting issues involving the application of ILO conventions have arisen in both countries, as they have in Argentina which has also a high number of ratifications (sixty as of 1 June, 1980). Mexico had ratified fifty-nine ILO conventions as of the same date and is of particular interest because it has continually contended that its constitutional provision on automatic incorporation guarantees the effective application of such conventions. The reaction of the ILO supervisory bodies to this contention and the resulting interaction with the Mexican government provides an important element in this case study.

Switzerland has ratified a smaller number of ILO conventions (thirty-nine as of 1 June, 1980) but its recent decision to adopt a more liberal policy concerning ratification of ILO conventions and its reason for that policy are of particular interest.[29] The Netherlands was chosen for the case study because of its advanced constitutional provisions giving primacy to international treaties in internal law. It was felt that the effect of these provisions on the practices of the Dutch Government in ratifying and applying ILO conventions would prove of interest. The Netherlands had ratified eighty-one ILO conventions as of 1 June, 1980. Italy had also ratified eighty-one ILO conventions by the same date.

5. Conclusion

A number of the specific features of international labour conventions primarily concern the elaboration and adoption of these conventions. Such features have little relevance to the question of the application of the conventions in municipal law. In particular, the following aspects are unrelated to internal application: the participation of nongovernmental elements in the drafting of conventions, the lack of signature by plenipotentiaries, the inadmissibility of reservations and the method of revising conventions. In addition, the procedure for submission, since it simply attempts to ensure consideration of the convention and publicity for its provisions, does not directly affect internal application nor does the system of informal opinions interpreting international labour conventions.

On the other hand, the generality of terms frequently used to provide flexibility in application and the multilateral law-making aspects of these conventions are relevant to internal application. The language in which the norms of treaties are couched has an important relationship to the incorporation of such conventions in national law. In particular, it is of great importance in the determination of whether a provision is considered to be self-executing and thus immediately applicable by courts and administrative agencies in states with the system of automatic incorporation.

The specific features of ILO conventions which distinguish them from other treaties do not relate primarily to national application. Thus, the conclusions of this study concerning national application of ILO conventions are relevant to the national application of other multilateral treaties laying down norms concerning social and economic policy.

NOTES

1. Lord A. D. McNair, *The Expansion of International Law* (Jerusalem: Magnes Press, Hebrew University, 1962), p. 29.

2. For general information concerning ILO conventions see C. Wilfred Jenks, *Human Rights and International Labour Standards* (London: Stevens and Sons, 1960), *Some Characteristics of International Labour Conventions*, 13 The Canadian Bar Rev. 448 (1935); E. A. Landy, *The Influence of International Labour Standards: Possibilities and Performance*, 101 I.L.R. 555 (1970); Ernest Mahaim, *Quelques questions de droit au sujet des conventions internationales du travail*, 20 R.I.T. 807 (1929), *Les conventions internationales du travail—à propos de débats récents*, 10 Revue de droit international et de législation comparée 669–734 (1929) and ibid., 11, 123–146 (1930); J. F. McMahon, *The Legislative Techniques of the International Labour Organization*, 41 Brit. Y. B. Int'l L. 1 (1965–66); Jean Morellet, *Un type original de traités: les conventions du travail*, 33 R.C.D.I.P. 1 (1938); Georges Scelle, *L'Organisation Internationale du Travail et le BIT* (Paris: Marcel Rivière, 1930); Nicolas Valticos, *Droit international du travail* (Paris: Dalloz, 1970), *Fifty Years of Standard-Setting Activities by the International Labour Organization*, 100 I.L.R. 201 (1969). See also *The Impact of International Labour Conventions and Recommendations* (Geneva: ILO, 1976).

3. See James T. Shotwell, *The Origins of the International Labour Organization* (New York: Columbia University Press, 1934), vol. 1, pp. 3–54, and *The Impact*, op. cit.

4. On 1 June 1980, 153 ILO conventions had been adopted by the International Labour Conference and 136 had received sufficient ratifications and were in force.

5. The International Covenant on Economic, Social and Cultural Rights, as well as the European Social Charter, covers in one instrument a number of matters covered in numerous separate ILO conventions.

6. *The Impact*, op. cit., pp. 13–14.

7. Article 3 (Convention No. 41), Convention Concerning Employment of Women During the Night (Revised 1934). The term "night" is defined in Article 2 of the Convention.

8. Article 1 (Convention No. 29), Convention Concerning Forced or Compulsory Labour, 1930. "Forced labour" is defined in Article 2.

9. 1973 R.C.E. 8–9.

10. McMahon, *Legislative Techniques*, 37.

11. Ibid., 39.

12. Advisory Opinion on the Interpretation of the Convention of 1919 Concerning Employment of Women During the Night, P.C.I.J., Ser. A/B, No. 50, p. 4, (1932).

13. McMahon, *Legislative Techniques*, 85–101. For general information on interpretation of ILO Conventions see C. Wilfred Jenks, *The Interpretation of International Labour Conventions by the International Labour Office*, 20 Brit. Y. B. Int'l L. 132–141 (1939) and Edward Yemin, *Interpretation of Treaties Adopted Within International Organizations* (with special reference to the UN and the ILO), unpublished manuscript.

14. Paul Reuter, *Introduction au droit des traités* (Paris: Armand Colin, 1972), p. 42 [translation]. Similarly, Scelle has pointed out that "the formal clauses of labour conventions may well require two or three or more ratifications for entry into force. It matters little from the juridical point of view—this is only a practical procedure or rather a hangover from the past. The coexistence of ratifications adds nothing to the voted text ... Each adherent is obligated, even if it is alone; it remains obligated even if other ratifying States violate their commitments. And if all the adherents but only one denounce the Convention, this last adherent remains bound by the obligations of the Convention." Scelle, *L'Organisation Internationale du Travail*, p. 181 [translation].

15. Article 19(5), *ILO Constitution*.

16. Nicolas Valticos, *Conventions internationales du travail et droit interne*, 44 R.C.D.I.P. 251, 265 (1955).

17. This point of view has had some practical relevance as is apparent from an early controversy concerning the modification or repeal of a convention on hours of work. Representatives at ILO Conferences in the twenties argued that ILO conventions did not create contractual obligations of states towards each other but rather created obligations towards the ILO itself, that ILO conventions were conditional international laws which states might accept or reject but could not amend (by reservations), and that, therefore, the Organization itself had the capacity to relieve Member States of their obligations by modifying or repealing a convention ratified by members. The opponents of these views prevailed, however. They insisted that what was intended at Versailles when the ILO was created was to set up a permanent organization to draft conventions and not to create a super-parliament. The setting up of a permanent organization, the new mode of elaboration of international labour conventions and the supervisory machinery created were means of avoiding some of the defects perceived in earlier efforts at elaboration and adoption of international labour conventions; it was not intended to undertake such a radical departure from current international practice as the creation of machinery for true international legislation. Mahaim, *Les conventions internationales du travail*, 10 Revue de droit international et de législation comparée 669, 722–732 (1929). In 1951 the Court of Appeal in Aix-en-Provence, France, held that a state of war between France and Italy did not have the effect of abrogating an international labour convention but simply of suspending its operation during hostilities. The reason given for the decision was that the ratification of such conventions does not result in bilateral or multilateral agreements but rather in affiliation to a régime instituted by an international organization and that the state of war between two members of the organization does not ipso facto cancel their commitments to the organization. Judgment, Court of Appeal, Aix-en-Provence, 7 May 1951, concerning the application of the Equality of Treatment (Accident Compensation) Convention, 1925 (ILO Convention No. 19), Etablissements Cornet v. Gaido, International Law Reports (1951), No. 155. See McNair, *The Expansion of International Law*, p. 42.

18. Scelle, *L'Organisation Internationale du Travail*, pp. 182–183.

19. Clive Parry, "The Law of Treaties," chapter 4 in Max Sorensen, ed., *Manual of Public International Law* (London: MacMillan, 1968), p. 197.

20. Scelle, *L'Organisation Internationale du Travail*, p. 184 [translation].

21. Article 19(5), *ILO Constitution.*

22. Mahaim, *Les conventions internationales du travail*, 10 Revue de droit international et de législation comparée 669, 718–722 (1929).

23. See Advisory Opinion of the Permanent Court of International Justice concerning the competence of the ILO: "The Organization has no legislative power. Each member is free to adopt or to reject any proposals of the Organization either for a national law or for an international convention." Competence of the International Labour Organization to Regulate, Incidentally, the Personal Work of the Employer, P.C.I.J., Ser. B., No. 13, pp. 1, 17 (1926).

24. For examples see C. Wilfred Jenks, "Human Rights, Social Justice and Peace, The Broader Significance of the ILO Experience," in Asbjorn Eide and August Schou, ed., *International Protection of Human Rights* (Stockholm: Almqvist and Wicksell, 1968), pp. 239–292.

25. *International Labour Code 1951* (Geneva: ILO, 1952), vol. I, p. 74. ILO recommendations (adopted by the International Labour Conference) often contain more advanced and detailed standards than those laid down in conventions. They are not intended to be ratified and do not create binding legal obligations. They are thus not included in this study.

26. Valticos, *Conventions internationales du travail*, 251, 265.

27. "They [ILO Conventions] seem to me to be typical *Vereinbarungen*, their object being to secure identical rules upon the topics regulated by them in the different countries which adopt them ... They are in fact permanent law-making treaties." Lord A. D. McNair, *The Law of Treaties* (Oxford: Clarendon Press, 1961), p. 752; Charles Rousseau, *Droit international public* (Paris: Dalloz, 5th ed. 1970), pp. 47–48; Reuter, *Introduction au droit des traités*, p. 42; D. P. O'Connell, *International Law* (London: Stevens and Sons, 2d ed. 1970), vol. II, pp. 757–758; Herbert W. Briggs, *The Law of Nations* (New York: Appleton-Century-Crofts, Inc., 2d ed. 1952), pp. 875–878, 884–890.

28. *U.N. Conference on the Law of Treaties, Official Records*, First Session, Vienna, 1968, A/Conf. 39/11, Eighth, Ninth and Tenth Meetings, pp. 42–58. Article 5 of the Vienna Convention on the Law of Treaties provides that "the present Convention applies to any treaty which is the constituent instrument of an international organisation and to any treaty adopted within an international organisation without prejudice to any relevant rules of the organisation." This Article, which permits the *lex specialis* of an international organization to prevail over any conflicting rules of the Vienna Convention, was particularly desired by the specialised agencies of the U.N. C. Wilfred Jenks, the ILO observer at the Conference which drafted the Vienna Convention, took the leading role in pushing for its adoption. His intervention at the Conference sets forth a number of rules and practices relating to international labour conventions which differ from the comparable rules eventually included in the Vienna Convention.

29. See chapter 2, sec. 4.3.

CHAPTER 2

The ILO Supervisory System and Problems of Automatic Incorporation

1. The ILO Supervisory System

Reciprocity has traditionally been the most important enforcement mechanism in international law. It fails to function, however, when states do not perceive their own immediate interests as threatened by another state's non-compliance with international law. Thus, inter-state complaints, either before judicial or quasi-judicial bodies, have not proved highly effective in regard to enforcement of treaties laying down social and humanitarian norms which consist of parallel rather than reciprocal or contractual obligations.[1]

The most effective present methods of enforcement of such treaties are supervisory systems by an international organization or procedures for individual complaints at the international level. States have been more willing to accept the development of supervisory systems involving reporting to an international body, and fact-finding by such bodies, than procedures for complaints by individuals. The phenomenon of the increasing adoption of treaties on social and economic matters has thus been paralleled by the increasing importance of international supervisory systems.[2] The ILO supervisory system is one of the oldest and most successful of such systems.[3] Landy has pointed out the need for supervisory systems:

> It is hardly surprising that, with this steady extension of the treaty as the main-stay of international organization, the question of actual performance should also have been raised with increasing insistence. For the adoption of international legislation and its formal acceptance by a growing number of countries cannot, by themselves, add to the stability of inter-State relations, unless there also exists some degree of assurance that the contracting parties really comply with their treaty obligations. This concern that governments respect their pledged word thus emerges as a crucial problem of the contemporary world. ... procedures have had to be developed in order to verify governmental compliance with ratified treaties.[4]

The ILO supervisory system consists of (1) procedures provided for in the ILO Constitution, (2) a special procedure instituted in collaboration with the United Nations for investigating allegations of violations of freedoms of association,[5] and (3) the "regular supervisory procedure." The latter has been the most significant of the procedures for the purposes of this study and will be described below in some detail.

The special procedures under the ILO Constitution have been used only to a limited degree. Article 26 of the Constitution provides that a state which has ratified a particular convention may file a complaint that another ratifying state is not effectively observing the provisions of the convention. The same Article provides for the ILO Governing Body to appoint a Commission of Inquiry to investigate the complaint if it sees fit. The Governing Body may also adopt the same procedure on its own motion or on receipt of a complaint from a delegate to the Conference. States have rarely filed complaints under this Article although in recent years several complaints have been filed by Conference delegates. Thus inter-state complaints in the ILO system, as is the case with enforcement procedures of other similar treaties, have not played an important role.

Article 24 of the Constitution provides that industrial associations of employers or workers may make "representations" that a Member State has failed to observe a convention. Between 1924 and 1970 only eight such representations were made. Since 1970 five representations have been made under Article 24. Representations are examined by a tripartite committee appointed by the Governing Body from among its members and the representation and the government's reply may be published if the Governing Body so decides.

The main burden of supervision has fallen on the "regular system" of supervision of conventions by two ILO Committees. States which have ratified international labour conventions presently submit reports on such conventions at yearly, two-yearly or four-yearly intervals. The International Labour Office provides a sample report form to assist governments in the preparation of these reports. The ILO Constitution requires the submission of the government reports (Article 22) but makes no provision for examination or criticism of the reports. It provides that the Director-General should lay a summary of the reports before the annual International Labour Conference. It was apparently originally assumed that the Conference itself would examine the reports. This proved to be impractical and eventually two Committees were established to examine the reports and to make comments to governments on their implementation of conventions. These two Committees, established in 1926, continue to function today and constitute what is referred to as the "regular system" of supervision of ILO conventions. The work of these Committees in highlighting problems involved in the constitutional system of automatic incorporation constitutes the core of the present study.

The two Committees which exercise this supervision are the Committee of Experts on the Application of Conventions and Recommendations (hereinafter referred to as the "Committee of Experts") and the Conference Committee on the Application of Conventions and Recommendations. The Committees differ significantly in composition and in methods of work. The Committee of Experts is an eighteen-member body of independent experts, appointed in their own capacity and not as government representatives, by the ILO Governing Body upon the proposal of the Director-General. With aid from the Secretariat of the International Labour Office it undertakes the initial examination of government reports to ascertain whether the law and practice of a ratifying state is in conformity with the convention on which the state is reporting. In addition to the reports the Committee considers legislative texts, labour inspection reports, judicial decisions, reports on technical cooperation projects and any comments of industrial organizations.

If discrepancies between the convention and a state's law or practice are noted the Committee directs comments to the government in the form of unpublished "direct requests" for minor discrepancies, or "observations" (published in the Committee's annual report) for more serious or continued discrepancies. In the event of eventual elimination of the law or practice which is not in harmony with a ratified convention the Committee publishes an expression of "satisfaction" for the government's action.

The work of the Committee of Experts is technical and quasi-judicial. Its report is presented each year to the International Labour Conference and serves as the basis for discussion by the Conference Committee on the Application of Conventions and Recommendations. In addition to comments directed to specific governments on specific conventions the Committee's report also includes general observations applicable to a number of governments or relevant to the application of a number of conventions.

The Conference Committee on the Application of Conventions and Recommendations (hereinafter referred to as the "Conference Committee") differs considerably from the Committee of Experts. It is one of the committees elected by the delegates to the annual ILO Conference and is composed of representatives of governments, employers and workers enjoying equal voting strength. It normally consists of more than 100 members. At the annual Conference, the Conference Committee selects for discussion a certain number of cases of serious discrepancies between conventions and national law or practice pointed out by the Committee of Experts in its annual report. The time available generally limits the consideration to not more than twenty-five percent of the observations made by the Committee of Experts. The Conference Committee discusses the cases in public meetings and government representatives are invited to provide oral and written information if they so desire. The composition and nature of the Committee gives it a more political and less technical tone than the Committee of Experts. The Conference Committee submits a report to the plenary session of the Conference which includes a paragraph referring to states which have failed to comply with reporting requirements or whose law or practice are not in conformity with conventions which they have ratified. The mention of a state in this paragraph (referred to as the "special list") is perceived as a condemnation if it relates to failure to carry out the obligations of ratified conventions. It is thus the most serious moral censure available within the ILO regular supervisory system. Although the report contains no recommendation for action by the full Conference, the Conference in plenary session has on occasion not adopted the Committee's report because of reservations about particular decisions taken by the Conference Committee.[6]

2. Development of Supervisory Committees' Concern Regarding Automatic Incorporation

An effective supervisory system for the implementation of ILO conventions must necessarily inquire into the incorporation of the norms of the conventions in the municipal law of the ratifying state.[7] The norms of these conventions are intended to have internal effects and if they do not become national law it is unlikely that they will be applied. By virtue of Article 19(5)(d) of the ILO Constitution, ratifying Member States are committed to "take such action as may be necessary to make effective the provisions" of conventions. One of the constant efforts of the ILO supervisory bodies over the years has been to ascertain the legal status of the provisions of treaties in the national law of ratifying states.

The ILO supervisory committees were forced at an early date to consider whether the constitutional technique of automatic incorporation per se guaranteed that the provisions of conventions were made "effective" in national law, when states reporting to the ILO on the application of a convention stated that the implementation of the convention was ensured because under their constitutional system treaties were automatically incorporated into their national law. As early as 1933, the Committee of Experts questioned in their annual report whether the system of automatic incorporation always guaranteed the effective application of treaties:

> The reports sent by certain countries [Greece, Spain and Lithuania] present a difficulty of a constitutional character. They appear to indicate that the fact of the due ratification of a Convention or of the passing of an Act of Parliament approving ratification and reproducing the text of the Convention concerned does in some way secure the putting into force of the Convention, even in the absence of other legislative or administrative measures ...[8]

Thus, at an early date, the Committee of Experts suggested doubts concerning the efficacy of automatic incorporation. The Committee's 1933 report continued by requesting governments to furnish more detailed information regarding the effect of ratification, particularly as to whether the mere act of ratification modified previously existing legislation. In the same year, the Conference Committeee wrote in its annual report:

> ... it must be pointed out that most of the Conventions are addressed to the States as such and oblige them to deal with a particular question in a particular way, but that they do not contain provisions such as would prescribe specific action for the individual citizens, quite apart from the fact that they do not supply the national authorities with any means for inflicting penalties.[9]

The Committee appears to be implying that the language of some ILO convention provisions, not being couched in terms of obligations or rights for citizens but simply obligations for states, are not suitable for direct application by courts but must be implemented by legislation. Thus, the Conference Committee raised the problem of the "non-self-executing" nature of convention provisions without using that expression. The Conference Committee report goes on to speak of the "confused legal situation" concerning automatic incorporation. This early reference to such confusion is particularly significant since it has remained a recurring theme in comments by ILO supervisory bodies since that time.

Little further mention appears to have been made of the non-self-executing problem by the Committee of Experts and the Conference Committee until the 1950s. From 1951 on the two Committees repeatedly drew the attention of governments to the problem of non-self-executing convention provisions and undertook a major attempt to clarify the problem for their interlocutors.[10] As part of this effort, the Governing Body in 1951 modified the sample report form furnished to governments in order to make somewhat more understandable the dimensions of the self-executing problem. It is unclear why the supervisory bodies emphasized the question so strongly only after 1950. Perhaps this late emphasis was due to the fact, pointed out by a number of commentators, that an understanding of the concept of self-executing treaty provisions only consciously entered into international legal concern in the 1950s following the United States case of *Sei Fujii* v. *California*[11] relating to the human rights provisions of the U.N. Charter. Aspects of the problem had been at issue at the international level, however, as early as the 1928 advisory opinion of the Permanent Court of International Justice in the *Jurisdiction of the Courts of Danzig* case.[12] A more plausible explanation for the increased concern of the ILO supervisory bodies was probably their own growing understanding, and that of the ILO secretariat, resulting from several important judicial decisions in Argentina, the United States and France between 1933 and 1950 relating to the direct application of ILO conventions.[13] This experience, added to an increased general awareness of the problem at the international level, might have led to the emphasis of the two ILO Committees.

Over a period of years the ILO Committees have become more specific in their questioning of governments concerning the status of conventions in the municipal legal system and more persistent in explaining problems involved in the automatic incorporation of treaties. In 1950 the Conference Committee reported that it had devoted particular attention to the question of states "where, in virtue of specific provisions of the national constitution, the ratification of the Convention confers on it force of law, or even of constitutional law." The Committee's report stated that it did not wish "to form a final judgment on this problem, which has involved juridical implications, and the details which may, in fact, vary from one country to another. ... It considers it essential, however, that in every case ratified Conventions be translated clearly in one way or another into the necessary national measures so as to give application to them."[14]

In 1951 the ILO Governing Body added more specific questions regarding automatic incorporation to the sample form provided to assist states in the preparation of their reports. This form (which is still in use) asks:

> If your country's ratification of the Convention gives the force of national law to its terms, please indicate by virtue of what constitutional provisions the ratification has had this effect. Please also specify what action has been taken to make effective those provisions of the Convention which require a national authority to take certain specific steps for its implementation, such as measures to define its exact scope and the extent to which advantage may be taken of permissive exceptions provided for in it, measures to draw the attention of the parties concerned to its provisions, and arrangements for adequate inspection and penalties.

In 1963, the annual report of the Committee of Experts considered the problems raised by the system of automatic incorporation in some detail.[15] The Committee treated the question under the heading of "practical application" rather than "legal application" of conventions. It pointed out that since its earliest years it had been concerned over the manner in which it could satisfy itself that Member States had, as required by Article 19 of the ILO Constitution, taken "such action as may be necessary to make effective" the provisions of such conventions. And it pointed out that it had emphasized repeatedly that the measures in question must have a bearing "both on the legal and on the factual position. It is not always easy however to distinguish between questions of law and of practice."

The 1963 report begins by pointing out the "most obvious aspect" of the problem regarding automatic incorporation—namely, that provisions which are not self-executing "even if introduced unchanged into internal law ... cannot be effectively applied in that form." The remainder of the report stresses the uncertainty existing in many countries in cases where a later law conflicts with an earlier treaty, the need for legislation where the convention requires penalties to be adopted and, finally, the need to avoid uncertainty as regards the legal position and to enable all persons concerned to be aware of the standards laid down in ratified conventions.

The Committee report points out that:

> A first aspect of this interdependence relates to the manner in which the standards laid down in ratified Conventions become applicable in internal law. Although this is, primarily, a juridical question, because the aim is to ensure that national legislation has really been brought into conformity with the Convention, the Committee has also often considered it (particularly as regards the incorporation of Conventions in internal law by virtue of their ratification) from the point of view of the practical application of Conventions; it has thus been concerned to see that there should be no uncertainty as regards the position in law in the field of the Convention and that all those concerned, judges, civil servants, labour inspectors, employers and workers, should be aware of the standards applicable, so that they can contribute to their implementation in practice.[16]

The report states that unless the internal standards which exist in a country are equal to or higher than those in the convention, it becomes important to ascertain what is the *practical* effect, internally, of the standards laid down in the convention. It points out that this problem has arisen mainly in respect of countries whose constitutional system provides that a convention which has been ratified and published (or promulgated) becomes immediately applicable in the internal law of the country but that it has also arisen in countries where the law authorizing ratification of the convention provides that it shall be incorporated in national law. The report continues:

> Clearly the Committee has always considered that the application of a Convention in a given country must be assessed in the light of the constitutional system or practice of that country, but the question arose whether incorporation of the Convention in national law by virtue merely of ratification of the Convention is sufficient to ensure its application in practice as well as in law.[17]

Although the Committee of Experts considers this to be a problem of "practical application" rather than a legal question, the problems on which it focuses concerning automatic incorporation are legal problems with the exception of the question of adequate publicity.

One can only conjecture concerning the reluctance of the Committee to treat the problem as a legal question and to continually refer to it as a *practical* one. As the Conference Committee pointed out in 1950, the question of automatic incorporation has "involved juridical implications" and varies from one country to another. It is possible that the Committee of Experts would find it difficult to be sufficiently "au courant" of the complexities of the constitutional systems in each of the countries which had raised the problem of automatic incorporation and would not wish to be involved in technical legal exchanges with an individual country over its own constitutional legal system. Hence while frequently pointing out *in general* the types of legal problems arising out of automatic incorporation and in some cases commenting on what appears to be the situation in a specific country the Committee of Experts has tended to move quickly on to different ground—namely, contending that, whatever the legal situation, there is a possibility of uncertainty and hence express amendment of conflicting legislation is advisable. Further, that when legal norms are contained in conventions they often remain unknown by administrators, judges, individuals, and hence there is need for adequate publicity of treaty provisions.

Again in its 1970 report, the Committee of Experts reiterated earlier statements:

> The Committee considers it necessary to refer at this stage to a problem which it has frequently encountered in connection with a number of countries and which it has examined repeatedly since 1933 and more recently in its general report in 1963 (paragraphs 21 to 35) and in observations concerning individual countries. This problem arises in cases in which governments indicate that under their national constitutional system ratified Conventions are automatically incorporated in internal law and consider that this is sufficient to give effect to such Conventions.
>
> The Committee recalls in this connection that in such cases the incorporation of the provisions of ratified Conventions in national law is not sufficient to give effect to them internally in the case of

> provisions which are non-self-executing, i.e., provisions which require legislative or other special measures to make them effective, in particular when it is necessary to make more specific provision in respect of certain standards, to establish administrative machinery or to provide for methods of supervision or penalties.[18]

3. States Invoking Automatic Incorporation as Guaranteeing Convention Implementation

3.1. *Mexico*

After the first reference to automatic incorporation in reports from Greece, Spain and Lithuania in the early 1930s, a number of other countries continued to mention automatic incorporation as guaranteeing the implementation of ratified conventions. Since 1937 Mexico has consistently called the attention of the ILO supervisory bodies to Article 133 of its Constitution and contended that it guaranteed implementation of conventions in Mexico. Article 133 declares that treaties which are in accordance with the Constitution shall be the supreme law of the land and take precedence over the constitutions and laws of states. The Mexican Government's reports for 1950–51 on ratified conventions included a letter from the Permanent Delegation of Mexico at the International Organizations in Geneva pointing out that "the provisions of Article 133 of the Constitution must be considered sufficient for the application of a Convention, the provisions of which modify the Federal Labour Act and are in themselves a body of labour legislation apart from the Act itself, but with the same binding force as the latter."[19] Subsequently, the Committee of Experts and the Conference Committee pointed out to the Mexican Government that a number of convention provisions required implementing legislation and thus could not be directly applied.

The government continued to contend, however, that there was no necessity for enacting legislation to implement ILO conventions; the constitutional provision was sufficient. Their insistence may have been due, in part, to political difficulties in amending the Federal Labour Act referred to in the letter from the Permanent Delegation of Mexico in Geneva.

The government reports to the ILO on ratified Conventions for 1954–55 contained the following standard paragraph:

> In accordance with section 133 of the Constitution of the United States of Mexico, the observance of the Convention is compulsory throughout the country since it has been ratified by the Senate of the Republic and published in the official gazette of the federation and

> since the instrument of ratification has been duly deposited in accordance with a Decree signed by the President of the Republic and countersigned by the Secretary of External Relations. The provisions of the Convention have the full force of a Mexican act; anything that is contained in other laws and is contrary to the provisions of the Convention now has no validity; and those of the Convention's principles that were not already embodied in Mexican legislation are now applicable. The implementation of the Convention was ensured by its promulgation, and in this case, as in that of any other law, any citizen may take advantage of the benefits provided he fulfills the obligations laid down in the instrument, the proper authorities being under an obligation to see to its implementation.[20]

Later government reports continued to refer to Article 133, although recognizing that some conventions, as pointed out by the Committee of Experts, did require the implementing legislation. The subsequent actions of the Mexican government in response to the ILO's requests for supplementary legislation are referred to elsewhere in this study.[21]

3.2. *Colombia*

In this same period questions arose regarding automatic incorporation of treaty provisions in other countries. In 1950 the United States government asked the ILO for an opinion regarding the self-executing nature of a provision of an ILO convention, since only self-executing provisions of treaties are applied by U.S. courts.[22] And in a 1949–50 report on a ratified convention the government of Colombia contended that an ILO convention was automatically incorporated into national law since it has been approved by Congress.[23] The government maintained that the Hours of Work Convention was thus fully applied in industrial establishments. At the 1956 International Labour Conference, a representative of the government of Colombia stated in the Conference Committee on the Application of Conventions:

> ... in accordance with the spirit of the national constitution, the jurisprudence of the Supreme Court of Justice has established the priority of international treaties over any internal legislation which might be contrary to the said instruments. The Court of Justice considered that a treaty which had been transformed into a law in virtue of the Constitution prevailed over any internal law, provided it had international implications.[24]

The subsequent interchange between the government of Colombia and the ILO supervisory bodies illustrates what the Conference Committee had earlier referred to as the often "somewhat confused legal situation" relating to automatic incorporation. It eventually appeared that international treaties were not automatically incorporated into Colombian law. In 1951 the government reiterated in a report on an ILO convention that the ratification of three ILO conventions had the effect of incorporating the terms of these conventions in national law.[25] At meetings of the Conference Committee in 1956 and 1962 a written communication from the government and a statement by a government representative both maintained that ratified conventions prevailed in Colombia over conflicting laws—even laws adopted after the treaty.[26]

In 1969, however, Alfonso Plata-Castilla in an article in the International Labour Review wrote:

> ... in contrast to the system in certain other countries, the Constitution of Colombia *does not provide* for automatic incorporation of ratified conventions in national legislation, with binding force for subjects of the country. In this it follows the dualist theory of international law, according to which treaties are merely a source of reciprocal obligations among the parties subject to international law, without any direct, intrinsic consequences for the internal law of those States. Their provisions cannot therefore be cited by citizens in their dealings with national authorities until such time as a specific enactment has given them force of law in the substantive sense, as binding requirements within the national legal system.
>
> Hence in Colombia neither the instrument of ratification of an international labour convention nor the act of approval ... gives the standards laid down by the convention validity under the national law. For the convention to be applied, substantive legislation must be passed, stating how the subject-matter is to be regulated in accordance with the relevant standards.[27] [italics added]

The earlier statements of the government conflicting with the above analysis are explained later by Plata-Castilla. In referring to a decree in 1934 laying down regulations implementing the Hours of Work Convention (No. 1) he wrote:

> ... it may be mentioned in passing that the fact of prior approval by a formal Act of Congress was considered at the time to mean that the provisions of a ratified Convention automatically became part of national law as would be the case for ordinary legislation, which is why the government issued a decree laying down regulations in the matter ... Present practice is based on the consideration that the provisions of a ratified Convention cannot become part of national law or be cited in dealings with the competent national authorities until legislation has passed which goes beyond the mere approval of such Conventions.[28]

3.3. *Guatemala*

The Guatemalan government also entered into a long series of communications with the ILO relating to automatic incorporation of treaties in national law. In reports on ratified conventions, written communications to the Conference Committee and remarks by government representatives before the Conference Committee, the government of Guatemala had contended since 1955 that conventions duly approved by Congress, ratified and published, had the force of law automatically. These communications had pointed out that, although the Guatemalan Constitution contained no article providing that treaties had the force of law upon ratification, it had nevertheless been considered that the requirement under the Constitution that treaties be approved by Congress had the effect (when they were so approved, ratified and published) of transforming them into national law.[29]

In 1969 the government communicated the following information to the Conference Committee:

> In a formal note, dated 8 May 1969, addressed to the Ministry of Labour and Social Welfare, the Council of State expressed the following opinion: a categorical statement should be forwarded to the International Labour Organization, through the proper channels indicating that international Conventions and treaties dealing with labour matters, when approved and ratified by Guatemala, become part of the law of the Republic and accordingly must necessarily be applied.[30]

The 1970 report of the Committee of Experts took note of the 1969 Council of State opinion but pointed out that even if treaties were automatically incorporated in national law, legislation was required to implement non-self-executing provisions or to provide penalties for violations of conventions and that it was essential that adequate publicity be given to ratified conventions where legislative provisions inconsistent with the conventions were on the statute books.[31] The Committee report went on to state its own understanding of the Guatemalan constitutional system relating to the relative priority of treaties and statutes, namely, that subsequent statutes prevailed over earlier treaties.[32]

In 1971, in discussion in the Plenary Session of the Conference, the spokesman for Guatemala stated that:

> We have taken note with interest of the observations made by the I.L.O. and despite our conviction that international labour conventions take precedence over and nullify any contrary legislation, we are nevertheless seeking to amend and modernise our legislation.[33]

This willingness not to rely solely on the efficacity of automatic incorporation seems to have been borne out subsequently. During direct contacts between a representative of the Director-General of the ILO and various Guatemalan government officials in 1972 concerning the possibility of improved implementation of ILO conventions no mention appears to have been made of automatic incorporation and decrees were subsequently adopted implementing a number of conventions.[34]

3.4. *Argentina*

Following two important Argentine Supreme Court cases involving the application of ILO conventions,[35] the Argentine government's reports to the ILO concerning automatic incorporation were confusing. In 1962, a government representative at the Conference Committee stated that there existed two schools of thought as to whether a ratified convention automatically became the law of the land: some considered that under the Constitution, ratified treaties became binding national law immediately, whereas others considered that internal measures were necessary to implement all conventions. The government representative stated that the Argentine government, not endorsing either theory, considered it more practicable to eliminate as far as possible any discrepancies between existing legislation and ratified conventions.[36] In 1963, however, a government representative at the Conference Committee stated that by virtue of Article 31 of the Argentine Constitution ratified conventions had the force of national law and if existing legislation was brought into line with conventions it was with a view to avoiding divergencies in interpretation and uncertainties in practical application.[37]

4. States Rarely Invoking Automatic Incorporation as Guaranteeing Convention Implementation

Although some countries contended in reports to the ILO that automatic incorporation guaranteed implementation of conventions, other countries, which also have the system of automatic incorporation, have seldom made such contentions. France, the Netherlands and Switzerland are all automatic incorporation states, yet they have rarely cited automatic incorporation as guaranteeing implementation.

4.1. *France*

Occasional references have been made by France to automatic incorporation as guaranteeing implementation and there are several judicial decisions involving ILO conventions which are relevant in this regard. Nevertheless, such references have been rare given the extremely high number of ILO conventions ratified by France. Valticos has written:

> Contrary to the practice in certain other countries with the monist system which invoke, sometimes excessively, the automatic incorporation of ratified conventions in their internal legal order, French practice in the application of international labor conventions has not generally been to rely on the "soft pillow" of monism, although France is one of the countries whose constitution most clearly incorporates monist doctrine.[38]

The reason for France's reticence in this regard appears to be the French practice referred to in a 1970 article by Morellet:

> The French Constitution embodies the monist principle. But it is in fact French legal practice in most cases to incorporate the provisions of a Convention by means of a formal amendment of internal law. This practice, which combines dualism with monism, has the advantage of calling the attention of public authorities, the courts and the general public to the law applicable.[39]

4.2. *The Netherlands*

The Netherlands is another country with the system of automatic incorporation which has seldom invoked it as guaranteeing application. In its reports on the numerous ILO conventions which it has ratified the Netherlands government has seldom referred to automatic incorporation, even in cases where the ILO supervisory bodies have referred to discrepancies between national legislation and ratified conventions or the lack of national legislation implementing the convention. It appears to be the policy of the Netherlands, as of France, not to ratify conventions unless, in general, national legislation has implemented them. In a communication to the ILO in 1974 relating to the non-ratification of conventions the Netherlands government stated that where national legislation was not in conformity or where there was no implementing legislation it did not intend to ratify certain conventions.[40]

4.3. *Switzerland*

Until recently Switzerland maintained a policy of not ratifying ILO conventions unless national legislation had been adopted to carry out the obligations of the convention. As a result the Swiss government rarely referred to automatic incorporation as ensuring implementation. A corresponding result of this policy, however, was that Switzerland ratified a relatively small number of ILO conventions in comparison with the number ratified by other Western European countries. In 1969, the Swiss government announced a change of policy in a report by the Swiss Federal Council to the Federal Assembly:

> Until the present time, in examining whether or not to ratify an ILO convention, we have adopted a more cautious attitude than the legal situation required. Whether it was a question of immediately applicable conventions or conventions requiring implementing national provisions, we have proposed ratification only in the case where our country already possessed the legislation required to satisfy the obligations imposed by the convention. In the future, we intend to go a bit further. When an immediately applicable convention coincides in major details with legislation in force in our country, we will submit it for your approval with the idea that the lacunae in our legislation will be automatically filled by the provisions of the convention, transformed by ratification into federal law.[41]

Thus, Switzerland signaled its intention to rely on automatic incorporation to ensure implementation of ILO conventions in the future unless there were serious discrepancies between national legislation and the convention. Following this decision two government reports on ratified conventions stressed that conventions were applied because they had been automatically incorporated in national law.[42]

5. Conclusion

The legal and practical problems involved in the automatic incorporation of conventions in national law became progressively more apparent to ILO Committees as they supervised the application of the conventions over a number of years. One of the most recurrent themes in the comments of ILO supervisory organs to national governments has related to these problems. National governments have been slow to perceive that automatic incorporation does not guarantee effective national application of treaties. This has required repeated patient efforts by the ILO Committees to demonstrate that the mere invocation of automatic incorporation is not sufficient evidence of national application of ILO conventions. As the exchanges with the governments of Argentina, Colombia and Guatemala illustrate there may even be confusion as to whether a particular country does or does not have the system of automatic incorporation.

The 1963 report of the Committee of Experts summarizes the problems which the Committee had observed over the years in the automatic incorporation of convention provisions:

(1) the non-self-executing character of some of the provisions of the conventions;
(2) the need in some cases for legislation providing for the imposition of penalties for violation of convention provisions;
(3) the situation in some countries where a later law supersedes an earlier treaty (the ILO supervisory bodies have not emphasized the largely theoretical question of the conflict of treaty provisions with national constitutions although the question has arisen with regard to the application of an ILO convention on one occasion);[43]
(4) the problem of ensuring adequate publicity for and application of treaty provisions, particularly when conflicting national legislation is on the books.

The ILO experience demonstrates that the complexities involved in the automatic incorporation of treaties are often little known and understood even in countries which have adopted the constitutional system of automatic incorporation.

NOTES

1. See Richard Bilder, *Rethinking International Human Rights: Some Basic Questions*, 1969 Wisconsin L. Rev. 171–217; Antonio Cassese, "A New Reservations Clause (Article 20 of the United Nations Convention on the Elimination of All Forms of Racial Discrimination)" in *Recueil d'études de droit international en hommage à Paul Guggenheim* (Genève: Imprimerie de la Tribune de Genève, 1968), pp. 266, 269–270. The number of inter-state complaints of violations of the European Convention on Human Rights has been extremely small in comparison with the number of individual complaints of violations. The reluctance of states to accept the jurisdiction of international judicial organs also frequently renders inter-state complaints futile.

2. See Antonio Cassese, *Il Controllo Internazionale* (Milano: A. Giuffré, 1971), pp. 35–36, 255–271, 303–307.

3. The information on the ILO supervisory system in this section is taken primarily from E. A. Landy, *The Effectiveness of International Supervision—Thirty Years of ILO Experience* (Dobbs Ferry, New York: Oceana Publications, Inc., 1966); Nicolas Valticos, *Un système de contrôle international: la mise en oeuvre des conventions internationales du travail*, 123 R.C.A.D.I. 315–407 (1968–I) and *Droit international du travail* (Paris: Dalloz, 1970); *The Impact of International Labour Conventions and Recommendations* (Geneva: ILO, 1976), pp. 47–77.

4. Landy, *Effectiveness of International Supervision*, pp. 1–2.

5. This procedure is not specifically linked to the supervision of the implementation of conventions in national law and hence will not be further referred to in this study. See *The Impact*, op. cit., pp. 69–73.

6. See 59 R.P. 747–762 (1974).

7. "... on ne saurait, en effet, apprécier si un Etat s'acquitte des engagements qu'il a assumés en ratifiant une convention sans rechercher si et de quelle manière les normes préscrites par cette convention ont été introduites dans le droit interne du pays considéré,"

Nicolas Valticos, *Conventions internationales du travail et droit interne*, 44 R.C.D.I.P. 251, 253 (1955).

8. 17 S.R. 486 (1933).

9. 17 R.P. 520 (1933).

10. See chapters 5, 6 and 7 for a detailed discussion of the problem of non-self-executing treaty provisions.

11. 38 Cal. 2d 718, 242 P.2d 617 (1952). This case is discussed in chapter 5.

12. Advisory Opinion, P.C.I.J., Ser. B, No. 15, March 3, 1928, 16–24.

13. See chapter 6 for a discussion of these cases.

14. 33 R.P. 460 (1950).

15. 1963 R.C.E. 8–16.

16. Ibid., 8.

17. Ibid.

18. 1970 R.C.E. 7–8.

19. Mexican Government Report for 1950–51 on the Unemployment Indemnity (Shipwreck) Convention, 1920 (No. 8). The first references to automatic incorporation appeared in the reports of the Mexican Government for 1937–38, 1938–39 on the Night Work of Young Persons (Industry) Convention, 1919 (No. 6).

20. Mexican Government Report for 1954–55 on the Forced Labour Convention, 1930 (No. 29). Translation ILO file.

21. Chapters 7, 8 and 9, infra.

22. See discussion of this request in chapter 7, sec. 2, infra.

23. Colombian Report for 1949–50 on the Hours of Work (Industry) Convention, 1919 (No. 1).

24. 39 R.P. 656 (1956).

25. Colombian Report on the Minimum Age (Sea) Convention, 1920 (No. 7), reference to conventions Nos. 7, 8 and 9; 34 R.P. 563 (1951).

26. 39 R.P. 656 (1956); 46 R.P. 690 (1962).

27. Alfonso Plata-Castilla, *International Labour Standards and Colombian Legislation*, 99 I.L.R. 137, 138 (1969).

28. Ibid., 142.

29. See, inter alia, Guatemalan Government Report for 1954–55 on the Medical Examination of Young Persons (Industry) Convention, 1946 (No. 77); 1971 Direct Request of the Committee of Experts addressed to Guatemala concerning the Migration for Employment Convention (Revised), 1949 (No. 97).

30. 53 R.P. 591 (1969).

31. 1970 R.C.E. 23–24.

32. Ibid., 24.

33. 56 R.P. 179 (1971).

34. 1974 R.C.E. 32.

35. Alonso, Gregorio c. Sociedad Anonima Haras "Los Cardos", Fallo de la Corte Suprema 186:258; No. 9033, 15 March 1940, *La Ley* t.XVII, p. 877, 30 March 1940 and Roa, Felix y otros c. Moschos, Constantino, Fallo de la Corte Suprema, 19 de mayo de 1961, R.383–XII. See chapter 6 for extensive discussions of these two decisions.

36. 46 R.P. 689 (1962).

37. 47 R.P. 521 (1963).

38. Nicolas Valticos, *Droit international du travail et droit interne français*, Travaux du comité français de droit international privé, 1973–75 (Paris: Dalloz, 1977), pp. 11, 18 [translation].

39. Jean Morellet, *The Influence of International Labour Conventions on French Legislation*, 101 I.L.R. 333 (1970).

40. ILO Ratification Prospects File, The Netherlands. The observations in the text are based on an extensive examination of ILO files on conventions ratified by the Netherlands.

41. Feuille fédérale. 1969 I 721, pp. 9–10 [translation]. Since this announcement by the Swiss Government on the 50th anniversary of the founding of the ILO, eight additional ILO conventions have been ratified by Switzerland (as of 1 June 1980). On the question of ratification of ILO conventions by Switzerland see Nicolas Valticos, *Les effêts des conventions internationales du travail en Suisse*, 50 Mémoires de la Faculté de Droit (Université de Genève) 327–345 (1975).

42. Report of the Swiss Government on the Hygiene (Commerce and Offices) Convention (No. 120) for 1968–70 and on the Minimum Age (Underground Work) Convention (No. 123) for 1968–70.

43. See chapter 8, sec. 2.1, concerning the denunciation of Convention No. 6 by Mexico.

CHAPTER 3

Elements of Automatic Incorporation

In an effort to bring intellectual clarity to a complex subject, Dominicé has suggested that an analysis of the relationship of treaties to municipal law should carefully distinguish the three aspects of the validity of treaties in municipal law, their direct application in national law and their rank in relation to national constitutions or legislation.[1] Dominicé's helpful distinctions are used in this study as the theoretical framework for elucidating the problems involved in the national application of international labour conventions. The term "status" is used, however, in preference to the term "validity", employed by Dominicé, in order to emphasize the distinction between the international validity of a treaty and its status in national law, i.e., its force as law within a national legal system.

This chapter is a brief introduction to the constitutional system of automatic incorporation of treaties in national law. It provides an outline of the basic elements of the system of automatic incorporation which will be developed in detail in subsequent chapters in relation to the application of labour conventions.

1. Status (Force of Law) of Treaties in National Legal Systems: Automatic Incorporation and Legislative Incorporation

International law determines the validity of treaties in the international legal system, i.e., when and how a treaty becomes binding upon a state as regards other State Parties. It also determines the remedies available on the international plane for its breach. But it is the national legal system which determines the status or force of law which will be given to a treaty within that legal system, i.e., whether national judges and administrators will apply the norms of a treaty in a specific case. International conventional law is not supra-national law and treaty norms are not immediately operative by virtue of the international legal system within particular states.[2] While a State Party may be able to invoke the provisions of a treaty against another State Party in international fora, individuals do not normally have access to such fora and may invoke the provisions of a treaty only within the national legal system and then only if the treaty provisions have become part of national law.[3] When the treaty norms become domestic law, national judges and administrators apply them, and individuals in the ratifying states may receive rights as a result of the treaty provisions. Thus, developed municipal legal systems supplement the more limited enforcement system of international law.

While the international legal system does not reach *directly* into the national systems to enforce its norms it attempts to do so *indirectly*. States are required under international law to bring their domestic laws into conformity with their validly contracted international commitments.[4] Failure to do so, however, results in an international delinquency but does not change the situation within the national legal systems where judges and administrators may continue to apply national law rather than international law in such cases. The work of the supervisory bodies of the International Labour Organization in influencing states to bring their law into conformity with ILO conventions is an example, however, of the increasing efficacy of the international legal system in this regard.

The status of treaties in national law is determined by two different constitutional techniques referred to in this study as "legislative incorporation" and "automatic incorporation". In some states the provisions of ratified treaties do not become national law unless they have been enacted as legislation by the normal method. The legislative act creating the norms as domestic law is an act entirely distinct from the act of ratification of the treaty. The legislative bodies may refuse to enact legislation implementing the treaty. In this case the provisions of the treaty do not become national law. This method, referred to as "legislative incorporation", is used, inter alia, in the United Kingdom, Commonwealth countries and Scandinavian countries. In other states, which have a different system, ratified treaties become domestic law by virtue of ratification. This method is referred to as "automatic incorporation"[5] and is the method adopted, inter alia, by France, Switzerland, the Netherlands, the United States and many Latin American countries and some African and Asian countries. It is important to note that in many of these states, proclamation or publication of the treaty may also be necessary for its force as national law. Even in such states, however, some treaty provisions require implementing legislation before they will be applied by the courts. Such provisions are categorized as "non-self-executing."

Some countries which have officially adopted the system of legislative incorporation also employ a technique which, in practice, accomplishes the same result as that of automatic incorporation. In these countries—of which Austria, the Federal Republic of Germany, and Italy are examples—the parliamentary act of approval of ratification or an "order of execution" accompanying this parliamentary act of approval accomplishes the incorporation of the treaty provisions in national law. This is to be distinguished from the usual system of legislative incorporation whereby the legislation enacting specific provisions of the treaty is not related to the act of ratification. This special technique is sometimes referred to as "global transformation" or "quasi-automatic incorporation." Since the practical effects of the use of this technique are similar in many respects to that of automatic incorporation it is assimilated to the technique of "automatic incorporation" for the purposes of this study.[6]

International law does not dictate that one or the other of the methods of legislative or automatic incorporation must be used. Either is satisfactory assuming that the norms of treaties effectively become part of national law. Conversely, neither method is ipso facto satisfactory under international law, if, in practice, the norms of ratified treaties are not applied by national judges and administrators. The method by which treaties become national law is a matter in principle to be determined by the constitutional law of the ratifying state and not a matter ordained by international law. The international community, lacking more effective means of enforcement, is often dependent on the constitutional system of particular states for the effective application of treaties intended for internal application.

Some national constitutions provide for automatic incorporation of treaty provisions.[7] In other states, judicial decisions have determined that treaties are to be automatically incorporated.[8] A correlation appears to exist between legislative consent to ratification and automatic incorporation. In states with the system of automatic incorporation, legislative consent by at least one house of the legislature is generally required before the executive may ratify treaties. In states with the system of legislative incorporation, ratification of treaties is frequently a purely executive act not requiring prior approbation of the legislature. In the United Kingdom, and other common law countries which have followed U.K. precedent in this regard, parliamentary consent to ratification is normally not required and express legislative enactment of treaty provisions is necessary before they become domestic law.[9]

The relationship between international law and national law has traditionally been discussed in the literature in terms of the monist and dualist theories. Proponents of monism maintain that international law and national law form part of the same legal system and generally proclaim the superiority of international law within that system. Dualists maintain that international law and national law form two unrelated systems with neither having priority over the other since they operate in separate spheres. Discussions of the relative merits of the dualist and monist positions have largely remained on the theoretical plane and have often been essentially sterile controversies.[10] The theories of monism and dualism have only limited relevance to the present study since this study is not a theoretical analysis of the two doctrines but a practical examination of the relationship between international treaties and national law. A state's choice of the method of automatic incorporation or legislative incorporation has been influenced in some cases by a preference for one or the other theory.[11] It has been contended that Italy and Germany chose the system of legislative incorporation of treaty provisions as a result of the influence of the outstanding jurists Anzilotti and Triepel, two of the most prominent advocates of the dualist theory.[12]

The choice of automatic incorporation frequently appears to have been dictated by a desire to apply international treaties more effectively in internal law and is considered to be the practical application of the monist theory. Since World War II a number of constitutions have provided for automatic incorporation of treaty provisions into national law. Holloway remarks that "a significant feature of most post-World War II constitutions is the express recognition of the primacy of international law and the adoption of provisions to secure its effective enforcement."[13] While the method of automatic incorporation has been one of the means adopted by states in order to ensure more effective implementation of international law in domestic legal systems, it has not always accomplished this result in practice. Problems relating to direct application and rank, referred to below and reverted to extensively in later chapters, have, in particular, created problems for the effective application of treaty provisions in automatic incorporation states.

2. Direct Application of Treaty Provisions (The "Self-Executing" Problem)

In countries with the system of automatic or quasi-automatic incorporation not all treaty provisions are directly applied by judges and administrators. Some treaty provisions are considered to be non-self-executing, i.e., to require implementing legislation before their norms may be applied. Some publicists use the term "direct application" to refer to this phenomenon. In U.S. legal literature the expression "self-executing" treaty provisions is commonly used and the American expression or its direct translation is often used in legal writing concerning other legal systems.[14]

Dominicé has pointed out that the aspects of validity (status) and direct application have often been confounded by judges and publicists. Although closely related, they are distinct since the question of direct application or the self-executing nature of treaty provisions only becomes relevant when it has been preliminarily determined that the treaty has been automatically incorporated in national law. No treaty is self-executing in legislative incorporation states.[15] Dominicé also points out that the status of treaties and their rank within the national legal system are solely determined by national law, whereas the problem of "direct application" requires a consideration of the aim and content of the treaty itself, and hence touches on questions of international law.[16] Wildhaber has also pointed out the distinction—and frequent confusion—between the domestic status of treaties and direct application. He writes:

> A treaty becomes incorporated in municipal law to the extent that it is capable of application. Here we encounter the bewildering problem of the self-executing nature of treaties—bewildering mainly because too many authors use the term without adequately defining it. The concept is used to describe two different situations:
>
> (a) Some authors assert that treaties are self-executing, in a given state, if the *state's constitution* provides that international conclusion and entry into force of treaties suffice to render treaties *municipally* binding and obligatory. In that sense one may say that in the United Kingdom "treaties are not self-executing", while in other countries here examined treaties are self-executing. This use of the term self-executing seems unfortunate. The notion of self-executing first evolved in the United States. Since it is clear that in the USA some treaties are self-executing, others not, although all treaties are the supreme law of the land, the concept, self-executing, obviously must mean something different from automatic incorporation of treaties in (American) municipal law.
>
> (b) According to other authors, a treaty is self-executing if *municipal courts can apply it immediately* and without further implementing acts, to individuals. This seems to me the proper use of the notion self-executing ...[17]

An individual may invoke the provisions of a treaty before national courts in automatic incorporation states in the absence of implementing legislation only when its provisions are considered to be self-executing and when he has standing to do so. The criteria for determining whether a provision is self-executing or directly applicable are not the same in each country and much confusion exists concerning the classification of provisions in this regard. A treaty provision may well be considered self-executing in one jurisdiction and not in another.[18] It suffices at this point to state that, in general, treaty provisions are considered by national courts and administrators as self-executing when they lend themselves to judicial or administrative application without further legislative implementation. The problem of the self-executing nature of treaty provisions is, however, far more complex than this simplistic definition would suggest, as will become apparent in subsequent chapters.

3. The Rank or Hierarchy of Treaty Provisions

A further complication may prevent even self-executing treaty provisions from being applied within automatic and quasi-automatic incorporation states. National courts have frequently been called upon to decide whether treaty provisions should be applied if they conflict with constitutional provisions or with national laws. Should the treaty provisions prevail over the constitution and national laws or vice-versa? Does it make a difference whether the treaty or the legislation was adopted at a later date? This problem is referred to as that of the "rank" or "hierarchy" of treaty provisions. As with the problem of the self-executing nature of treaty provisions it arises only in states with automatic or quasi-automatic incorporation systems.

A strong preference for the monist theory and the supremacy of international law would dictate the priority of treaty provisions over municipal constitutions and laws whether later or earlier and regardless of whether the issue arose in the international or municipal legal system. The dualist position would support the proposition that international law should prevail in the international legal system and municipal law in the municipal legal system.[19] In practice, the solutions adopted by various states are less absolute than either the extreme dualist or monist theories. Paul de Visscher has classified the solutions adopted by various states in cases of conflict between self-executing treaty provisions and municipal legal norms.[20] He points out that in one group of states, treaty provisions and national legislation are considered to be of equal rank and, in accordance with the maxim *lex posterior derogat priori*, the latest in time of the two norms will prevail over the earlier. The courts in such states often attempt to interpret the municipal legislation or the treaty in such a manner that conflict is avoided. In federal states adopting this solution, treaties prevail over state or provincial constitutions or laws, even though the state laws may have been adopted subsequent to the treaty. They do not, however, prevail over later federal legislation.

In another group of states, the constitution provides that treaties are superior to municipal legislation but since there is no judicial review of the validity of legislation the supremacy of treaties is not always upheld by the courts. If conflicting legislation is enacted after the treaty the courts have a tendency to apply the municipal legislation.

Another method appears to have been adopted only by the Netherlands. Its Constitution provides for the supremacy of treaties not only over Dutch legislation but over the Constitution itself in certain cases.

4. Conclusion

Through the technique of automatic incorporation, treaties in many countries become the "law of the land" immediately upon ratification (and upon proclamation or publication in some countries). This technique or system has been widely adopted since World War II as a more effective method of providing for national implementation of treaties than the system of legislative incorporation.

Nevertheless, the mere fact that a state has adopted the system of automatic incorporation does not guarantee that treaty provisions will have direct effect in national law. The courts of states which employ the system of automatic incorporation refuse to directly apply non-self-executing treaty provisions. These provisions require implementing legislation. In considering whether a treaty provision will have municipal effect in a particular country, it is essential to determine whether or not it will be considered self-executing by the courts of that country. Since the criteria for determining the self-executing character of a treaty provision differ from country to country, it is difficult to determine in the abstract whether a particular provision is or is not self-executing. Each national legal system must be examined in this regard.

A further limitation on the direct application of treaty provisions results from the problem of the rank or hierarchy of treaty provisions in national law. In some states, a subsequent national law may have priority over an earlier self-executing treaty provision.

Differing national treatment of the problems of the self-executing character of treaty provisions and the rank of treaty provisions suggests that it is simplistic to classify all automatic incorporation states into a common category. Detailed consideration of the legal system in a particular state is necessary in determining whether treaty provisions will be effectively applied therein.

NOTES

1. Christian Dominicé, *La Convention européenne des droits de l'homme devant le juge national*, 28 A.S.D.I. 9, 10 (1972).

2. For general information regarding treaties and national law see Kaye Holloway, *Modern Trends in Treaty Law* (London: Stevens and Sons, 1967); Pierre Lardy, *La force obligatoire du droit international en droit interne* (Paris: R. Pichon et R. Durand—Auzias, 1966); Lord A. D. McNair, *The Law of Treaties* (Oxford: Clarendon Press, 1961); Paul de Visscher, *Les tendances internationales des constitutions modernes*, 81 R.C.A.D.I. 516 (1952–I).

3. Within the European Economic Community (EEC) a provision of the Treaty of Rome may be directly applicable to private parties. The EEC constitutes a "new legal order,"

however, which must be distinguished from the general international legal system. N.V. Algemene Transport—en Expeditie Onderneming Van Gend & Loos c. Administration Fiscale Néerlandaise, Court of Justice of the European Communities, 9 Recueil 1 (1963), Case No. 26–62; 1963 C.M.L. Rep. 105. See Note, Stefan A. Riesenfeld and Richard M. Buxbaum, *N.V. Algemene Transport—en Expeditie Onderneming Van Gend & Loos c. Administration Fiscale Néerlandaise: A Pioneering Decision of the Court of Justice of the European Communities*, 58 Am. J. Int'l L. 152 (1964). Exceptions may also exist within particular treaty communities, e.g., individuals may invoke the provisions of the European Convention on Human Rights before the European Commission on Human Rights if their state has accepted the right of individual petition: European Convention for the Protection of Human Rights and Fundamental Freedoms (1950), 213 U.N.T.S. 221, Article 25.

4. See Vienna Convention on the Law of Treaties (1969), U.N. Doc. A/Conf. 39/27, Article 27; Advisory Opinion on Exchange of Greek and Turkish Populations, P.C.I.J., Ser. B, No. 10, p. 20 (1925); McNair, *Treaties*, p. 78: "It is the duty of a party to a treaty to see to it that its municipal law enables it to give effect to the treaty and that the organs—executive and judicial—are properly equipped with the powers required for that purpose; if that is not already the case, the defect must be remedied, for no State can plead a deficiency in its municipal law or organization against a complaint of a breach of a treaty obligation ..."

5. The term "automatic incorporation" is used herein because it is the expression employed by the Committee of Experts of the International Labour Organization, 1974 R.C.E. 21, 1963 R.C.E. 8. The terms "immediate validity" and "automatic reception" are, however, sometimes used in the same sense in which the term "automatic incorporation" is used in this study. Georges Malinverni, *L'Application de la Convention européenne des droits de l'homme en Suisse*, Mémoires publiés par la Faculté de Droit de Genève, Quinzième Journée Juridique (1977), p. 4; Rosalyn Higgins, "Compliance with United Nations Decisions on Peace and Security and Human Rights Questions," in Stephen M. Schwebel, ed., *The Effectiveness of International Decisions* (Leyden: A. W. Sijthoff, 1971), p. 36.

6. Dominicé, *La Convention européenne*, 13.

7. E.g., Argentina, France, Mexico, the Netherlands and the United States. See chapter 4.

8. E.g., Switzerland.

9. Le Parlement belge, 4 P.D. 129 (1876); McNair, *Treaties*, pp. 81–110.

10. For an excellent summary of the monist and dualist theories, see Lardy, *La force obligatoire*, pp. 15–34. See generally Dionisio Anzilotti, *Cours de droit international* (Paris: Sirey, 3rd ed. 1929); Hans Kelsen, *Les rapports de système entre le droit interne et le droit international public*, 14 R.C.A.D.I. 231–331 (1926–IV); D. P. O'Connell, *International Law* (London: Stevens and Sons, 2d ed. 1970), vol. I, pp. 38–46; Georges Scelle, *Précis de droit des gens* (Paris: Sirey, 1932–34); Heinrich Triepel, *Droit international et droit interne* (Paris: A. Pédone, 1920), *Les rapports entre le droit interne et le droit international*, 1 R.C.A.D.I. 77–118 (1923); Michel Virally, "Sur un pont aux ânes: les rapports entre droit international et droits internes" in *Mélanges offerts à Henri Rolin* (Paris: Pedone, 1964), pp. 488–504.

11. The choice of automatic incorporation has not always been dictated by a preference for the theory of monism. In some cases, historical experience has been more important than theory. See section on the United States constitutional system, chapter 4, sec. 1.1.

12. Holloway, *Modern Trends*, p. 238: "Domestic provisions concerning the application or performance of international law and in particular of conventional law within the municipal legal order reveal the direct or indirect influence of the dualist and monist conceptions of the relations between international law and municipal law ... The influence of dualist theory has been strongest in Germany and Italy through two of its most distinguished exponents—Triepel and Anzilotti." It should be recalled that although both Italy and Germany have, in theory, adopted the method of legislative incorporation inspired by dualism their system of

"global transformation" or "quasi-automatic incorporation" in practice closely resembles the method of "automatic incorporation" inspired by monism.

13. Holloway, *Modern Trends*, p. 249. See also de Visscher, *Les tendances internationales*, 571–573; Lardy, *La force obligatoire*, pp. 9–10.

14. A distinction has been made in the literature concerning European community law between "direct application" and "direct effect." See J. A. Winter, *Direct Applicability and Direct Effect: Two Distinct and Different Concepts in Community Law*, 9 C.M.L. Rev. 425 (1972). For the purposes of this study the terms "direct application" and "self-executing nature" are considered to be interchangeable.

15. It is sometimes said, however, that treaties are self-executing in countries of legislative incorporation if implementing legislation has already been adopted before ratification. See Lawrence Preuss, *On Amending the Treaty-Making Power: A Comparative Study of the Problem of Self-Executing Treaties*, 51 Mich. L. Rev. 1117, 1124 (1953): "In view of this practice of securing enabling legislation in advance of ratification, treaties in the United Kingdom are self-executing ... From the moment the treaty becomes binding *internationally*, the British Government is in a position to give effect to it *internally*. The treaty is, in effect, self-executing by virtue of prior legislative action, or by reason of the fact that legislation adequate for its internal enforcement was already in existence at the time of the ratification of the treaty." The use of the term "self-executing" in this sense is confusing since in such cases it is the legislation and not the treaty which is applied directly.

16. Dominicé, *La Convention européenne*, 12.

17. Luzius Wildhaber, *Treaty-Making Power and Constitution* (Basel und Stuttgart: Helbing & Lichtenhahn, 1971), pp. 226–227 [footnotes omitted].

18. Examples of conflicting determinations by national courts of the self-executing nature of provisions of ILO conventions are provided in chapter 6, infra. Conflicting decisions on the self-executing nature of provisions of the European Convention on Human Rights are referred to in numerous studies of the domestic application of that convention. See also Note, Stefan A. Riesenfeld, *The Doctrine of Self-Executing Treaties and GATT: A Notable German Judgment*, 65 Am. J. Int'l L. 548 (1971), for examples of differing opinions by German and U.S. courts on the self-executing nature of Article III of GATT.

19. International law does, of course, prevail over municipal law within the international legal system. See references n.2 supra.

20. de Visscher, *Les tendances internationales*, 563 et seq. Examples of states which have adopted the various solutions are given in chapter 4, infra.

CHAPTER 4

The System of Automatic Incorporation in Selected States

An introduction to the constitutional systems of the countries selected for this case study is essential to an understanding of the problems referred to in subsequent chapters concerning the application of ILO conventions in such countries. The general outline of the constitutional systems of automatic incorporation of the United States, Argentina, Mexico, France, the Netherlands, Switzerland, and Italy will be provided in this chapter. Later chapters will consider the problems of the self-executing nature of treaty provisions and the rank of treaty provisions in those countries.

1. Constitutional Provisions for Automatic Incorporation

1.1. *The United States, Argentina, and Mexico (Federal States with Similar Constitutional Provisions)*

The United States, Argentina, and Mexico have substantially similar constitutional provisions on the incorporation of treaties in national law. Article VI(2) of the United States Constitution, providing that treaties "shall be the supreme Law of the Land," was the first of the provisions adopted and served as a model for the provisions in the Argentine and Mexican Constitutions.[1] Argentina and Mexico, like the United States, are federal states. Article VI(2) of the U.S. Constitution (referred to as the "Supremacy Clause") provides for the supremacy of the federal constitution, federal laws, and treaties over state constitutions and laws. Its importance in relation to federalism may account for its influence on the adoption of similar provisions in the two "civil law" countries of Argentina and Mexico. The similarities between the various provisions are evident. The respective provisions state:

> *United States Constitution, Article VI(2) (1787)*
> "This Constitution, and the Laws of the United States which shall be made in Pursuance thereof; and all Treaties made, or which shall be made under the Authority of the United States, shall be the supreme

> Law of the Land; and the Judges in every State shall be bound thereby, any Thing in the Constitution or laws of any State to the Contrary notwithstanding."[2]
>
> *Argentine Constitution, Article 31 (1975)*
> "The Constitution, the laws of the Nation enacted by the Congress in pursuance thereof, and treaties with foreign powers are the supreme law of the Nation; and the authorities in every Province are bound thereby, notwithstanding any provision to the contrary which the provincial laws or constitutions may contain ..."[3]
>
> *Mexican Constitution, Article 133 (1917) (amended 1934)*
> "The Constitution, the laws of the Congress of the Union that emanate therefrom and all treaties that have been made and shall be made in accordance therewith by the President of the Republic, with the approval of the Senate, shall be the supreme law of the whole Union. The judges of each State shall conform to the said Constitution, the laws, and treaties, in spite of any contradictory provisions that may appear in the constitutions or laws of the States."[4]

In these three states the executive must obtain the approval of the federal legislature in order to ratify treaties (the Senate in the United States and Mexico, both Houses of Congress in Argentina).[5] In each of the countries the Constitution provides that treaties shall prevail over state or provincial laws or constitutions. In none of them does the constitutional provision state whether treaties prevail over federal legislation. In all of them in the event of such a conflict the norm which is later in time, whether incorporated in a treaty or federal law, prevails over the earlier provisions.[6] The courts in such cases make considerable efforts by interpretation to reconcile apparently conflicting treaties and laws. In Mexico, but not in Argentina and the United States, the Constitution states that treaties are the supreme law of the land *only* when made in accordance with the Constitution. All three countries have a system of judicial review whereby the courts determine the application of the appropriate constitutional provision, treaty provision or federal law in the event of a conflict.[7]

The system of automatic incorporation was not adopted in the U.S. because of a theoretical preference for monism over dualism, but because of historical experience under the Articles of Confederation.[8] The important doctrinal discussions concerning the theories of monism and dualism developed long after the U.S. Constitution was adopted and U.S. legal literature rarely treats the problem of incorporation of treaty provisions from this theoretical point of view. Following the American Declaration of Independence from England and prior to the adoption of the Constitution of 1787, the thirteen American colonies were loosely united under the Articles of Confederation. Difficulties developed during this period concerning the method of negotiating and approving treaties as well as actions by the colonies negating by legislation or judicial decision the application of treaties entered into by the Congress under the Articles of Confederation. The primary purpose of the inclusion of Article VI(2) in the Constitution, therefore, was to ensure the supremacy of federal law (including treaties) over state law, but it contained no explicit provision relating to the relative supremacy of treaties and federal legislation. Erades and Gould have pointed out that this problem was not in the forefront of the minds of the drafters of the U.S. Constitution.[9]

One aspect of U.S. law relating to treaties is not yet clearly settled. Legal commentators, reflecting the lack of a clear determination by the courts, differ on whether proclamation of a treaty by the President is essential for the treaty to become binding internally in the U.S. Henkin writes "For domestic purposes the treaty becomes law only upon proclamation by the President" citing *Haver* v. *Yaker*.[10] Wildhaber states that proclamation is not essential to the status of the treaty in U.S. law; ratification and entry into force internationally are sufficient.[11] Erades and Gould, while pointing out the divergent opinions on the need for proclamation for treaties to become binding U.S. law, are of the opinion that only ratification and international entry into force are necessary.[12]

Treaties may be directly applied by courts in Argentina in accordance with Article 31 of the Argentine Constitution.[13] A dissimilarity between Article VI(2) of the U.S. Constitution and Article 31 of the Argentine Constitution should be noted. The latter provides that "treaties *with foreign powers*" [italics added] are the supreme law of the land. No limitation similar to the above italicized portion of Article 31 exists in the U.S. constitutional provision. This provision has resulted in a question being raised as to whether ILO conventions should be considered "treaties with foreign powers" and thus the supreme law of the land or whether they are rather commitments to an international organization and thus are not included in the scope of the "Supremacy Clause." The Argentine Supreme Court has never clearly decided the question.[14]

The main elements of Article 133 of the Mexican Constitution of 1917 were first incorporated in the Mexican Constitution of 1857.[15] Article 133 has an important variation from Article VI(2) of the United States Constitution on which it was modeled. In a 1934 constitutional reform the phrase italicized below was added to the text:

> The Constitution, the laws of the Congress of the Union that emanate therefrom, and all treaties that have been made and shall be made *in accordance therewith* by the President of the Republic, with the approval of the Senate, shall be the Supreme Law of the whole union. [italics added]

This addition, which is not present in the U.S. constitutional provision, was expressly added to establish the supremacy of the Constitution over a treaty in case of conflict.[16]

Article 133, like the comparable U.S. and Argentine provisions, asserts that treaties have priority over state constitutions or laws but includes no provision relating to the relative priority of treaties and federal law.

1.2. *France*

A number of provisions of the French Constitution of 1958 relate to treaties.[17] The President negotiates and ratifies treaties.[18] Most treaties require legislative consent before they are ratified.[19] If a treaty is considered to be unconstitutional by the Constitutional Council it may be ratified only after amendment of the Constitution.[20] Automatic incorporation of treaty provisions is provided for by Article 55:

> Article 55. Treaties or agreements duly ratified or approved shall, upon their publication, have an authority superior to that of laws, subject, for each agreement or treaty, to its application by the other party.[21]

The French constitutional provisions thus differ to a considerable degree from those of Argentina, Mexico and the United States. As France is a unitary state there is no provision relating to the primacy of federal law and Article 55 specifically provides that treaties (upon publication and subject to reciprocity) have an authority superior to laws.[22] Thus, the French Constitution gives a higher rank to treaties than the other three Constitutions. As Lardy has pointed out, however,

> efforts undertaken in this country to achieve the effective primacy of international law still today face resistance which is difficult to overcome. As we shall see, the domestic judge, believing himself to be the servant of French law, hesitates to control the conformity of that law in relation to a superior norm—whether international or constitutional—because he believes that to do so would be beyond his competence and violate the principle of separation of powers. The law is regarded as the expression of the popular will and appears to the French judge to have supreme validity by virtue of a long democratic tradition; it is not surprising that this judge, despite the constitutional provision favorable to international law, still hesitates to apply the norms of this law in preference to internal law.[23]

The notion of judicial review thus differs from that of the other three countries discussed previously. Although the French Constitution in principle embodies the monist theory, since there is no effective judicial review, it falls within the second category of de Visscher's classification of automatic incorporation states mentioned previously. It appears that it is "French legal practice in most cases to incorporate the provisions of a Convention by means of a formal amendment of internal law."[24]

Article 55 of the French Constitution provides that treaty provisions are superior to other laws, subject to their application by the other party to the treaty. Valticos has pointed out that this provision relates to contractual treaties and, therefore, does not play any role with regard to "traités-lois" such as ILO conventions, which "are not agreements between states giving rise to reciprocal commitments and thus belonging strictly to the states who are parties, but instruments of an institutional character having a common aim and whose obligations are governed by the constitution of this organization."[25]

1.3. *The Netherlands*

The Netherlands Constitution accords a greater supremacy to treaties than any other constitutional system.[26] It expressly recognizes the supremacy of self-executing treaties over national legislation (whether adopted earlier or later than the treaty) but much more strikingly, it permits treaties to derogate from the Constitution in certain instances.

The relevant provisions of the Constitution are as follows:[27]

> Article 63. If the development of the international legal order requires this, the contents of an agreement may deviate from certain provisions of the Constitution. In such cases only explicit approval can be given; the Chambers of the States-General shall not approve a Bill to that effect but with a two-thirds majority of the votes cast ...
>
> Article 65. The provisions of agreements the contents of which may be binding on anyone[28] shall have this binding effect as from the time of publication. Rules with regard to the publication of agreements shall be laid down by law.
>
> Article 66. Legal regulations in force within the Kingdom shall not apply if this application should be incompatible with provisions—binding on anyone—of agreements entered into either before or after the enactment of the regulations.

Other articles provide that treaties shall be ratified by the King with the approval, explicit or implicit, of the States-General.[29]

While similar to the French constitutional provisions in recognizing the supremacy of treaties over legislation, the Netherlands constitutional provisions differ in four important respects from the French provisions:

(1) in providing that treaties may, on occasion, derogate from the Constitution;
(2) in expressly limiting the automatic incorporation and hierarchy of treaties to self-executing treaties only;[30]
(3) in making it clear that legal regulations in conflict with treaty provisions need not be applied by the courts;
(4) in not including the limitation of reciprocity contained in the French provisions.

2. Automatic Incorporation Without Express Constitutional Provisions

2.1. *Switzerland*

The Swiss system for the incorporation of treaty provisions in national law differs from that of the other countries described above since there is no constitutional provision providing for automatic incorporation of treaties.[31] It is, nevertheless, settled doctrine and practice that validly concluded treaties have internal validity in Switzerland immediately upon promulgation by the executive authority.[32] Treaties are ratified in the name of the Swiss Confederation by the Federal Council after approval of ratification by both divisions (councils) of the Federal Assembly.[33] In certain instances treaties are subject to acceptance or rejection by referendum of the people of Switzerland.[34]

2.2. *Italy (Quasi-Automatic Incorporation)*

In theory, Italy has adopted the dualist system for incorporation of treaties.[35] The Italian Constitution has no provision relating to the incorporation of treaties in national law and it is settled doctrine that ratification and international entry into force of a treaty alone do not make the treaty provisions national law.[36] In practice, however, the Italian system functions as other systems for the automatic incorporation of treaties. This results from the practice in Italy of attaching "an order of execution" (also referred to as "implementing order") to the act of the legislature authorizing the President to ratify treaties. This order of execution provides that full and entire effect is given to the provisions of the treaty. From a formal point of view the order of execution is separate from the law authorizing ratification and it is not mentioned in the Italian Constitution. In practice, it is always attached to the law authorizing ratification and the practical result is that upon ratification and international entry into force the order of execution ensures that the treaty becomes national law.[37] The Italian system thus conforms to the system of "global transformation" or "quasi-automatic incorporation" referred to in chapter 3.

3. Conclusion

Six of the seven countries included in this case study (Argentina, France, Mexico, the Netherlands, Switzerland and the United States) have adopted the system of automatic incorporation and Italy has adopted a quasi-automatic incorporation system considered (for the purposes of this study) to be an automatic incorporation state. In five of the countries (Argentina, France, Mexico, the Netherlands and the United States) automatic incorporation results from a constitutional provision. In Italy and Switzerland, the Constitution has no provision concerning the status of ratified treaties in national law. In Italy, incorporation results from an "order of execution" adopted at the time of the legislative act approving ratification of the treaty, and, in Switzerland, the courts have held that ratified treaties are automatically incorporated in national law.

The system of automatic incorporation may thus be adopted in various countries by different constitutional techniques. The method used to adopt the system does not seem to create significant differences in the application of conventions. Questions of judicial review, separation of powers and judicial receptivity to international law have, however, resulted in significant variations in application of conventions in the states examined in this study.

NOTES

1. The United States Constitution (including Article VI(2)) was adopted in 1787. The similar provision of the Argentine Constitution (Article 31 of the Constitution of 1975) was first included in the Constitution of 1853. The essential elements of the similar provision of the Mexican Constitution (Article 133 of the Constitution of 1917) were first included in the Constitution of 1857. A substantive addition to Article 133 in 1934 provided that treaties are the supreme law of the land only if made in accordance with the Constitution. "Indiscutiblemente el origen del artículo 133 Constitucional debe buscarse en el párrafo 2 del artículo VI de la Constitución de los Estados Unidos de Norteamérica. Nuestro artículo 133 Constitucional no solamente está inspirado en la Constitución Norteamericana, sino que está copiada de ella. La Constitución Argentina, en idéntica forma que la Mexicana, tomó de la Norteamericana esa importantisima parte del Artículo VI y la incluyó dentro de su artículado." Mauricio Valdés Villareal, *Relaciones entre El Derecho Interno y El Derecho Internacional* (México: Tesis, Universidad Nacional de México, Facultad de Derecho y Ciencias Sociales, 1944), p. 42. See also Enrique Paez Stille, *Interpretación del Artículo 133 de la Constitución* (México: Tesis, Universidad Nacional de México, 1945), pp. 17–23.

2. Amos J. Peaslee, *Constitutions of Nations* (The Hague: Nijhoff, rev. 3rd ed. 1970), vol. IV, p. 1204.

3. Ibid., vol. IV, p. 12.

4. Ibid., vol. IV, p. 951.

5. Article II(2), United States Constitution (1787); Article 67, Argentine Constitution (1975); Article 33, Mexican Constitution (1917).

6. See chapter 8, infra.

7. See Keith Rosenn, *Judicial Review in Latin America*, 35 Ohio St. L. J. 785 (1974).

8. On incorporation of treaty provisions in U.S. law see Louis Henkin, *Foreign Affairs and the Constitution* (Mineola, New York: The Foundation Press, Inc, 1972), chapter V; L. Erades and Wesley L. Gould, *The Relation Between International Law and Municipal Law in the Netherlands and in the United States* (Leiden: Sijthoff, 1961); Lawrence Preuss, *The Execution of Treaty Obligations Through Internal Law—System of the United States and Some Other Countries*, 45 Proc., Am. Soc. Int'l L. 82 (1951); Marjorie Whiteman, ed., *Digest of International Law*, vol. 14, (Washington, D.C.: Government Printing Office, 1970), chapter XLII, sections 27–31, pp. 282–331.

9. "However certain their intentions in regard to states and treaties, just what the provisions concerning the three forms of the 'supreme Law of the Land' happened to mean in the treaty-federal statute relationship was not clear to the Founding Fathers. Indeed to many who expressed opinions about the new Constitution this did not appear to be a problem. Treaties were supposed to deal with external affairs and statutes with internal affairs ... But aside from a rather commonly held view that treaties must conform to the Constitution, there was no certainty whether even in commercial matters a treaty could override an earlier conflicting federal statute without the aid of an Act of Congress ... The records of the Federal Convention are of no help in ascertaining what the relationship between treaties and statutes was intended to be ..." Erades and Gould, *Relation Between International Law and Municipal Law*, p. 373.

10. 9 Wall. 32 (1829). Henkin, *Foreign Affairs*, p. 131. In the case of Haver v. Yaker, Justice Davis for the Court, wrote: "As the individual citizen, on whose rights or property it [the treaty] operates has no means of knowing anything of it while before the Senate, it would be wrong in principle to hold him bound by it, as the law of the land, until it was ratified and proclaimed." 9 Wall. 32, 55. See also Whiteman, *Digest of International Law*, vol. 14, sections 13–14, pp. 113–122.

11. Luzius Wildhaber, *Treaty-Making Power and Constitution* (Basel und Stuttgart: Helbing & Lichtenhahn, 1971), p. 194; Henry Reiff, *The Proclaiming of Treaties in the United States*, 30 Am. J. Int'l L. 63 (1936); Roy v. United States and the Ogallala Tribe of Sioux Indians, 45 Ct. Cl. 117, 181 (1910).

12. See Erades and Gould, *Relation Between International Law and Municipal Law*, pp. 305–307, for an extensive discussion of this issue.

13. See, in general, regarding Argentine constitutional law: German J. Bidart Campos, *Manual de Derecho Constitucional Argentino* (Buenos Aires: Ediar, 1974), *El Derecho Constitucional del Poder*, 2 vols. (Buenos Aires: Ediar, 1967), *Derecho Constitucional*, 2 vols. (Buenos Aires: Ediar, 1964–66); Salvador Maria Lozada, *Derecho Constitucional Argentino Segun El Metodo de Casos* (Buenos Aires: Abeldo-Perrot, 1972), *Instituciones de Derecho Publico* (Cordoba, Argentina: Editions Macchi, 1966).

14. See discussion of Haras "Los Cardos" case, chapter 6, sec. 2.1, infra. A somewhat similar provision was included in the French Constitution of 1946 but not in the 1958 Constitution. Article 26 of the 1946 Constitution provided: "Les traités *diplomatiques* régulièrement ratifiés et publiés ont force de loi ..." See Nicolas Valticos, *Conventions internationales du travail et droit interne*, 44 R.C.D.I.P. 251 (1955), for a discussion of the implications of the 1946 Constitution as regards ILO conventions.

15. For information concerning the constitutional system of Mexico see Ignacio Burgoa, *Derecho Constitucional Mexicano* (México: Porrua, 1973); Felipe Tena Ramírez, *Derecho Constitucional Mexicano* (México: Porrua, 11th ed. 1972); Paez Stille, *Interpretación del Artículo 133*; Valdés Villareal, *Relaciones entre El Derecho Interno.*

16. *Diario de los Debates de la Camara de Senadores del Congreso de los Estados Unidos Mexicanos*, de 3 de octubre 1933; Valdés Villareal, *Relaciones entre El Derecho Interno*, pp. 43–45.

17. For detailed information concerning the French Constitution and treaties see Pierre Lardy, *La force obligatoire du droit international en droit interne* (Paris: R. Pichon et R. Durand—Auzias, 1966), pp. 97–163 and Jean Morellet, *The Influence of International Labour Conventions on French Legislation*, 101 I.L.R. 331 (1970).

18. Article 52. Peaslee, *Constitutions of Nations*, vol. III, p. 322.

19. "Article 53. Peace treaties, commercial treaties, treaties or agreements relative to international organization, those that imply a commitment for the finances of the State, those that modify provisions of a legislative nature, those relative to the status of persons, those that call for the cession, exchange or addition of territory may be ratified or approved only by a law ..." Ibid.

20. Article 54. Ibid., p. 323.

21. Ibid. The essential aspects of this article were contained in Article 26 of the Constitution of 1946. Prior to 1946 there was no constitutional provision regarding international treaties. The relationship of treaties and national law had been determined by judicial decision prior to that time; the courts applied the treaty if it was later in time than a conflicting law and divided over whether the treaty should be applied if the conflicting law was later in time. Lardy, *La force obligatoire*, p. 107.

22. Prior to the Constitution of 1958 promulgation was required to give the treaty internal effect in France. This requirement was dropped in the 1958 Constitution. For information concerning promulgation and publication in French law see Lardy, *La force obligatoire*, pp. 123–126.

23. Ibid., p. 97 [translation]. Lardy emphasizes the importance of the monist theories of Georges Scelle on the development of the French constitutional system for the incorporation of treaties in national law. Ibid., p. 107.

24. Morellet, *Influence of International Labour Conventions*, 333.

25. Nicolas Valticos, *Les conventions internationales du travail devant le juge français*, 53 R.C.D.I.P. 41, 46–47 (1964).

26. See, inter alia, Erades and Gould, *Relation Between International Law and Municipal Law*; Lardy, *La force obligatoire*, pp. 163–179; Jonkheer H. F. van Panhuys, *The Netherlands Constitution and International Law—A Decade of Experience*, 58 Am. J. Int'l L. 88 (1964); "Rapport néerlandais" in *Deuxième colloque international de droit européenne* (Zwolle: N.V. Uitgeversmaatschappij W. E. J. Tjeenk Willink, 1966); Menno J. van Emde Boas, *The Impact of the European Convention of Human Rights and Fundamental Freedoms on the Legal Order of the Netherlands*, 13 Neth. Int'l L. Rev. 337 (1966) and 14 Neth. Int'l L. Rev. 1 (1967). The information concerning the Netherlands in this study is taken solely from sources available in English and French.

27. Peaslee, *Constitutions of Nations*, vol. III, p. 660.

28. The words "the contents of which may be binding on anyone" in Articles 65 and 66 were included to designate that only self-executing treaties would have binding effect and prevail over other legal regulations. van Panhuys, *Netherlands Constitution and International Law*, 100.

29. Articles 60 and 61.

30. This may be a case in which Dominicé's distinction between validity and direct

application (see chapter 3) does not apply since the Netherlands Constitution expressly limits the validity of treaties in national law to self-executing treaties only.

31. For information concerning the incorporation of treaty provisions in Swiss law see Lardy, *La force obligatoire*, pp. 182–244; William J. Rice, *The Position of International Treaties in Swiss Law*, 46 Am. J. Int'l L. 641 (1952); Jacques Secretan, *Swiss Constitutional Problems and the International Labour Organisation*, 56 I.L.R. 1 (1947); Alexandre Berenstein, *The Influence of International Labour Conventions on Swiss Legislation*, 77 I.L.R. 1 (1958); Michel Waelbroeck, *L'effêt direct de l'accord rélatif aux échanges commerciaux de 22 juillet 1972, entre la Communauté Economique Européenne et la Confêderation Suisse*, 29 A.S.D.I. 113 (1973); Lucius Caflisch, ed., *Les rapports entre le droit international et les ordres juridiques nationaux, Pratique Suisse*, 26 A.S.D.I. 91 (1969–70) and 30 A.S.D.I. 110 (1974); Luzius Wildhaber, *Bemerkungen zum Fall Schubert betrefend das Verhältnis von Völkerrecht und Landesrecht*, 30 A.S.D.I. 195 (1974); Georges Malinverni, *L'Application de la Convention européenne des droits de l'homme en Suisse*, Mémoires publiés par la Faculté de Droit de Genève, Quinzième Journée Juridique (1977); Wildhaber, *Treaty-Making Power*, p. 202; Paul Guggenheim, *Traité de droit international public* (Genève: Georg, 2d ed. 1967), vol. I, pp. 73–74.

32. Message of the Swiss Federal Assembly of 10 December 1920 concerning the resolutions of the First Session of the International Labour Conference, Feuille fédérale, vol. V, No. 51, 15 décembre 1920, 457: "In Switzerland, the treaty takes immediate effect from the act of promulgation, which gives the treaty the status of a legislative act and incorporates its content as an integral part of Federal law without the necessity of any other expression of legislative will. The Federal Assembly is, therefore, competent to create Federal law by means of international agreements ... even on a subject on which the Confederation has no express power to legislate." Reprinted in English in Secretan, *Swiss Constitutional Problems*, 4. See also Lardy, *La force obligatoire*, p. 197. Publication of treaties in the *Recueil Officiel* is required but is simply a means of making the treaty known rather than a constitutive element of its force in Swiss law (Lardy, ibid., p. 196).

33. See Articles 8, 9, 10, 89 and 102 of the Federal Constitution of the Swiss Confederation, Peaslee, *Constitutions of Nations*, vol. III, p. 932 et seq.

34. This provision of the Swiss Constitution (Article 89), which was amended in 1977, is of no relevance in this study since ILO conventions do not fall within the class of treaties subject to referendum.

35. "Rapport italien" in *Deuxième colloque*, op. cit., p. 115. Preuss, *Execution of Treaty Obligations*; Angelo P. Sereni, *The Italian Conception of International Law* (New York: Columbia University Press, 1943); Marino Offeddu, *Le Convenzioni Internazionali del Lavoro e l'Ordinamento Giuridico Italiano* (Padova: Cedam, 1973); Luigi Condorelli and Georgio Gaja, ed., *Relationship Between Municipal Law and International Law, Judicial Decisions*, Italian Yearbook of International Law 365 (1976).

36. The suggestion has been made that international treaties should prevail over national laws in view of Article 10(1) of the Italian Constitution of 1943 (relating specifically only to customary international law) which provides that "Italy's legal system conforms with the generally recognized principles of international law." Preuss, *Execution of Treaty Obligations*, 91, n.81.

37. "Rapport italien" in *Deuxième colloque*, op. cit., pp. 115–117.

CHAPTER 5

The Concept of Self-Executing Treaty Provisions

The ILO Committee of Experts has emphasized that only self-executing convention provisions are directly applied in automatic incorporation states. Non-self-executing provisions require implementing legislation and are not applied by courts or administrators unless such legislation has been adopted. The determination of whether implementing legislation is required is important to the ILO supervisory bodies who are charged with ascertaining whether conventions are effectively applied in national law. It is also important to national administrative agencies but particularly to individuals (the ultimate beneficiaries of ILO conventions) since individuals may not invoke convention provisions in automatic incorporation states if they are non-self-executing and implementing legislation has not been adopted.

Whether a treaty provision is or is not self-executing within a particular national legal system is a matter to be decided under the national law of that country and the criteria for making such a determination may differ in various countries. Succeeding chapters will treat in detail the specific problems which have arisen regarding the self-executing nature of provisions of ILO conventions. Before considering those problems, however, it is useful to examine more generally the criteria courts and legal scholars in the countries selected for this case study have used in determining whether any treaty provision is self-executing.

The first section of this chapter is devoted to a survey of the criteria for self-executing treaties in United States law. The second section will consider more briefly the concept of self-executing treaty provisions in the other countries considered in this case study. A study of the concept of self-executing treaty provisions in the United States cast considerable light on the problems the ILO Committees have perceived in this regard. The term "self-executing" to describe treaty provisions originated in United States constitutional law and its meaning has been considered on many occasions by U.S. courts and legal scholars—more extensively, it appears, than in any other legal system. Other countries have also adopted the term "self-executing"—or its direct translation—to describe treaty provisions which are directly applied in their law. It seems appropriate, therefore, to consider at greater length the concept of self-executing treaty provisions in the United States, the country where the concept originated.

1. The Doctrine of Self-Executing Treaty Provisions in the Law of the United States

1.1. *Origin of the Doctrine*[1]

Article VI(2) of the United States Constitution provides that:

> ... all Treaties made, or which shall be made, under the Authority of the United States, shall be the supreme Law of the Land; and the Judges in every State shall be bound thereby, any Thing in the Constitution or Laws of any State to the Contrary notwithstanding.

As early as 1829, however, the U.S. Supreme Court decided in the case of *Foster* v. *Neilson*[2] that not all ratified treaties create, immediately upon ratification, rights and obligations which will be enforced by the U.S. courts. Only those treaties which do not require legislative action, subsequently referred to as self-executing treaties, will be enforced by the courts. Thus, the doctrine of self-executing treaty provisions is a judicial interpretation of Article VI(2) of the Constitution. In oft-quoted words, commonly cited as the origin of the doctrine of self-executing treaties in U.S. constitutional law, Chief Justice John Marshall, delivering the opinion for the Court, wrote:

> A treaty is in its nature a contract between two nations, not a legislative act. It does not generally effect, of itself, the object to be accomplished, especially so far as its operation is infra-territorial; but is carried into execution by the sovereign power of the respective parties to the instrument.
>
> In the United States a different principle is established. Our Constitution declares a treaty to be the law of the land. It is, consequently to be regarded in the courts of justice, as equivalent to an act of the legislature, whenever it operates of itself without the aid of any legislative provision. But when the terms of the stipulation import a contract, when either of the parties engages to perform a particular act, the treaty addresses itself to the political, not the judicial department; and the legislature must execute the contract before it can become a rule for the Court.[3]

In applying this rule in *Foster* v. *Neilson* the Supreme Court held that a provision of the Florida Purchase Treaty of 1819 with Spain providing that grants of land in the ceded territories "shall be ratified and confirmed to the persons in possession of the lands" was non-self-executing because the words "shall be ratified" implied futurity and were thus in the form of a contract. The plaintiff in *Foster* v. *Neilson* had sought to recover a tract of land in Louisiana, relying in part on the Florida Purchase Treaty. The Court's holding that the relevant provision of the treaty was non-self-executing meant that his claim could not be upheld in the absence of congressional action. Marshall's opinion has been criticized. Quincy Wright has pointed out that "if all treaty provisions are in the nature of a contract it is difficult to see how treaty provisions which import a contract can be distinguished from those 'equivalent to an act of the legislature'."[4] In reference to the above quotation from Chief Justice Marshall's opinion, Schachter has commented:

> It is, however, evident that this statement does not in itself provide a workable test to determine whether a provision in a treaty requires legislative action. In almost all treaties one of the "parties engages to perform a particular act" but in many of these treaties the particular acts can be performed by judicial or administrative officers without the aid of legislative action.[5]

The Court itself implicitly overruled its earlier decision four years later in *United States* v. *Percheman.*[6] Chief Justice Marshall, again writing the opinion for the Court, stated, upon examining the Spanish text of the Treaty:

> Although the words "shall be ratified and confirmed" are properly the words of contract, stipulating for some future legislative act, they are not necessarily so. They may import that they "shall be ratified and confirmed" by force of the instrument itself. When we observe that in the counter part of the same treaty [Spanish text] ... they are used in this sense, we think the construction proper, if not unavoidable.[7]

Thus confusion lay at the very origin of the doctrine in U.S. law and subsequent cases have led to further confusion. Reiff has written that "theoretically, a self-executing and an executory provision should be readily distinguishable. In practice it is difficult. John Marshall found it so and the courts since then have had similar experiences."[8]

1.2. *Definition of Self-Executing Treaty Provisions*

In attempting to define self-executing treaty provisions, legal scholars in the United States have stated that a self-executing provision of a treaty is one which the courts will apply directly and a non-self-executing provision is one which requires implementing legislation and which the courts will, therefore, not apply directly.[9] It is evident that this definition is a *petitio principii*. It begs the question since it provides no guidance as to which treaty provisions require implementing legislation and which do not. Some provisions of treaties state unequivocally that implementing legislation should be adopted; in such cases, they are clearly non-self-executing. But the type of situation which arose in the *Foster* v. *Neilson* and the *Percheman* cases is not uncommon. In those cases the U.S. Supreme Court found a treaty provision so unclear that on one occasion it held that it required implementing legislation and on another occasion that the same language did not so require. In an effort to clarify the self-executing nature of treaty provisions, U.S. courts and scholars have referred to three relevant criteria: (1) the intention of the parties, (2) the precision and detail of the language employed, and (3) whether the subject matter relates to powers belonging to the legislative or executive branches rather than to the judicial branch.[10] These criteria will be considered below.

1.3. *Criteria for Determination*

1.3.1. *Intention of the Parties*

According to the *Restatement of Foreign Relations Law of the United States* a treaty "that manifests an intention that it shall become effective as domestic law of the United States at the time it becomes binding on the United States ... is self-executing in that it is effective as domestic law of the United States."[11] This authoritative interpretation of American law thus emphasizes the intention of the parties as a primary criterion for determining whether a provision is self-executing.[12]

In the important case of *Sei Fujii* v. *California*, Judge Gibson, delivering the opinion for the California Supreme Court and citing a number of U.S. Supreme Court cases, wrote that "in order for a treaty provision to be operative without the aid of implementing legislation and to have the force and effect of a statute, it must appear that the framers of the treaty intended to prescribe a rule that, standing alone, would be enforceable in the courts."[13] The search for intention begins with the language of the treaty. "When inquiring into the 'intention' of the treaty's drafters, a court will, of course, look carefully at the text of the agreement. It will consider the verbs used—'does hereby' versus 'shall undertake' as well as other textual indications."[14]

A number of problems are apparent in using intention as a criterion for determining the self-executing nature of a treaty provision. The language of the treaty may be inconclusive. One U.S. legal commentator has pointed out that even language of futurity does not necessarily indicate that the intention of the parties is that the provision should be non-self-executing:

> Some courts have misinterpreted the future language text, holding that an agreement containing any language of future action cannot be self-executing. For instance, contract language necessarily speaks of future action. But only reference to future action by the political branches should cause an agreement to be deemed non-self-executing. Language directed toward the future activity of individuals is not necessarily used with the intent that the agreement be non-self-executing. As an illustration, an international agreement stating that the "citizens of [each of] the [signatory countries] shall have the liberty to ... travel ... in the territories of the other" is self-executing. Even though future language is used, it calls for no action by the political branches and will prescribe a rule enforceable in domestic courts, if it meets any other applicable language tests.[15]

Treaty provisions expressing prohibitions (negative stipulations) would seem to be self-executing but it has also been suggested that even in such cases the prohibition may be too non-specific to be enforced by the courts and may thus not indicate an intention that the provision should be self-executing.[16]

Finally, as both Schachter and Riesenfeld have pointed out, it is difficult to determine whether the parties to a multilateral agreement intended a particular provision to be self-executing or not since the question may be irrelevant for State Parties using the system of legislative incorporation of treaty provisions.[17] Riesenfeld has written: "Although the doctrine looking to the intent of the parties is widely supported by practice and theory, it seems much more reasonable to consider the self-executing or executory nature of international conventions a matter depending primarily upon the constitutional law of each nation rather than upon a dubious intent of the parties."[18]

1.3.2. *Precision and Detail of Language*

U.S. courts and commentators have also referred to the degree of precision and detail of the language employed in the treaty as a criterion for determining the self-executing nature of a provision. This criterion is closely related to that of the intention of the parties, since it is frequently said that lack of precision and detail demonstrate that the parties did not intend the provision to be self-executing.

This criterion was important in the above-mentioned case of *Sei Fujii* v. *California*,[19] whose notoriety contributed to spreading knowledge of the U.S. doctrine of self-executing treaties. The California Supreme Court held, in this case, that the California Alien Land Law prohibiting aliens ineligible for citizenship from owning land in California was contrary to the "equal protection" clause of the 14th Amendment of the U.S. Constitution, while refusing to hold, as a lower court had, that the Law violated Articles 55 and 56 of the U.N. Charter ratified by the U.S. The Court held that Articles 55 and 56 of the Charter were not self-executing because, inter alia, these provisions were not sufficiently precise and detailed.

Article 55 of the Charter provides that "the United Nations shall promote ... universal respect for, and observance of human rights and fundamental freedoms for all without distinction as to race, sex, language or religion." Article 56 states that "all members pledge themselves to take joint and separate action in cooperation with the Organization for the achievement of the purposes set forth in Article 55." The Court held that these provisions were too general to be applied by a court. Chief Justice Gibson, delivering the opinion for the Court, wrote:

> The provisions in the Charter pledging cooperation in promoting observance of fundamental freedoms lack the mandatory quality and definiteness which would indicate an intent to create justiciable rights in private persons immediately upon ratification. Instead, they are framed as a promise of future action by the member nations ...
>
> In other instances treaty provisions were enforced without implementing legislation where they prescribed in detail the rules governing rights and obligations of individuals or specifically provided that citizens of one nation shall have the same rights while in the other country as are enjoyed by that country's own citizens.[20]

This criterion for determining the self-executing nature of a treaty provision has also been criticized. In an article written before the California Supreme Court decision but after the lower court decision, Schachter pointed out that Article 56 of the U.N. Charter is no more vague than certain provisions of the U.S. Constitution such as the "equal protection" clause of the 14th Amendment (applied in the *Sei Fujii* case) or the provisions of some statutes:[21]

> These concepts [contained in Articles 55 and 56 of the U.N. Charter] ... do have specific content based on the Charter itself and on precedent and practice; the important and recognized rights and freedoms are no vaguer than any number of well-known constitutional and statutory expressions which have been left to courts to apply ... It cannot be said that a greater degree of precision is required in a treaty provision than in an act of Congress ...[22]

In 1974 the Ninth U.S. Circuit Court of Appeals in *People of Saipan* v. *U.S. Department of Interior* held a provision of the Trust Agreement for the Trust Territory of the Pacific Islands self-executing despite the generality of its language.[23] Judge Goodwin, delivering the opinion for the Court, stated:

> Admittedly, the substantive rights guaranteed through the Trusteeship Agreement are not precisely defined. However, we do not believe that the agreement is too vague for judicial enforcement. Its language is no more general than such terms as "due process of law," "seaworthiness," "equal protection of the law," "good faith" or "restraint of trade" which courts interpret every day.[24]

It is thus apparent that U.S. courts and scholars have differed widely on the question of the precision and detail of language necessary in order to characterize a treaty provision as self-executing.

1.3.3. *Subject Matter as Criterion—Separation of Powers Question*

Regardless of the intent of the parties and the precision and detail of the language employed—both of which may lead to the view that a treaty provision in question is self-executing—the courts of the United States may refuse to consider it as self-executing, and thus refuse to apply it without implementing legislation, if it concerns a subject matter within the constitutionally enumerated powers of other branches of the government. This fact is of capital importance and introduces a further element of complexity into the determination of the self-executing nature of treaty provisions. According to the *Restatement*, "a treaty cannot be self-executing ... to the extent that it involves governmental action that under the Constitution can only be taken by Congress."[25] The usual examples concern the appropriation of money and the laying down of criminal sanctions. In *Turner* v. *American Baptist Missionary Union*, the Circuit Court (D. Mich.) held:

> A treaty under the Federal Constitution is declared to be the supreme law of the land. This unquestionably applies to all treaties, where the treaty-making power, without the aid of Congress, can carry it into effect. It is not, however, and cannot be the supreme law of the land, where the concurrence of Congress is necessary to give it effect. Until this power is exercised, as where the appropriation of money is required, the treaty is not perfect. It is not operative, in the sense of the Constitution, *as money cannot be appropriated by the treaty-making power*. This results from the limitations of our government.[26] [italics added]

In the case of *The Over the Top*, Judge Thomas, delivering the opinion for the federal District Court in Connecticut, wrote:

> The learned judge speaks of the treaty as self-executing. The significance of the phrase in this connection is somewhat obscure. As a treaty, there was no need of Congressional legislation to make it effective, and in this sense all treaties are self-executing. But if it was the intent of the Government to make it a crime for a ship of British registry to unlade liquor within a sea zone on our coast, traversible in one hour, then that intent was not effectuated by the mere execution of the treaty. *It is not the function of treaties to enact the fiscal or criminal law of the nation.* For this purpose no treaty is self-executing. Congress may be under a duty to enact that which has been agreed upon by treaty, but duty and its performance are two separate and distinct things.[27] [italics added]

The doctrine of self-executing treaty provisions has appeared to some scholars to be linked to the amorphous doctrine of "political questions" in U.S. constitutional law. Quincy Wright has written:

> It [the doctrine of self-executing treaty provisions] affirms that certain treaty provisions, like certain provisions of customary international law and certain provisions of the Constitution are of such character that the Court leaves their interpretation and application to the political organs of the Government—the President or Congress—and applies whatever decisions these organs may make.[28]

Despite technical considerations regarding intent and precision of language, highly subjective considerations enter into play in determining the self-executing nature of treaty provisions in U.S. law when it must be determined whether a matter is within the province of the political branches. Steiner and Vagts have pointed out that

> having exhausted such data [concerning intention and language] it [the Court] may examine the broader context of the agreement including the feasibility of construing the treaty to be self-executing in the light of *the administrative and political problems inherent in creating operative rules without implementing or reinforcing legislation.*[29] [italics added]

The involvement of sensitive political problems in the determination of the self-executing character of treaty provisions was apparent in the *Sei Fujii* case. A three-judge California lower court had unanimously held in that case that the California Alien Land Law was contrary to the human rights provisions of the U.N. Charter and hence was abrogated as a result of U.S. ratification of the Charter. Two justices of the U.S. Supreme Court had suggested previously in a concurring opinion in the *Oyama* v. *California* case[30] that the human rights provisions of the Charter might abrogate the California Alien Land Law. These statements probably influenced the decision of the California lower court. Upon appeal, the California Supreme Court held, as mentioned previously, that the human rights provisions of the U.N. Charter could not be applied directly by U.S. courts.

The California lower court decision as well as the remarks of the Justices of the U.S. Supreme Court triggered a major constitutional conflict in the United States. Fear that internationally drafted human rights treaties might result in the direct abrogation of the U.S. laws precipitated Senator John W. Bricker and others to propose the so-called "Bricker Amendment" to the U.S. Constitution providing, inter alia, that no treaties would be self-executing in U.S. law. After a bitter dispute, the Bricker Amendment failed by one vote in 1954 to receive the necessary two-thirds majority in the U.S. Senate.[31] It should be recalled that there were a number of laws on the books in the states of the U.S. at this time permitting racial discrimination. Most of these laws were subsequently struck down by the U.S. Supreme Court as contrary to the U.S. Constitution but the suggestion that "outside interference" in the form of the direct application of treaties by U.S. courts might accomplish this same object resulted in outraged reaction from a substantial group of lawyers and lawmakers. The California Supreme Court's invocation of the U.S. Constitution to outlaw the Alien Land Law rather than the invocation of the U.N. Charter may have helped avoid an ultimate decision to amend the U.S. Constitution rendering all treaties non-self-executing. In any event, a contrary decision by the California Supreme Court would surely have had immense political consequences. The Bricker controversy undoubtedly forewarned judges of the serious repercussions which might arise from the direct application of certain treaty provisions.

The sequelae of the Bricker Amendment are still evident in the United States. In 1978 the Department of State, in submitting four major human rights treaties to the President for his transmission to the Senate for advice and consent to ratification, recommended that U.S. ratification of the treaties should be accompanied in each case by a U.S. declaration that the substantive provisions of the treaties are not self-executing.[32] No implementing legislation is proposed by the Department of State, however, and there is no analysis provided of the language or subject matter of the treaty provisions which would justify the mere declaration that they are all non-self-executing. Since such a declaration would have no international effect (as it does not attempt to vary the obligations of the parties) it seems clear that it is intended to allay fears that these human rights treaties might be directly applied by U.S. courts. Whether the courts would uphold such a broad and unsubstantiated declaration of the non-self-executing character of all these treaty provisions by the Executive or the Senate is questionable.[33]

Experience regarding the self-executing nature of provisions of human rights treaties in U.S. law emphasizes that policy considerations may be as important as purely technical legal considerations in determining the self-executing character of treaty provisions.

1.4. *Confusion Regarding the Doctrine*

U.S. case law on the doctrine of self-executing treaties provides very little guidance to an individual or administrative agency attempting to determine if a treaty provision will be held directly applicable by the courts. Neither the criterion of intent, nor precise language, nor subject matter—all employed at various times by the courts to determine the self-executing nature of a provision—seem to have been applied with sufficient consistency to make an accurate prediction likely. On the basis of an extensive consideration of the doctrine of self-executing treaty provisions, Evans has written:

> ... any attempt to generalize, e.g., to state ... that all treaties touching upon the enumerated powers of Congress are non-self-executing will usually involve so many exceptions to the attempted rule that the effect must be of limited value. This does not mean that the courts pursue a haphazard course in their consideration of the matter, but rather that they have considerable latitude in reaching a decision with regard to an issue which has been controversial since pre-Republic days.[34]

In 1948, an Attorney Adviser in the Legal Adviser's Office of the Department of State prepared a memorandum on the "Definition of 'Self-Executing' Treaty". He concluded that "an examination of adjudicated cases and of some treatises and of some of the law reviews has failed to disclose a clear definition of the term 'self-executing treaty'."[35]

Schachter has also pointed out the difficulty of generalizing in this area:

> An examination of the cases reveals that there are only two clear situations where a treaty provision requires legislative action before it can become effective: (1) where the treaty has an explicit provision to this effect and (2) where the power to deal with the subject of the treaty is vested solely in the legislature, as for example a provision calling for criminal penalties or requiring a direct appropriation of money. Outside of these categories it does not seem possible to generalize regarding the kind of treaties which require legislative implementation; each case must be examined on its own merits in order to determine whether the treaty provision may become presently effective without awaiting further legislation.[36]

It is important, however, for individuals and administrative agencies to know how the law applies to them and how they should apply the law. The lack of precision in the definition of self-executing treaties can be extremely confusing, leaving them in the dark as to whether a particular treaty provision, not implemented by legislation, provides a rule for them or not. Reiff has suggested that

> if there were a system of prior advisory opinions for use in the Federal courts, enforcement of treaties generally might be facilitated by securing early definitive judicial pronouncements upon the character of a treaty stipulation. In the absence of such a system, the character of a provision cannot be definitively determined until litigation brings it to the Supreme Court. That often is an unfair burden upon private litigants and it also unduly delays proper enforcement in some instances.[37]

He goes on to point out that, in the absence of definitive pronouncement by the Court, subjective determinations must nevertheless be made:

> Aware of this situation, and with special reference to the particular agreements under discussion, various agencies of the Federal Government, aside from the courts, have from time to time in practice made preliminary determinations upon the character of a provision, deciding, until reversed by a court, that the provision is either self-executing or executory. Congress does this regularly when adopting enforcing legislation; the President does it implicitly when in his messages he asks Congress for legislation to enforce a treaty; the Secretary of State has undertaken to do it in diplomatic correspondence with other governments; special commissions established by the President or by Congress for the purpose of studying existing legislation in relation to treaty obligations have on occasion done so; and the Attorney General on request and administrative authorities frequently in the routine course of their work, have also made such determinations. One agency defers to another. There appears to be no rule of law conferring upon a single agency apart from the Supreme Court, authority to make a final determination ...[38]

If one looks to the U.S. judicial system for guidance as to the meaning of self-executing treaty provisions one is left in a quandary. The meaning of the concept is not clear in the judicial system where it originated and where it has received the greatest amount of judicial interpretation and comment. The difficulty in determining whether a treaty provision will be directly applied in U.S. law has led Myres McDougal to state, "this word 'self-executing' is essentially meaningless, and ... the quicker we drop it from our vocabulary the better for clarity and understanding."[39] It appears that the only possible working definition of self-executing treaty provisions in U.S. law is the one given by most commentators which, as stated earlier, is a *petitio principii* and is not helpful in resolving problems as to whether treaties will be directly applied: A self-executing treaty is one which is applied directly by the courts without implementing legislation; a non-self-executing treaty is one which requires implementing legislation.

It has been contended that U.S. courts have been reluctant to find treaty provisions to be self-executing.[40] This negates to a considerable degree the common assumption that in the U.S. legal system treaties are directly applicable upon ratification. The implications arising from the confused legal situation in the U.S. are useful in understanding the attitude of the various supervisory organs of the ILO when faced with the contention that treaty provisions are directly applicable in a particular constitutional system.

2. The Concept of Self-Executing Treaties in Other Automatic Incorporation States

While the concept of self-executing treaty provisions is generally known in automatic incorporation states the degree to which it plays a role in the application of treaties and occasions scholarly comment varies greatly from country to country. In few countries has it been considered as extensively by courts and scholars as in the United States. This section will consider the meaning of the concept in countries other than the U.S. in which the application of ILO conventions is being examined in this case study.

2.1. *The Netherlands*

The concept of self-executing treaties in the Netherlands is discussed first in this section since it plays an important role in the application of treaties in that country. Under Articles 65 and 66 of the 1956 amendments to the Dutch Constitution, only treaty provisions "the contents of which may be binding on anyone" have binding effect and have priority over statutes. According to van Panhuys, the expression "binding on anyone" was included in Articles 65 and 66 to refer to self-executing treaties.[41] In view of the generally very liberal provisions of the Dutch Constitution relating to the application of treaties in Dutch law[42] it might be assumed that the expression "the contents of which may be binding on anyone" was not intended to limit unduly the application of conventions in the Netherlands. The courts in the Netherlands, however, have construed this expression narrowly in some instances.

In the 1956 case of *Institut national des appellations d'origine des vins et eaux de vie* v. *J. Mettes* the Supreme Court gave a restrictive interpretation to "binding on anyone" and refused to apply directly a provision of a treaty.[43] Article 11 of the French-Netherlands Commercial Treaty of 1935 provided that each party would undertake to protect products from the territory of the other party against unfair competition by "maintaining or taking" prohibitive measures against the use of wrong indications as to the geographical origin of such products. The Supreme Court held that this provision imposed an obligation on the ratifying states but did not create an obligation for individuals ("anyone") to abstain from the acts referred to. Hence, it was considered as non-self-executing.

This decision of the Supreme Court has been criticized by one Dutch commentator. Van Panhuys has pointed out that "this Article [11 of the French-Netherlands Commercial Treaty] was so worded that it could easily be applied by the courts in conjunction with legal proceedings in force."[44]

In 1968, the Dutch Supreme Court held in the case of *In re the Portalon* that the Hague Rules on Bills of Lading contained in the International Convention for the Unification of Bills of Lading (Brussels Convention of 1924) were non-self-executing because the Protocol to the Convention stated that the parties could give effect to the Convention either by force of law or by legislative incorporation.[45] The Court concluded that this language indicated that the Hague Rules were not intended to be self-executing. Erades has criticized this decision on several grounds. He points out:

> At the time when the above Brussels Convention was being drafted the concept of self-executing treaties was still a purely American affair, a matter of federal constitutional law. The so-called "self-executing" character of a treaty was an issue which hardly attracted attention in international law. This is in itself an indication that the Protocol may not have the significance which the Supreme Court attributed to it.[46]

Erades goes on to point out that the legislative history does not support the Dutch Supreme Court interpretation. He also cites the influence of the U.S. law on self-executing treaties:

> Some twenty-five years later the attention of international lawyers was drawn, largely as a result of the discussions in the United States around the Californian *Sei Fujii* case, to the American doctrine of "self-executing" treaties. The doctrine spread itself rapidly throughout the Continent. It was said to be part of international law in general and it became an important issue in the European communities. In 1956 it was prematurely petrified in Articles 65 and 66 of the Netherlands Constitution ...

> The purpose of the revisions of the Netherlands Constitution in 1953 and 1956 has been to open up the Netherlands legal order to international law. The introduction of the doctrine of "self-executing" treaties in the Constitution in 1956 has however in practice proven to have a contrary effect. The present case clearly demonstrates that it has become an overinflated balloon which it is now the proper time to puncture.[47]

In contrast to the cases mentioned above the Dutch courts have considered most of the provisions of the European Convention on Human Rights as "binding on anyone"—thus self-executing.[48] In Dutch legal thinking the theory predominates that the aim of that Convention is "the granting of rights and freedoms, of which the individual may avail himself within the municipal legal order."[49]

Scholars referring to the criteria for determining the self-executing nature of treaties in Dutch law have mentioned "intention" and "need for further legislative or administrative action."

> The Supreme Court has stated that the question of whether a provision of an international treaty is of such a [self-executing] nature depends, so far as Dutch law is concerned, solely upon an interpretation of the treaty concerned. The courts will have to interpret the relevant treaty, whenever such a case arises, taking into account the phrasing and the economy of the treaty concerned.[50]

Thus, taking into account the aim of the European Convention on Human Rights, it appears that the courts have considered its provisions to be self-executing in the main.

Questions of separation of powers and sensitive political questions as elements in determining the self-executing nature of treaty provisions—important in U.S. law—appear less important in the Netherlands because of the express language of Articles 65 and 66.[51] The language of the treaty appears to be the essential element as well as the intention of the parties to create rules "binding on anyone."

While the Dutch courts have defined "binding on anyone" narrowly in some cases they have appeared to be more liberal with regard to the European Convention on Human Rights for the reasons previously mentioned. Their tendency to interpret narrowly the notion of "self-executing" treaties has been criticized not only by Erades and van Panhuys but also by Lardy who considers it a dangerous tendency which puts in question the entire Dutch system giving primacy to international treaties over national law.[52]

2.2. *Switzerland*

The question of whether a treaty provision is or is not self-executing has apparently not been a major problem in the application of treaties in Swiss law. Wildhaber has written, "Swiss practice has hardly exhibited any awareness of the distinction between self-executing and non-self-executing treaties. Courts apply a treaty unhesitatingly even if it contains criminal penalties."[53] Malinverni states that the Swiss Federal Tribunal (the Supreme Court of the Confederation) has a broad conception of the notion of direct effect.[54] In the 1972 decision in the case of *Banque de Credit International* c. *Conseil d'Etat du Canton de Genève*,[55] the Federal Tribunal referred to self-executing provisions as follows:

> International treaties approved by the federal assembly are incorporated into federal law, and when they create legal rules are obligatory for the authorities ... and citizens, provided that they are directly applicable ... Thus, an individual may invoke a treaty before an administrative body and the courts if it contains rules of law which are sufficiently precise to be applied as such in a particular case and to provide the basis for a concrete decision, the major premise of a legal syllogism of which the decision will be the conclusion. This is not the case with a treaty provision which announces a program or lays down general principles which should guide the legislation of contracting states and which is addressed not to the administrative and judicial authorities but to the national legislature.[56]

The Federal Tribunal has thus not emphasized the intention of the parties to the treaty as an important element in determining the self-executing nature of treaty provisions. It has rather considered whether the treaty provision could be applied by a court and has applied provisions which the courts of other states might have considered non-self-executing. In the *Banque de Credit International* case the Federal Tribunal held that Article 16(1) of the Stockholm Convention instituting the European Free Trade Association could be directly applied. This article required non-discriminatory treatment for nationals of Member States and is worded in general terms. The Tribunal held it to be self-executing despite the generality of language and the fact that a paragraph of the same article provided for the adoption of additional provisions giving effect to the principles contained in paragraph 1.[57]

2.3. *France*

Scholars who have examined extensively the application of treaties in France have given relatively little importance to the question of the self-executing nature of treaty provisions in French law. In his excellent treatise *Treaty-Making Power and Constitution*, Wildhaber does not refer to the question of self-executing provisions in France although he does so in considering the application of treaties in the U.S., Switzerland, and Austria.[58] Lardy states tersely that "non-self-executing agreements, i.e., those which do not possess the necessary precision for a direct application, are evidently an exception to the constitutional rule [in France]; their application depends on legal provisions implementing their terms."[59]

A lengthy report on the application in France of the Treaty of Rome instituting the EEC discusses the problem of the self-executing nature of treaties in general and refers to specific problems relating to the Treaty of Rome but makes no reference to problems regarding the self-executing nature of other treaties in France.[60]

In a 1973 communication concerning the application of ILO conventions in France, Valticos devotes considerably more attention to the question of the self-executing nature of ILO conventions than in two previous articles on the same subject. He refers in particular to the increased interest in the question of direct application of treaties as a result of the development of European law.[61] It is significant that these two lengthier treatments of the question of the self-executing nature of treaty provisions in France appeared to be influenced by the importance of the subject in relation to the application of the Treaty of Rome.[62]

2.4. *Italy*

A treaty becomes national law in Italy by virtue of an "order of execution" or "implementing order" adopted by Parliament at the same time as the Act approving ratification. Thus, it is not the ratification itself which incorporates the treaty in national law. Nevertheless, the same problems exist concerning self-executing treaty provisions in Italian law as in automatic incorporation states:[63]

> [I]f the treaty has been "incorporated" into Italian law through an implementing act (that is, a law which ... establishes that "full and entire implementation is given to the treaty ...") it is then fully effective but limited to those provisions "which are complete in their essential elements"; ... on the other hand, the provisions of the treaty which lack "completeness" remain ineffective (in spite of the implementing Act) until the national legislator takes the necessary measures to complete them.[64]

Italian judges apparently have the tendency to give a liberal interpretation to the concept of self-executing treaty provisions. Three 1972 Italian judgments have been cited as showing "that the implementing order—a precise legislative act ordering the implementation of a specific treaty—induces the Italian judge to make every effort to put the provisions of the agreement into effect, persuading him to consider the latter as being as self-executing as possible."[65]

Condorelli has commented on the criteria used by Italian courts in deciding on the self-executing character of a treaty provision as compared with the criteria employed by the European Court of Justice. He writes:

> I think the [above] comments made clearly demonstrate the existence of two conceptions of the phenomenon of self-executing international agreements. In Luxembourg an individual provision of a treaty is appraised in the light of the general principles of the whole of the treaty of which it forms a part. In Rome, on the other hand, each individual provision is taken into account and a decision is taken both on the extent to which it is specific and to which it can be applied by the national courts.[66]

Condorelli thus emphasizes that a treaty provision may be self-executing under one legal system and not under another due to differing criteria applied by courts.

2.5. *Argentina and Mexico*

As pointed out in chapter 4 Argentina and Mexico have adopted constitutional provisions based on the U.S. Constitution "Supremacy Clause." Thus, it is normal that the concept of self-executing treaty provisions should exist in Argentine and Mexican law. Bidart Campos has referred to the concept of self-executing treaties in Argentine law[67] and Paez Stille and Evans have referred to the existence of the concept in Mexican law.[68] No extensive analyses of the concept have been found, however, in the cases or in the writings of scholars in those two countries. Presumably an interpretation of the concept in those countries would rely heavily on U.S. sources given the origin of their constitutional articles on the incorporation of treaties.

3. Conclusion

The term "self-executing", used to describe treaty provisions which will be directly applied by courts, originated in U.S. law. The term or its translation is used in other legal systems in the same sense. Nevertheless, the reality behind the expression varies widely in different legal systems. In some states, the courts have appeared reluctant to find treaty provisions to be self-executing. In others, the tendency appears to be the opposite.

Courts of various countries apply different criteria (or the same criteria differently) in deciding whether a provision is self-executing. As a result, the same provision may be applied directly by the courts of one country and not be applied directly by courts in another country. It is difficult to predict in advance whether a treaty provision will be considered self-executing by the courts of a particular country.

Judges occasionally state that the intention of the parties is determinative in deciding whether a particular provision is self-executing. This criterion is subject to criticism since the concept of self-executing treaty provisions is irrelevant in states with the system of legislative incorporation. Courts in some countries stress the language of the treaty provision and tend to find provisions which lack detail and specificity to be non-self-executing. Other courts appear to find no difficulty in applying general provisions. In some legal systems, courts have paid particular attention to the aim of the treaty in determining its self-executing aspect. Within the same legal systems, courts have not always been consistent in applying these various criteria.

Thus, although the term "self-executing" is widely employed in automatic incorporation states, it appears difficult to define it beyond stating that it refers to treaty provisions which will be applied by the courts. The lack of consistent content given to the concept of self-executing treaty provisions provides little help in determining whether a particular provision will be directly applied by courts.

NOTES

1. The term "doctrine" is used in this section, although "concept" might seem more appropriate, since the expression "doctrine of self-executing treaty provisions" is commonly employed in U.S. legal writing. Some provisions of a treaty may be self-executing and other provisions of the same treaty may be non-self-executing. Thus, reference is generally made in this study to the self-executing nature of treaty *provisions* rather than of the treaty as a whole.

2. Foster and Elam v. Neilson, 27 U.S. (2 Pet.) 253 (1829).

3. Ibid., 314.

4. Quincy Wright, *National Courts and Human Rights—The Fujii Case*, 45 Am. J. Int'l L. 62, 65, n.12 (1951).

5. Oscar Schachter, *The Charter and the Constitution: The Human Rights Provisions in American Law*, 4 Vand. L. Rev. 643, 645 (1951).

6. 32 U.S. (7 Pet.) 51 (1833).

7. Ibid., 89.

8. Henry Reiff, *The Enforcement of Multipartite Administrative Treaties in the United States*, 34 Am. J. Int'l L. 661, 669–670 (1940).

9. "A self-executing treaty refers in American constitutional law to a treaty provision which imposes an obligation upon the United States of such character as to be applied by the courts." Wright, *National Courts*, 63; "It seems apparent, however, from the cases which

have been examined that treaties which require implementing legislation are not self-executing while those which can be enforced by the courts *ex proprio vigore* are self-executing." Attorney Adviser Diven to Legal Adviser Gross, Department of State, Memorandum, "Definition of 'Self-Executing Treaty'," 22 April 1948, MS. Department of State, file 711.009/4–2248, quoted in Marjorie Whiteman, ed., *Digest of International Law*, vol. 14 (Washington, D.C.: Government Printing Office, 1970), pp. 304–305.

10. The material presented in this section is necessarily a brief survey of U.S. decisions and writings on self-executing treaty provisions. For more detailed information see Edwin Dickinson, *Are the Liquor Treaties Self-Executing?*, 20 Am. J. Int'l L. 444 (1926); Ronald A. Brand, *Security Council Resolutions: When Do They Give Rise to Enforceable Legal Rights? The United Nations Charter, the Byrd Amendment and a Self-Executing Treaty Analysis*, 9 Cornell Int'l L. J. 298 (1976); Alona E. Evans, *Self-Executing Treaties in the United States of America*, 30 Brit. Y. B. Int'l L. 178 (1953); Edwin F. Feo, *Self-Execution of United Nations Security Council Resolutions Under United States Law*, 24 U.C.L.A. L. Rev. 387 (1976); Louis Henkin, *The Treaty Makers and the Law Makers: The Niagara Reservation*, 56 Colum. L. Rev. 1151 (1956); Leslie Henry, *When is a Treaty Self-Executing?* 27 Mich. L. Rev. 776 (1928–29); Henry Reiff, *The Enforcement of Multipartite Administrative Treaties in the United States*, 34 Am. J. Int'l L. 661 (1940); Stefan A. Riesenfeld, *The Doctrine of Self-Executing Treaties and GATT: A Notable German Judgment*, 65 Am. J. Int'l L. 548 (1971); Jean Russotto, *L'Application des traités self-executing en droit américain* (Montreux: Imprimerie Ganguin et Laubscher, S.A., 1969); Oscar Schachter, *The Charter and the Constitution: The Human Rights Provisions in American Law*, 4 Vand. L. Rev. 643 (1951); Bernhard Schlüter, *The Domestic Status of the Human Rights Clauses of the United Nations Charter*, 61 Calif. L. Rev. 110 (1973); Jack Solomon, *When are Treaties Self-Executing?*, 31 Neb. L. Rev. 463 (1952); Charles W. Stotter, *Self-Executing Treaties and the Human Rights Provisions of the United Nations Charter: A Separation of Powers Problem*, 25 Buffalo L. Rev. 773 (1976); Whiteman, op. cit., pp. 302–316; Luzius Wildhaber, *Treaty-Making Power and Constitution* (Basel und Stuttgart: Helbing & Lichtenhahn, 1971), pp. 199–202; Quincy Wright, *Treaties as Law in National Courts: The United States*, 16 Louisiana L. Rev. 755 (1956), *National Courts and Human Rights—The Fujii Case*, 45 Am. J. Int'l L. 62 (1951). See also Eric Stein, "When is an International Agreement 'Self-Executing' in American Law?" in Stein, Hay and Waelbroeck, *European Community Law and Institutions in Perspective* (Indianapolis: The Bobbs-Merrill Company, Inc., 1976), p. 102.

11. *Restatement (Second) of the Foreign Relations Law of the United States* (St. Paul, Minnesota: American Law Institute Publishers, 1965), pt. III, "International Agreements," sec. 141, p. 432.

12. See also Dickinson, op. cit., 449: "Generally unless a treaty contains an express stipulation for legislative execution, or belongs to that exceptional category of treaties which cannot from their nature be given effect as law *ex proprio vigore*, it would appear that the question is simply one of construction. If the treaty was intended to be self-executing, it has immediately the effect of law. If not, it requires legislation before it can become a rule for the courts."

13. Sei Fujii v. California, 38 Cal. 2d 718, 242 P.2d 617, 620 (1952).

14. Henry J. Steiner and Detlev F. Vagts, *Transnational Legal Problems* (Mineola, New York: The Foundation Press, Inc., 2d ed. 1976), p. 584. See also Head Money Cases (Edye v. Robertson), 112 U.S. 580, 598 (1884); Whitney v. Robertson, 124 U.S. 190 (1888); Cook v. United States, 288 U.S. 102, 118–119 (1933); Valentine v. United States, 299 U.S. 5, 10 (1936); Bacardi Corp. v. Domenech, 311 U.S. 150, 161 (1940).

15. Feo, op. cit., 394 [footnotes omitted]. See also Schachter, op. cit., 645.

16. Feo, op. cit., 395.

17. "... it is not possible to find in the history of the [U.N.] Charter evidence regarding the

'intent' of the parties in regard to the self-operative effect of Article 56. For it was clear to the representatives at San Francisco that the methods and procedures for carrying out the Charter obligations in municipal law had to be left to the varying constitutional systems of Member States. There is therefore no point in seeking or attempting to postulate a specific legislative intent on the question of whether Article 56 was or was not to be automatically operative in municipal law." Schachter, op. cit., 654.

"The cases illustrate the difficulty of applying to multilateral treaties the doctrine that the self-executing nature of international agreements is to be determined from the expressed intent of the parties ... But what of multilateral treaties with states whose constitutions, written or unwritten, require formal transformation by statute? Does it make sense to search for the intent of the parties, if some of the parties could not have had such an intent with respect to their own sphere?" Riesenfeld, op. cit., 550 [footnotes omitted].

18. Riesenfeld, op. cit., 550.

19. 38 Cal. 2d 718, 242 P.2d 617 (1952).

20. 242 P.2d 617, 621–622. The Sei Fujii case was not appealed to the U.S. Supreme Court.

21. A statute, however, may also be non-self-executing: "An examination of the decisions of the Supreme Court on this topic will show there is no practical distinction whatever as between a statute and a treaty with regard to its becoming presently effective, without waiting further legislation. A statute may be so framed as to make it apparent that it does not become practically effective until something further is done, either by Congress itself or by some officer or commissioner intrusted with certain powers with reference thereto. The same may be said with regard to a treaty. Both statutes and treaties become presently effective when their purposes are expressed as presently effective." Putnam, J., for the Circuit Court of Appeals (1st Circuit), United Shoe Machinery Company v. Duplessis Shoe Machinery Co., 155 Fed. 842, 845 (1907).

22. Schachter, op. cit., 655–656.

23. 502 F.2d 90 (9th Cir. 1974). The Trust Agreement implemented Article 79 of the U.N. Charter relating to non-self-governing territories. The provision of the Trust Agreement (Article 6) which the Court held self-executing required the United States to "promote the economic advancement and self-sufficiency of the inhabitants, and to this end ... regulate the use of natural resources" and to "protect the inhabitants against the loss of their lands and resources."

24. Ibid., 99.

25. *Restatement*, op. cit., sec. 141(3). See also Louis Henkin, *Foreign Affairs and the Constitution* (Mineola, New York: The Foundation Press, Inc., 1972) and Stotter, *Self-Executing Treaties and the Human Rights Provisions of the U.N. Charter*, 25 Buffalo L. Rev. 773 (1976).

26. 24 Fed. Cas. 344, 345, No. 14,251 (C.C.D. Mich. 1852).

27. 5 F.2d 838, 845 (D. Conn. 1925).

28. Wright, *National Courts*, 64–65. It has been pointed out that the "political questions" doctrine does not entirely justify the law on self-executing provisions since "the preservation of the federal legislature's constitutional rights should end where the treaty contains clearly justiciable norms." Schlüter, op. cit., 133.

29. Steiner and Vagts, *Transnational Legal Problems*, p. 584.

30. Oyama v. California, 332 U.S. 633 (1948).

31. See Louis B. Sohn and Thomas Buergenthal, *International Protection of Human Rights* (Indianapolis: The Bobbs-Merrill Company, Inc., 1973), pp. 948–971 for information concerning the Bricker Amendment.

32. Message from the President of the United States Transmitting Four Treaties Pertaining to Human Rights, Senate, 95th Cong., 2d Sess., Executives C, D, E & F, February 23, 1978. The treaties transmitted were the International Covenant on Civil and Political

Rights, the International Covenant on Economic, Social and Cultural Rights, the American Convention on Human Rights and the International Convention on the Elimination of All Forms of Racial Discrimination.

33. See David Weissbrodt, *United States Ratification of the Human Rights Covenants*, 63 Minn. L. Rev. 35, 66–72 (1978) and Charles H. Dearborn III, *The Domestic Legal Effect of Declarations that Treaty Provisions are not Self-Executing*, 57 Texas L. Rev. 233 (1979). Cf. Henkin, *Foreign Affairs and the Constitution* (Mineola, New York: The Foundation Press, Inc., 1972), p. 158. Henkin states that courts will give "great weight" to executive views on whether treaties are self-executing or not. See also discussion in Steiner and Vagts, *Transnational Legal Problems*, pp. 585–587, relating to the U.S. ratification of the 1962 International Coffee Agreement. The determination of whether a treaty provision is self-executing or not would properly seem to be a question for judicial decision. Given the tendency of American courts, however, to refuse to decide sensitive questions relating to the separation of powers on the grounds that they are "political questions" it seems possible that U.S. courts might find a treaty provision "non-self-executing" if the executive had previously stated it to be so.

34. Evans, op. cit., 190.

35. Diven Memorandum, Whiteman, *Digest of International Law*, vol. 14, p. 304.

36. Schachter, op. cit., 645–646.

37. Reiff, op. cit., 670.

38. Ibid., 670–671.

39. 45 Proc., Am. Soc. Int'l L. 102 (1951).

40. C. H. McLaughlin, *The Scope of the Treaty Power in the United States*, 42 Minn. L. Rev. 709, 748–750 (1958). See Taylor v. Morton, 23 Fed. Cas. 784, No. 13,799 (C.C.D. Mass. 1855); Vanity Fair Mills, Inc. v. T. Eaton Co., 133 F. Supp. 522 (S.D.N.Y. 1955).

41. Jonkheer H. F. van Panhuys, *The Netherlands Constitution and International Law—A Decade of Experience*, 58 Am. J. Int'l L. 88, 100 (1964).

42. See chapter 4, sec. 1.3, for information concerning the Dutch constitutional provisions.

43. Hoge Raad (1 June 1956), N. J. 1958, No. 424 with annotation by D. J. Veegens, in English in 6 Neth. Int'l L. Rev. 399 (1959). This case involved an action for damages brought by a French association of vinegrowers against a Dutch subject who had sold bottles labeled "Cognac" which did not contain French cognac.

44. Van Panhuys, op. cit., 102. To the same effect see Menno J. van Emde Boas, *The Impact of the European Convention of Human Rights and Fundamental Freedoms on the Legal Order of the Netherlands*, 13 Neth. Int'l L. Rev. 337, 344 (1966): "This provision when read in conjunction with the ordinary civil law of torts (Article 1401 of the Civil Code) might seem to permit of direct application" [footnotes omitted].

45. In re the Portalon, 8 November 1968, N. J. 1969, No. 10; reported in 16 Neth. Int'l L. Rev. 97 (1969). The case involved the interpretation of a bill of lading incorporating the Hague Rules rather than the application of the Brussels Convention itself.

46. L. Erades, *The 1924 Brussels Convention on Bills of Lading is Non-Self-Executing*, 16 Neth. Int'l L. Rev. 99 (1969).

47. Ibid., 99–100.

48. See van Emde Boas, *The Impact of the European Convention of Human Rights and Fundamental Freedoms on the Legal Order of the Netherlands*, Part II, 14 Neth. Int'l L. Rev. 1, 13 (1967): "As a rule, the Dutch courts have never doubted that the provisions of the [European] Convention [on Human Rights] are binding on everyone. Otherwise, the courts would have confined themselves to stating that, since Article 66 of the Constitution was not applicable to the case under consideration, they were not competent to investigate whether Dutch law was in conformity with the Convention." See remainder of this paragraph for

remarks relating to the non-self-executing character of Article 13 and Article 5(4) of the European Convention on Human Rights.

49. Van Emde Boas, *The Impact of the European Convention of Human Rights and Fundamental Freedoms on the Legal Order of the Netherlands*, 13 Neth. Int'l L. Rev. 337, 342 (1966).

50. Ibid., 343.

51. But see in this regard, van Emde Boas, ibid., 345: "There is, however, some doubt about the extent of the courts' powers to examine the conformity of Dutch law with the Treaty [European Convention on Human Rights]. According to a well established principle of public law, Dutch courts are not empowered to give judgment on matters of political expediency or the manner in which the legislative and administrative authorities exercise their discretion." Thus, in 1962 the Dutch Supreme Court refused to consider whether Article 183 of the Dutch Constitution prohibiting religious processions was compatible with Article 9(2) of the European Convention on Human Rights guaranteeing freedom of religion on the ground that the balancing of the interests of public order versus freedom of religion was the province of the legislator and not the courts. Hoge Raad, 19 January 1962, N. J. 1962, No. 107 annotated by B. V. A. Roling, in English in 9 Neth. Int'l L. Rev. 319 (1962). It has been contended that this decision renders Article 9(2) of the European Convention on Human Rights non-self-executing in the Netherlands. Duynstee, N. J. 1964, 121.

52. Pierre Lardy, *La force obligatoire du droit international en droit interne* (Paris: R. Pichon et R. Durand—Auzias, 1966), p. 173.

53. Wildhaber, *Treaty-Making Power and Constitution*, p. 206 [footnotes omitted].

54. Georges Malinverni, *L'Application de la Convention européenne des droits de l'homme en Suisse*, Mémoires publiés par la Faculté de Droit de Genève, Quinzième Journée Juridique (Genève: Georg, 1977), p. 16.

55. Chambre de droit administratif, 13 octobre 1972, ATF 98 I b 385.

56. Ibid. [translation]. Reproduced in 30 A.S.D.I. 121, 122 (1974).

57. In an article referring to the application of the European Convention on Human Rights in Switzerland, Malinverni suggests that the European Convention on Human Rights might be given constitutional rank in Switzerland as it has been in Austria in view of the similarity between many of the liberties guaranteed by the Constitution and those guaranteed by the Convention. Constitutional guarantees of freedoms are frequently couched in generalities and yet applied by the courts. Elevating the broad provisions of certain treaties, such as human rights treaties, to constitutional rank might provide a further incentive to a liberal interpretation of the term "self-executing" in Switzerland as regards such provisions. Malinverni, op. cit., 13–15, 29–35.

58. Wildhaber, *Treaty-Making Power and Constitution*, pp. 198–234.

59. Lardy, *La force obligatoire*, p. 112 [translation].

60. "Rapport français" in *Deuxième colloque international de droit européen, 1963* (Zwolle: N.V. Uitgeversmaatschappij W. E. J. Tjeenk Willink, 1966), p. 235.

61. Nicolas Valticos, *Droit international du travail et droit interne français*, Travaux du comité français de droit international privé, 1973–75 (Paris: Dalloz, 1977). Cf. Valticos, *Les conventions internationales du travail devant le juge français*, 53 R.C.D.I.P. 41 (1964) and *Conventions internationales du travail et droit interne*, 44 R.C.D.I.P. 251 (1955).

62. The criteria (cited by Valticos) used to determine the self-executing nature of treaty provisions will be referred to in Chapter 7 relating to the self-executing character of ILO conventions.

63. See "Rapport Italien" in *Deuxième colloque international de droit européen, 1963*, op. cit., p. 115; Luigi Condorelli, *Il Giudice Italiano e i Trattati Internazionali* (Padua: Cedam, 1974), p. 32; Luigi Condorelli and Giorgio Gaja, *Judicial Decisions*, Italian Yearbook of International Law 365 (1976).

64. Condorelli and Gaja, loc. cit., 365.

65. Ibid., 371.

66. Condorelli, *EEC Treaty and GATT*, Italian Yearbook of International Law 21–22 (1977).

67. German J. Bidart Campos, *Manual de Derecho Constitucional Argentino* (Buenos Aires: Ediar, 1974), p. 26. See also Salvador Maria Lozada, *Instituciones de Derecho Publico* (Cordoba, Argentina: Editions Macchi, 1966), pp. 287–288 and discussion concerning the case of Haras "Los Cardos," chapter 6, sec. 2.1 infra.

68. Enrique Paez Stille, *Interpretación del Artículo 133 de la Constitución* (México, Tesis, Universidad de México, 1945), pp. 31–32; Evans, op. cit., 178, 205.

CHAPTER 6

National Courts and the Self-Executing Nature of ILO Convention Provisions

The close link between the right of individuals to invoke the provisions of treaties and the problem of the self-executing nature of treaties has been referred to previously. Individuals may claim rights under treaties before national courts in countries of automatic incorporation if such treaties are considered self-executing and if the individuals have standing to invoke the treaty.[1]

Although cast in the form of agreements between states, ILO conventions are intended ultimately to benefit individuals within countries. The aim of these conventions relating to social security, safety and health of workers, trade union rights and discrimination in employment is to improve the lot of individual workers within ratifying states. Judicial decisions in national courts relating to the direct application or self-executing character of provisions of ILO conventions have not been frequent. Some interesting cases involving this issue have arisen, however, in the United States, Argentina and France. These cases are discussed in some detail in this chapter. They are highly instructive in pinpointing problems in determining the self-executing nature of provisions of these conventions.

1. United States—The *Warren* Case

In the 1940s a case was brought in a United States federal court concerning the application of the Shipowners' Liability Convention.[2] Walter Warren, a messman on the S.S. *Anna Howard Shaw*, a ship owned by the United States, broke his leg while on shore leave in Naples. He had gone to a dance hall with other crew members and, in the course of the evening, had stepped onto an unprotected ledge overlooking the sea off a room adjoining the dance hall. While on the ledge, Warren grasped an iron rod which seemed to be attached to the building and leaned forward to look. The rod broke loose and the seaman lost his balance and fell, breaking his leg. He filed suit in the District Court for the Southern District of New York against the United States as shipowner, seeking "maintenance and cure" (a suit in U.S. admiralty law for salary and medical expenses). After a decision by the District Court allowing Warren "maintenance" and a reversal by the Second Circuit Court of Appeals, the Supreme Court granted certiorari and decided in the 1951 case of *Warren* v. *United States* that Warren was entitled to "maintenance and cure."[3]

At issue was the interpretation of Article 2 of the Shipowners' Liability Convention on which Warren based his claim:

> Article 2. 1. The shipowner shall be liable in respect of
> (a) sickness and injury occurring between the date specified in the articles of agreement for reporting for duty and the termination of the engagement;
> (b) death resulting from such sickness or injury.
>
> 2. Provided that national laws or regulations may make exceptions in respect of
> (a) injury incurred otherwise than in the service of the ship;
> (b) injury or sickness due to the wilful act, default or misbehavior of the sick, injured or deceased person;
> (c) sickness or infirmity intentionally concealed when the engagement is entered into.

Warren claimed that paragraph 1 of Article 2 was self-executing and provided for absolute liability on the part of the shipowner.[4] He also claimed that paragraph 2 was not self-executing and, therefore, the exceptions referred to therein were not operative until a statute enacted them. No statute to that effect had been enacted, although the general maritime law of the U.S., developed by decisional law of the courts, provided for the same exceptions referred to in paragraph 2. In an opinion written by Justice Douglas, the Court held that the exceptions referred to in paragraph 2 of Article 2 were operative without the necessity for an Act of Congress since they were part of U.S. common law developed by judicial decision.

Douglas wrote that paragraph 2 of Article 2 did not require implementing legislation in order to be applied directly by the Court since the term "national laws or regulations" covered court decisions as well as legislative acts. And he pointed out that the exceptions permitted by paragraph 2 were operative by virtue of the general U.S. maritime law which provided that serious misconduct by the seaman such as gross negligence or wilful disobedience could bar recovery. The Court's finding that the expression "national laws or regulations" referred to the common law as well as to statutes was consistent with an interpretation provided to the U.S. government by the International Labour Office. While the Warren case was pending in the courts, the U.S. government asked the International Labour Office about the meaning of "national laws or regulations" as used in the Convention. The Office replied:

> No record has been found of any case in which it has been necessary for the International Labour Organization to express an opinion whether the term "national laws or regulations" which is frequently included in International Labour Conventions refers solely to statutes or can be regarded as also including the principles of general maritime law. The expression has, however, unquestionably been used for the purpose of leaving certain aspects of the questions dealt with in the Convention to national discretion, and it would appear to be consistent with this general purpose to interpret the provisions as allowing each party to the Convention to make the exceptions provided for either by specific enactment or by the application of some existing legal principle or rule ...
>
> It is, of course, for the courts of each country to decide what effect the incorporation of the terms of the Convention in national law as the direct result of ratification, by specific statutory enactment, or otherwise may have had, but from an international point of view, it would appear legitimate for a Member of the Organization to rely upon and have recourse to the exceptions provided for in paragraph 2 of Article 2 of the Shipowners' Liability (Sick and Injured Seamen) Convention, 1936, irrespective of whether these exceptions have been specifically enacted or are applicable in virtue of existing customary law.[5]

This advice was communicated to the U.S. government on 13 November 1950. The *Warren* case was argued before the Supreme Court on 2 January 1951 and the decision handed down on 26 February 1951. Although no mention is made of the ILO reply in Justice Douglas' opinion it had been communicated to the Court by the government's brief. The Court's interpretation of "national laws or regulations" conformed to that of the ILO.[6]

The ILO had also been asked at the same time whether paragraphs 1 or 2 of Article 2 of the Convention were self-executing or whether implementing legislation was required to give them effect. Although the ILO replied concerning the meaning of "national laws or regulations"—which Warren and the U.S. Government apparently felt was determinative of whether paragraph 2 was self-executing or not—it did not take a position on whether that paragraph could be classified as self-executing.[7]

Warren had contended that even if paragraph 2 were self-executing his conduct was not due to a "wilful act, default or misbehaviour", hence, maintenance should be granted. The Court agreed with Warren, finding that he had been negligent but not guilty of "wilful ... misbehaviour" such as to bar recovery. The Court further found that, although Warren's injury occurred during shore leave, it was incurred "in the service of the ship."[8]

Justice Douglas did not use the term "self-executing" to describe either paragraph 1 or paragraph 2 of Article 2. He thus sensibly avoided the intellectual confusion which had resulted from attempting to determine whether paragraph 2 was or was not self-executing: Warren had claimed that paragraph 2 was non-self-executing; Chief Justice Stone found that paragraph 2 was not operative in the absence of legislation in his concurring opinion in *Waterman Steamship Corp.* v. *Jones.*[9] The Chief Justice in that opinion had relied on the report of the Secretary of State to the President recommending ratification of the Convention which had stated that paragraph 1 was self-executing but that if the U.S. were to avail itself of the exceptions in paragraph 2 it would have to do so by statute.[10] (Such an interpretation was taken to mean that paragraph 2 was non-self-executing.) Douglas explicitly rejects the view that legislation was required to carry out the Convention but does not use the expression "non-self-executing" to categorize paragraph 2. The majority opinion of the Court of Appeals in the *Warren* case had held that if paragraph 1 were self-executing so also was paragraph 2 *unless* the phrase "national laws or regulations" were interpreted to exclude decisional law and refer only to legislation, in which case, presumably paragraph 2 could be considered non-self-executing.[11] The Court of Appeals found that paragraph 2 was not so limited and that decisional law was included within the purview of "national laws or regulations." It is suggested below that the essential issue in the *Warren* case was not the question of whether the characterization "self-executing" should be applied to Article 2 and that focusing on terminology created confusion.

Article 2 of the Shipowners' Liability Convention is typical of many similar articles of ILO conventions. In paragraph 1 it lays down a general rule and in paragraph 2 it provides that exceptions may be made by "national laws or regulations." An understanding of the question at issue in the *Warren* case is thus relevant in the application of other ILO conventions.

The controversy concerning the self-executing character of paragraph 2 centered on the question whether the exceptions permitted by that paragraph could be made by statutory law and decisional law or only by statutory law. Persons arguing that the exceptions could be made only by statute found the paragraph to be non-self-executing. Those who believed that under the Convention exceptions could also be made by decisional law found paragraph 2 to be self-executing. A correct understanding of the legal obligations contained in Article 2, however, leads to the determination that paragraph 2 is either self-executing or it is inapplicable—but, in any event, it should not be considered to be *non*-self-executing. This is so, even if "national rules or regulations" is taken to cover only statutory law.

One helpful method of analyzing Article 2 is to consider it as containing two alternate rules—one or the other to be applied in differing circumstances. Rephrasing Article 2 as follows in order to clarify this alternate rule aspect is useful in determining its self-executing character:[12]

(1) In the event that no national laws or regulations make the exceptions permitted in (3) below, the shipowner shall be absolutely liable in respect of (a) sickness or injury ... (b) death ...
(2) In the event that national laws or regulations make the exceptions permitted in (3) below, the shipowner shall not be liable if the sickness, injury or death was due to one of the permitted exceptions.
(3) The exceptions permitted to be made are [same as (a) (b) (c) in paragraph 2 of Article 2].

The Convention thus imposes different obligations on ratifying states depending upon whether their "national laws or regulations" permit the exceptions. If there are no such national laws or regulations, rule no. 1 of absolute liability applies; if there are such laws or regulations permitting exceptions and the injured or deceased person's actions fall within the exceptions (whether or not national laws or regulations means only statutory law or also decisional law) rule no. 2 applies and the shipowner shall not be liable. When the Article is reworded in this form the obligations in both cases are clearly and specifically expressed and could easily be applied by a court. Thus, both paragraph 1 and 2 would appear to be self-executing. In one case the shipowner "'*shall be*' absolutely liable; in the other case, he '*shall not*' be liable if ..."

In either event, the first question in both situations is to determine whether "national laws or regulations" include decisional law but this is a question of interpretation and not of the self-executing character of the provision. Even if decisional law is not covered by this expression the second rule appears self-executory if applicable at all. Under this interpretation if a statute is in effect which makes the approved exceptions then rule no. 2 is applied by the court and the shipowner shall not be liable. If "national laws and regulations" means only statutory law and there is no statute permitting exceptions, rule no. 1 is applied and the shipowner shall be liable.

What is significant is that the ratifying state is under no obligation under the convention to adopt common law rules or statutes to enact the exceptions. The usual meaning of a *non*-self-executing provision is that it is a provision which imposes a legal obligation on a state but one which can only be carried out by enacting a statute. This is not the case in paragraph 2 of Article 2. If it applies at all—even if limited to exceptions made by statute—it would be self-executing. In the situation in which it does not apply it imposes no obligation on ratifying states. The various persons searching for a characterization of paragraph 2 as self-executing or non-self-executing seem to have been thrown off the track by the reference to possible statutory enactment in order that the exceptions might be availed of. They had in mind that a non-self-executing rule is one which requires statutory enactment. But they failed to note that it must be a *rule* first, i.e., it must first be determined that it imposes an obligation and, then, that in order for the obligation to be discharged a statute must be enacted. Here, the Convention imposed no obligation to create exceptions to the rule of paragraph 1.

Another method of analyzing Article 2 would be to consider paragraph 2 as being simply a saving clause which by definition merely acquiesces in what is done but in itself produces no effect. In that analysis also there would be no interest in characterizing paragraph 2 as self-executing or non-self-executing.

2. Argentina

2.1. *The* Haras "Los Cardos" *Case*

The problem of self-executing treaty provisions became well known in Argentine law as the result of the efforts of individuals to invoke the provisions of an ILO convention in federal and provincial courts. Between 1936 and 1940 a number of persons injured in agricultural work based their claims for compensation on the effect of ratification by Argentina of the Workmen's Compensation (Agriculture) Convention (ILO Convention No. 12). In 1940, the Argentine Supreme Court, after a number of conflicting lower court decisions, held in the case of *Alonso* v. *Haras "Los Cardos"* that the Convention did not modify existing workmen's compensation legislation.[13] The Supreme Court decision provoked an unusual amount of controversy, discussion and confusion among legal scholars and government officials concerning the application of treaties in Argentine law.[14]

Article 1 of the Workmen's Compensation Convention provides that a ratifying state "undertakes to extend to all agricultural wage-earners its laws and regulations which provide for the compensation of workers for personal injury by accident arising out of or in the course of their employment." Argentine Act No. 9688 of 1915 provided workmen's compensation for occupational injuries but excluded from its scope compensation for injuries in agricultural work except those arising from the use of power-driven machinery. Following the ratification of the ILO Convention in 1936 a number of persons injured in agricultural work not involving the use of power-driven machinery claimed compensation, contending that by virtue of Article 31 of the Argentine Constitution, the law ratifying the Convention had had the effect of automatically extending the provisions of Act No. 9688 to cover *all* injuries arising out of agricultural work.

Agricultural workers claiming compensation on the basis of the ILO Convention contended that the Convention as a duly ratified treaty was "the supreme law of the land" under Article 31 of the Constitution and should thus modify the national law concerning workmen's compensation. These claims raised two problems: (1) was the ILO Convention to be considered a treaty "with foreign powers" within the terms of Article 31[15] and (2) should the treaty be directly applied by the courts to amend existing legislation (the self-executing problem)? In the years 1936 to 1940 a number of conflicting decisions on these points were made by lower Argentine federal and provincial courts. Some found that ILO Conventions were not "treaties with foreign powers" or that Article 1 was not self-executing because of the language employed. Other courts found that the Convention was self-executing and thus Act No. 9688 had been modified to cover all agricultural workers.[16]

In the 1940 *Haras "Los Cardos"* decision the Argentine Supreme Court settled the controversy by deciding that legislation (which had not been adopted) was necessary to implement the Convention. Gregorio Alonso, an agricultural worker, had been injured while operating a horse-pulled mowing machine. He brought an action for compensation against his employer, the enterprise Haras "Los Cardos", basing his claim on the contention that Act No. 12,232 approving the ratification of the ILO Convention automatically extended Act No. 9688 by virtue of Article 31 of the Constitution. The Supreme Court decided that he could not succeed in his claim in the absence of implementing legislation.

The Court's decision that legislation was required was based on several grounds: (1) the language of the Convention and (2) the intention, or understanding, of the legislature (not the parties to the Convention) at the time it passed the Act approving ratification that legislation was necessary and (3) that such legislation was all the more necessary in a country such as Argentina where the existing legislation on workmen's compensation excluded certain persons required to be covered under the Convention. The Court also said that in view of its decision on other grounds it was unnecessary for it to decide whether ILO conventions were "treaties with foreign powers." The expression "non-self-executing" was not used by the Court but has been employed by commentators on the decision.

Soon after the *Haras "Los Cardos"* decision the Argentine legislature passed Act No. 12,631 implementing the Convention by specifically providing workmen's compensation for all injured agricultural workmen.

It might appear from its terms that Article 1 of the Convention is a non-self-executing provision; hence, that the Argentine Supreme Court had correctly interpreted it. The phraseology that a Member State "undertakes to extend" could be taken to indicate that the state committed itself to take some future action.[17] Article 1 does not appear to be worded in terms of immediate obligation. Nevertheless, the Supreme Court did not base its decision on these words of Article 1 alone but also on more dubious grounds relating to other terminology in the Convention and on the debates in the legislature at the moment of the adoption of the Act approving ratification.

The Argentine Supreme Court had held in an earlier case that a duly ratified treaty could have the effect of amending existing legislation, specifically, in that case, the Argentine Commercial Code.[18] In the *Haras "Los Cardos"* case they held otherwise. The Court referred in its opinion to the language of Article 1 but placed particular emphasis on the language of Article 5 as indicative of the need for the adoption of implementing legislation. Article 5 states:

> Subject to the provisions of Article 3 [referring to the coming into force of the Convention upon the ratification of two Member States] each Member which ratifies this Convention agrees to bring the provisions of Article 1 into operation not later than 1 January 1924, and to take such action as may be necessary to make these provisions effective.

The Court found that the International Labour Conference which adopted the Convention in 1921 has indicated by this provision that ratifying countries should take some future action in addition to ratification in order to implement the Convention, despite the fact that the law approving ratification in Argentina was adopted in 1935, eleven years after the 1924 limitation date. The Court's interpretation of Article 5 is erroneous. A provision similar to Article 5, but with varying dates, was commonly included in most ILO conventions drafted before 1927. It is clear from a 1927 article by Jean Morellet, then ILO Legal Adviser, that the ostensible, although misguided, *raison d'être* for this provision had nothing to do with whether the Convention was self-executing or not:

> It seems beyond doubt that the clause fixing the latest date for the application of the Conventions was adopted by the First Session of the Conference at Washington with a view to speeding up the process of bringing the Convention into force. In drafting it the intention probably was to make sure that the application of the Conventions should not be postponed beyond a certain limit. But in reality the effect of this provision is precisely the opposite of its intention.[19]

When it was found that this provision was ineffective and even counter-productive in this regard it was dropped from subsequently drafted conventions. From 1927 on, this provision was not included in later conventions but was replaced by a provision stating that a convention came into force for a country twelve months after ratification. In addition, the phrase in Article 5 requiring ratifying states "to take such action as may be necessary to make these provisions effective" is simply a reaffirmation of a requirement contained in Article 19(5)(d) of the ILO Constitution, and, as such, does not lend itself to an interpretation that the provisions of a particular convention are or are not self-executing. In the ILO Constitution, as well as in the convention, it is a phrase which could simply refer to the necessity of ensuring practical implementation in automatic incorporation states.

Such a clearly erroneous interpretation of an ILO convention could have been avoided had the International Labour Office been asked to provide an interpretation of Article 5.

The Supreme Court also stressed that in interpreting a law—in this case, the Act approving ratification of the Convention—primary importance must be given to the intention of the legislators. Its decision referred to a report of a Senate Commission at the time of the adoption of the law approving ratification of the Convention stating that when the process of ratification has been completed Congress would make the necessary adjustments in national legislation to bring it into harmony with the provisions of the Convention and to a similar remark from a member of the Chamber of Deputies. These were taken as indicating that the legislators did not intend ratification alone of Convention No. 12 to extend the provisions of Act No. 9688 to all agricultural workers.

Thus, a national court, in giving primacy to "intention" in the determination of the self-executing nature of a treaty provision referred not to the intention of the parties to the treaty but to the intention of the national legislators involved in the approval of the Convention. One could assume that the legislators had in mind the intention of the drafters of parties to the Convention as evidenced by the language of the treaty in voicing their own opinions regarding the need for legislation. They may, however, have had in mind the need for clarity within their own legal system in view of the existence of a statute on the books which was less extensive than the provisions of the Convention. They could have been thinking as well of policy considerations which made the adoption of legislation advisable.

While one result of the decision in *Haras "Los Cardos"* was the clarification of the immediate legal situation by the adoption of a law specifically implementing the Convention, another result was considerable doctrinal controversy concerning the implications of the Court's holding.

The Argentine Government itself reporting to the ILO supervisory organs seemed to be confused concerning the import of the decision.[20]

In a number of its reports to the ILO on ratified conventions for the 1951–1952 period, the Government stated that according to the Supreme Court opinion in *Haras "Los Cardos"* the mere fact of ratification implied nothing more under the Argentine Constitution than an undertaking to pass laws to put the principles contained in the Convention into effect. This same interpretation of the Argentine constitutional provision was adopted by Unsain, an Argentine jurist.[21] A number of other Argentine jurists—Ruiz Moreno, Ramírez Gronda, Krotoschin, Cortés Funes, and Perez—disagreed with Unsain's interpretation and with the Court's holding in the *Haras "Los Cardos"* case.[22] In their view the Argentine Constitution provided for automatic incorporation of treaties and ILO conventions were "treaties with foreign powers" and within the purview of the constitutional provision if their provisions were self-executing. The obligation of states ratifying ILO conventions "to take such action ... as may be necessary to make these provisions effective" did not require that legislation be adopted.

Ramírez Gronda considered that, contrary to the Supreme Court opinion in the "*Los Cardos*" case, Article 1 of the Workmen's Compensation (Agriculture) Convention was self-executing. He apparently considered the phrase "undertakes to extend" as not necessarily implying that legislation need be adopted since Article 1 could be applied by a court. He cited the fact that prior to the Supreme Court's decision a number of provincial courts had no difficulty in applying that Article. They simply considered it as extending the scope of Act No. 9688 to cover *all* agricultural workers.

Although Ramírez Gronda disagreed with the Court's holding that Article 1 of the Workmen's Compensation (Agriculture) Convention was non-self-executing he did recognize that some ILO conventions required implementing legislation—in particular, Article 3(c) of the Maternity Protection Convention (ILO Convention No. 3) which provides that a woman shall be paid maternity benefits either from public funds or by means of a system of insurance. He states that Argentine legislation is required to implement this convention since it would be necessary to establish a government or insurance system (which did not then exist) to provide the benefits.[23]

Benito Perez found that the Supreme Court decision in the "*Los Cardos*" case was not based on an exegesis of the text nor on the purpose of the Act but on the confused and contradictory parliamentary discussion preceding its adoption and on an inadequate understanding of what he referred to as "laws of a social character" which should result in immediate benefits for persons covered by the Convention.[24] Perez noted that in particular cases a treaty might encroach on fundamental rights reserved to the Provinces and this could be a problem with automatic incorporation; he pointed out, however, that this factor should be taken into account by the National Congress at the moment of ratification.[25]

Despite the confused reporting by the Argentine Government on the implications of the *Haras "Los Cardos"* decision, the majority of commentators have not considered the decision as implying that treaties in general are not automatically incorporated in Argentine law but rather that the particular Convention at issue was non-self-executing and thus an exception to the automatic incorporation of treaties.[26]

Without taking a position on the self-executing nature of Article 1 of the Workmen's Compensation (Agriculture) Convention, Ruiz Moreno stated that the provisions of ILO conventions could be self-executing if they were clear and precise. As an example he cited a convention provision which reads that "the working hours of a person ... shall not exceed eight in the day and forty-eight in the week." Surprisingly, however, he found Article 2 of the Convention concerning Equal Remuneration for Men and Women Workers for Work of Equal Value (No. 100) to be self-executing. That Article provides that ratifying states should promote the application of the principle of equal remuneration for work of equal value and ensure its application to the extent that national methods of wage determination permit. The Article is frequently cited as an example of a promotional obligation only and presumably thus not one that would be directly applied by a court.[27] Ruiz Moreno believed that the provision was sufficiently clear and complete to be self-executing, considered in conjunction with an Argentine Act which provided that collective agreements should not alter legal provisions intended for the protection of the general interest.[28]

2.2. *The* Roa *Case*

In 1961, the Argentine Supreme Court decided in the case of *Roa* c. *Moschos* that the provisions of the ILO Unemployment Indemnity (Shipwreck) Convention (ILO Convention No. 8) did not ipso facto modify the Argentine Commercial Code—in other words, were not directly applicable or self-executing.[29] Article 2 of this Convention provides that in case of shipwreck of any vessel the owner shall pay an unemployment indemnity to each seaman employed thereon at the same rate as wages payable under the contract but limited to a period of two months. The Argentine Commercial Code provided for indemnity in such an event only until the ship would normally have reached port. In the *Roa* case, a member of the crew of the shipwrecked vessel "Irene" asked for an unemployment indemnity of two months' salary, contending that the Convention had the effect of altering the provisions of the Commercial Code. The Court held otherwise, citing the *Haras "Los Cardos"* decision. Article 8 of the ILO convention at issue in the *Roa* case is substantially similar to Article 5 of the Convention which was at issue in the *Haras "Los Cardos"* case. The Supreme Court decision in that case cited Article 5 as indicating that legislation should be adopted to implement the Convention.

Cortés Funes has criticized the *Roa* decision contending that neither Article 8 of the Unemployment Indemnity (Shipwreck) Convention nor Article 5 of the Workmen's Compensation (Agriculture) Convention were intended to signify the need for implementing legislation. He also maintained that the legislature has the opportunity when it considers approval of ratification to compare the provisions of the convention with national law and if it does not wish national law to be modified to refuse approval of ratification of the convention. Cortés Funes appeared to consider both the Workmen's Compensation (Agriculture) Convention and the Unemployment Indemnity (Shipwreck) Convention as self-executing, contrasting the decisions in the *Haras "Los Cardos"* and *Roa* cases with the earlier decision of the Supreme Court declaring that the ratification of a convention resulted in the automatic amendment of the relevant article of the Commercial Code.[30]

In 1969, the ILO Committee of Experts recognized "with satisfaction" the adoption by Argentina of an Act implementing the Unemployment Indemnity (Shipwreck) Convention.[31]

3. France

3.1. *The* Klaiss *Case*

In the early 1960s a Frenchwoman, Madame Klaiss, invoked the provisions of the ILO Maternity Protection Convention (No. 3). Relying on the Convention, which was ratified by France in 1950, she requested an indemnity of ten additional days beyond the indemnity to which she would have been entitled as an employed worker under Article 298 of the French Social Security Code. The Code was adopted in 1956 but Article 298 simply reproduced the text of a 1945 ordinance whose origins were even earlier. The Code provided for payment of a daily indemnity to pregnant women for a period of six weeks before the presumed date of delivery. The Convention, on the other hand, provided for payment of an indemnity for the period of six weeks before the presumed date of delivery plus during the actual period until delivery, which, in the case of Madame Klaiss, amounted to ten additional days beyond the presumed date of delivery.

The relevant provision of the Maternity Protection Convention reads:

> Article 3: In any public or private industrial or commercial undertaking, or in any branch thereof, other than an undertaking in which only members of the same family are employed, a woman— …
>
> (c) shall, while she is absent from her work in pursuance of paragraphs (a) and (b), be paid benefits sufficient for the full and healthy maintenance of herself and her child, provided either out of public funds or by means of a system of insurance, the exact amount of which shall be determined by the competent authority in each country, and as an additional benefit shall be entitled to free attendance by a doctor or certified mid-wife; no mistake of the medical adviser in estimating the date of confinement shall preclude a woman from receiving these benefits from the date of the medical certificate up to the date on which the confinement actually takes place;

The French administrative bureau in charge of social security questions contended that the Convention did not concern matters of social security and, hence, should not prevail over a provision of the Social Security Code. Thus, the Code should govern the claim of Madame Klaiss and she should not receive the ten extra days indemnity. The *Cour d'appel* of Paris, considering Madame Klaiss' claim, requested an official interpretation from the French government concerning the scope of the Convention. The government provided an official interpretation that the Convention was of a general scope which included social security matters. The *Cour d'appel* of Paris considering that it was bound by the government's interpretation found that the Convention rather than the Code provision should apply in Madame Klaiss' case.[32] In 1962 the *Cour de Cassation* rejected the petition to quash basing its decision on the necessity of following the government's interpretation of the Convention, thus upholding the decision of the *Cour d'appel* that Madame Klaiss was entitled to ten additional days of maternity indemnity in accordance with the Convention.[33]

Implicit in the rejection of the petition to quash by the *Cour de Cassation* and the upholding of the decision of the *Cour d'appel* is the determination that Article 3(c) of the Convention is self-executing—i.e., it did not require any additional legislation in order to be applied by the courts. It would seem from its terms that Article 3(c) is non-self-executing since it entails the establishment of a government system of benefits or an insurance system. It will be recalled that Ramírez Gronda had referred to this provision as an example of a non-self-executing provision (since it entailed the establishment of some type of system) when he commented on the application of the Workmen's Compensation (Agriculture) Convention in Argentina.[34] At the time of Madame Klaiss' suit, a system for the payment of maternity benefits already existed in France. The only impact of the Convention was a difference in the period during which benefits were to be paid. It would not have been possible to apply the Convention directly in a country which did not already have a system. Hence, Article 3(c) is directly applicable in France but might not be in another legal system.[35]

3.2. *The* Castanié *Case*

The ILO Equality of Treatment (Accident Compensation) Convention (No. 19) has also given rise to court cases in France. Article 1(1) of this Convention provides that each ratifying state

> undertakes to grant to the nationals of any other Member which shall have ratified the Convention, who suffer personal injury due to industrial accidents happening in its territory, or to their dependents, the same treatment in respect of workmen's compensation as it grants to its own nationals.

France ratified the Convention in 1928. A French law of 1898 provided that foreign workers were entitled to equality of treatment for workmen's compensation only if bilateral agreements existed with their country of origin. In its early reports to the ILO on the Convention, the government contended that, by virtue of the ratification and publication of the Convention, nationals of other countries which had ratified the Convention were entitled to equality of treatment under French law even if no bilateral agreement existed.[36] The Ministry of Labour had inserted in the *Journal Officiel* a note so indicating and the Ministry of Justice circulated a similar memo to the *procureurs généraux*. In the early 1930s, however, lower court decisions were conflicting as to whether Article 1(1) was immediately applicable or whether implementing legislation was required. In 1934, the question was settled by the *Cour de Cassation* in the case of *Castanié* c. *Dame veuve Hurtado* in which the Court found this provision of the Convention directly applicable without legislation.[37]

In the *Castanié* case, the widow of a Spanish worker in Oran who had been killed in an industrial accident claimed compensation under the Convention. There was no bilateral agreement between Spain and France providing reciprocity in such cases but Spain had ratified the ILO

Convention. The Court held that the treaty ratified by both France and Spain prevailed over the earlier law of 1898 which provided for equality of treatment only in the case of bilateral agreements. No reference was made to the self-executing character of Article 1(1) of the Convention but it is implicit in the Court's decision. It is interesting to note that Article 1(1) contains the word "undertakes" which is also contained in the Workmen's Compensation (Agriculture) Convention and was relied on, in part, by the Court in the Argentine case of *Haras "Los Cardos"* (discussed in the preceding section) to indicate the non-self-executing character of the provision.[38]

3.3. *The* Compan-Vaquer *Case*

Another case arose in the 1970s in France under the same Equality of Treatment (Accident Compensation) Convention. *Fonds commun des accidents du travail* c. *Compan-Vaquer* was the subject of proceedings in the *Cour de Cassation* in 1971 and in the *Conseil d'Etat* in 1975. A Spaniard had been injured in industrial accidents in Algeria in 1933 and 1945. He received accident insurance by virtue of a French law which had been extended to Algeria. Following independence he returned to live in France. A French act adopted in 1964 provided for an increase in indemnity for Frenchmen who had lived in Algeria and further provided that administrative decrees should be adopted regulating the application of the Act to foreigners who lived in Algeria before independence. The decree adopted in 1965 essentially limited the increased indemnity to foreigners who had served in the Army or assisted France in some way. Compan-Vaquer, the claimant in this case, was not covered by any of the categories of the 1965 decree.

France had ratified the Equality of Treatment (Accident Compensation) Convention in 1928 and declared it applicable to Algeria in 1930. Spain had also ratified the Convention. As mentioned above, Article 1(1) of the Convention provides that a ratifying state undertakes to give to the citizens of any other country which has ratified the Convention the same treatment as regards workmen's compensation as it gives to its own citizens. Compan-Vaquer brought a civil action claiming that he was entitled as a result of the ratification of the Convention by both France and Spain to the increased indemnity provided Frenchmen by the 1965 Act. The *Fonds comnun* contended that the 1964 Act was a social assistance law and not a social security (workmen's compensation) law and hence its benefits were not extended to foreigners of ratifying states by virtue of Article 1(1) of the Convention.

The lower court held that the 1964 Act was a social security (workmen's compensation) act and not just a social assistance act and thus was inconsistent with the Convention. It held that that Act could not derogate from the Convention and, therefore, Compan-Vaquer was entitled to the increased indemnity. The *Cour de Cassation* quashed this decision on the ground that the judicial proceedings should be stayed until the administrative tribunal determined whether the 1965 decree was illegal or not.[39] The issue of the legality of the decree was decided in 1975 by the *Conseil d'Etat* which found that the 1964 Act was not incompatible with the Convention because it did not explicitly exclude foreigners such as Compan-Vaquer and thus the decree was not illegal.[40] The *Conseil d'Etat* found that nothing in the legislative history showed that it was intended to exclude from the benefits of the Act foreigners who were entitled under the ILO Convention to the benefits of equality of treatment in social security legislation. Hence the Act and the decree although not explicitly including Compan-Vaquer in their coverage did so implicitly.

Although the decision of the *Conseil d'Etat* concerned only the legality of the decree which it found compatible with the Convention and did not expressly consider whether Article 1(1) of the Convention was or was not self-executing, a determination that it was self-executing is implicit in the court proceedings in this case.

4. Conclusion

The cases discussed in this chapter illustrate that the determination of whether a provision of an ILO convention is self-executing is not an easy matter for national courts. In each of the cases discussed lower courts came to conflicting decisions and a final decision was made only by the highest court of the country. While this may be the situation for most disputed legal points it is especially difficult with regard to the application of treaty provisions. In such cases the problem is not so much the application of a particular law to a concrete situation but rather whether or not the treaty provision is law at all. It seems unfortunate that individuals must carry their claim to the highest court in the land before ascertaining whether or not ILO conventions are legal norms in their country.

The cases also illustrate that it may well be difficult for ILO supervisory bodies to assume in advance that a particular provision either will or will not be considered self-executing in a particular country. Decisions on the same provision vary from country to country and seem to be based on criteria not easily apparent from the language of the convention.

NOTES

1. Some treaty provisions which impose obligations on the executive branch which can be carried out without further legislation may be considered self-executing although they could not be interpreted as implying the creation of rights for individuals.

2. ILO Convention No. 55, 1936. The Convention was ratified by the United States in 1938.

3. 340 U.S. 523 (1951).

4. The Government agreed that paragraph 1 was self-executing. The Government brief stated: "In clear and concise language, paragraph 1 lays down a rule of law which determines the rights and duties of seamen and shipowners. Legislation by Congress could do no more than enact its terms verbatim." Brief for the United States, In the Supreme Court of the United States, October Term, 1950, No. 87, Walter K. Warren, Petitioner v. United States of America, p. 32.

5. *International Labour Code 1951* (Geneva: International Labour Office, 1952), vol. I, p. 864.

6. The Court's opinion points out that the term "law" in American jurisprudence usually includes the rules of court decisions as well as legislative acts, citing Erie Railroad Company v. Tompkins, 304 U.S. 64 (1938), and stated that "no reason is apparent why a more restricted meaning should be given 'national laws or regulations'." Thus, the Supreme Court referred to U.S. judicial precedents to clarify the meaning of a term in an international treaty rather than to the interpretation provided by the international organization responsible for the drafting of the treaty. The Court did analyze the purpose of the Convention, however, in attempting to interpret it. In support of its perception of the purpose it cited the "travaux préparatoires" and a report of the U.S. Secretary of State who, in recommending ratification emphasized that the Convention (1) would not materially change American legal standards and (2) would raise standards of member nations to the American level and thus equalize operating costs. 340 U.S. 523, 527–528.

7. *International Labour Code*, op. cit., vol. I, p. 864. See chapter 7, sec. 2 infra, for further discussion of the ILO's reply.

8. Justices Jackson and Clark dissented on the grounds that the injury did not occur "in the service of the ship" and Justice Frankfurter also dissented on the grounds that the Court of Appeals' finding that Warren's injury was caused by a "deliberate act of indiscretion" should not be disturbed.

9. Reported in Aguilar v. Standard Oil Co. of New Jersey, 318 U.S. 724, 738 (1943).

10. The Secretary stated that paragraph 1 was self-executing because (1) ... it establishes liability, although no definite amount is provided; and (2) that it will not be held in the courts to conflict with present law in this country. House of Representatives Report No. 1328, 76th Cong., 1st Sess., p. 6, 1938.

11. Petition for rehearing denied, Warren v. United States, 179 F.2d 919, 922–923 (1950).

12. This analysis has been suggested to this writer by a 1957 article in which Professor Ramírez Gronda of Argentina referred to a decision of an Argentinian court in which a dissenting judge had pointed out that Article 10(1) of the Workmen's Compensation (Accidents) Convention, 1925 (ILO Convention No. 17) allowing national laws or regulations to make exceptions to the general rule of the Article contained, in effect, two different rules to be applied in different circumstances. Article 10(1) of Convention 17 reads as follows:

Injured workmen shall be entitled to the supply and normal renewal, by the employer or insurer, of such artificial limbs and surgical appliances as are recognized to be necessary; provided that national laws or regulations may allow in exceptional circumstances the supply and renewal of such artificial limbs and appliances to be replaced by the award to the injured workman of a sum representing the probable cost of the supply and renewal of such appliances, this sum is to be decided at the time when the amount of compensation is settled or revised.

The similarity of this provision with Article 2 of the Shipowner's Liability Convention is evident. See Juan D. Ramírez Gronda, *Validez y Vigencia de los Convenios Internacionales del Trabajo Ratificados*, 17 Derecho del Trabajo 5, 9–10 (1957).

13. Gregorio Alonso c. Sociedad Anonima Haras "Los Cardos," Fallos de la Corte Suprema 186:258; No. 9033, 15 March 1940, La Ley, t. XVII, p. 877, 30 March 1940.

14. See text relating to notes 21–26 of this section.

15. Article 31 of the Constitution provided that "treaties with foreign powers are the supreme law of the nation."

16. These conflicting decisions are referred to in Ernesto Krotoschin, *Tratado Práctico de Derecho del Trabajo* 2 vols. (Buenos Aires: Depalma, 2d ed., 1965), vol. II, p. 1056, n.42, as well as in reports by Argentina to the ILO during this period on the implementation of Convention No. 12, e.g., 25 S.R. 99 (1939).

17. See chapter 7, sec. 4, for a discussion of the expression "undertakes" in relation to determination of the self-executing nature of a provision.

18. Fallos de la Corte Suprema 150:84.

19. Jean Morellet, *At What Moment do the International Labour Conventions Become Applicable?*, 16 I.L.R. 765 (1927).

20. See chapter 2, sec. 2, for discussion of conflicting statements made by the Government following this decision.

21. See Alejandro M. Unsain, *Ratificación de Convenciones Internacionales del Trabajo*, 9 Derecho del Trabajo 497–501 (1949).

22. Hector Ruiz Moreno, *La Organización Internacional del Trabajo*, 13 Derecho del Trabajo 5–22 (1953); Ramírez Gronda, op. cit., 7–9; Krotoschin, op. cit., pp. 1056–1059; Gerónimo Cortés Funes, *Regimen de Incorporación de las Convenciones Internacionales a la Legislación Positiva Nacional*, Doctrina Judicial (26 de junio de 1961), No. 1372, 693–694 (this comment relates to the 1961 Roa case referred to in the text, infra, but the reasoning of the commentator applies equally to the Haras "Los Cardos" case); Benito Perez, *Alcance de las Convenciones de la OIT Ratificados por el Congreso*, 21 Derecho del Trabajo 635–637 (1961).

23. Ramírez Gronda, op. cit., 5–6. Cf. the Klaiss decision referred to in this chapter, sec. 3.1, where the French *Cour de Cassation* considered this provision of the Maternity Protection Convention as directly applicable since a system for maternity benefits already existed in France.

24. Perez, op. cit., 635.

25. Ibid., 636.

26. In commenting on the Haras "Los Cardos" decision, Valticos has written: "... si elle [la Cour suprême d'Argentine] décida que la ratification de la Convention sur la réparation des accidents du travail (agriculture), 1922, n'avait pas eu pour effêt de modifier la législation jusque-là en vigueur, elle le fit uniquement en raison des termes de cette convention, qui lui parurent ... dénués du caractère de dispositions *self-executing*. Cet arrêt ne constitue donc pas, comme on l'a parfois pensé, un arrêt de principe refusant d'une manière générale de reconnaître que, comme dans le cas des traités, la ratification d'une convention internationale du travail introduit celle-ci automatiquement dans le droit interne." Valticos, *Conventions internationales du travail et droit interne*, 44 R.C.D.I.P. 251, 262–263 (1955).

27. According to McMahon, the obligations contained in this Convention are "so minimal and amorphous as to be barely discernible," J. F. McMahon, *The Legislative Techniques of the International Labour Organization*, 41 Brit. Y. B. Int'l L. 37–38 (1965–66). In 1977 the Swiss Federal Tribunal refused to apply directly Convention No. 100, pointing out that this

Convention was not self-executing and required implementing laws or orders of execution. *Demoiselle Loup*, Tribunal fédéral (Chambre de Droit Public), La Semaine Judiciaire, No. 29, 457 (26 septembre 1978).

28. Ruiz Moreno, *Ratificación de Convenios Internacionales de Trabajo*, 16 Derecho del Trabajo 440–441 (1956). In 1974 an Argentine law came into force which provided for equal remuneration for men and women for work of equal value. An editorial in La Ley Laboral y Previsional, 3 (1 junio 1973), pointed out that this law rendered operative both Article 14 of the Argentine Constitution and the ILO Equal Remuneration Convention (ratified by Argentina in 1956). In doing so it supported the contested view that the Supreme Court had held that ILO conventions could not be automatically incorporated into national law: "Sin embargo, en virtud de la conocida doctrina de la Corte Suprema, sobre la necessidad de que una ley expresa integre en el derecho positivo, los principios de los tratados internacionales ratificados, la misma, no tenia en los hechos operatividad." Ibid.

29. Felix Roa y otros c. Constantino Moschos, Fallo de la Corte Suprema, 19 de mayo de 1961; reproduced in Salvador Maria Lozada, *Derecho Constitucional Argentino Segun El Metodo de Casos* (Buenos Aires: Abeldo-Perrot, 1972), vol. 1, pp. 847–848 and in 21 Derecho del Trabajo 635–637 (1961).

30. Cortés Funes, op. cit., 694.

31. 1969 R.C.E. 38.

32. *Bulletin jur. de la fédération nationale des organismes de sécurité sociale* No. 23–1961, F-4 rose.

33. L'arrêt Klaiss, Cass. civ., 2 sect. civ. 28 Mars 1962, Bul. Jur. 1a), No. 47–1962, F-4.

34. See sec. 2.1 of this chapter.

35. The question of the date of the adoption of the Social Security Code and the date of the ratification of the Convention in relation to the question of the priority of the one over the other in the Klaiss case is discussed in chapter 8. The administrative followup to the decision is discussed in chapter 9.

36. International Labour Conference, 15th session (1931), vol. II, pp. 371 and 381.

37. Req., 27 fevr., 1934, D. H., 1934.203, S., 1935, I.1 et note Niboyet.

38. See chapter 7, sec. 4, regarding the use of the term "undertakes" in Article 1(1) of Convention No. 19.

39. Fonds communs des accidents du travail c. José Compan-Vaquer, Cass. soc., 11 fevr., 1971, Clunet, 1971.568, obs. D. Ruzié. D.S., 1971, Somm. p. 121. Bull. civ. V, No. 109, p. 88.

40. Conseil d'Etat (2e et 6e sous-sect. réunies)., 25 juillet 1975, 65 R.C.D.I.P. 60 (1976) et note Valticos.

CHAPTER 7

ILO Supervision and the Self-Executing Nature of Convention Provisions

Whether a particular provision of a treaty is self-executing or not is, in general, a question of municipal law. The courts of a particular jurisdiction decide under their constitutional system whether or not they will apply a provision without implementing legislation.[1] Nevertheless, ILO supervisory organs, charged with the responsibility of ascertaining whether ratifying states have taken action necessary "to make effective" the provisions of conventions have themselves examined the question of whether a particular provision of an ILO convention is or is not self-executing within a specific legal system when there has not been a determination by the courts of the state concerned.

In examining this question, the supervisory Committees have obviously assumed that in every country with the system of automatic incorporation some treaty provisions cannot be directly applied by courts or administrators because they necessarily require implementing laws or regulations. In some cases, inquiries and comments by the supervisory bodies have led to a difference of opinion between them and the government over the necessity for implementing laws or regulations.

1. Non-Self-Executing Provisions of ILO Conventions

It has been pointed out frequently that a considerable number of ILO convention provisions appear to be non-self-executing. Valticos writes:

> From examining only the terms of international labour conventions, it can be said without hesitation that most of their provisions are non-self-executing.[2]

An examination of the Committee of Experts' observations and requests directed to governments over the years discloses that one of the most reiterated comments relates to the non-self-executing character of treaty provisions and the resultant need for the adoption of national laws or regulations.

A number of ILO conventions contain provisions referring specifically to the need for national laws or regulations. In such cases it is obvious that action implementing the convention must be taken by the government. Article 2(5) of the Holidays with Pay Convention, 1936 (No. 52) is typical of those that the supervisory Committees have considered to be non-self-executing:

> The duration of the annual holidays with pay shall increase with the length of service under conditions to be prescribed by *national laws or regulations*. [italics added]

The Committee of Experts suggested to Mexico in 1956 that laws or regulations be adopted to implement this provision.[3]

ILO convention provisions frequently include a reference to the "competent authority." The supervisory Committees have found such provisions to be non-self-executing, presumably on the theory that the governments must specifically designate the "competent authority" by laws or regulations. The Committee of Experts has referred to the following provision as requiring national implementation:

> Every employer shall be required ... (c) to keep a record in the form prescribed by the *competent authority* of all additional hours worked in pursuance of Article 3 of this Convention and of the compensation granted in respect thereof.[4] [italics added]

The Committee of Experts also referred to Article 8(1) of the Weekly Rest (Commerce and Offices) Convention, 1957 (No. 106) as requiring implementation. This Article provides that temporary exceptions to the requirement of a weekly rest period may be granted by the competent authority. The Committee of Experts asked Mexico in 1963 what measures had been taken under Article 8(1) and in what circumstances temporary exceptions are authorised. In a 1965 direct request, the Committee took note of regulations which had been adopted implementing Article 8(1). Numerous other examples of convention provisions referring to "national laws or regulations" or "competent authority" could be cited which the Committee of Experts has considered as non-self-executing. In general, the classification of the above type of provision as non-self-executing by the supervisory Committees has not resulted in substantial disagreement from the states concerned, undoubtedly because the need for implementing legislation is obvious in most cases.

Another common convention provision which has been considered non-self-executing is one which requires the adoption of penal sanctions. Such a provision implies the adoption of national legislation and the Committee of Experts has pointed this out to governments on occasion.[5]

In many countries one of the main considerations in determining that a treaty provision is non-self-executing is the generality of its terms. Few references have been found of comments by the Committee of Experts or Conference Committee citing this reason for their determination that a particular provision was non-self-executing. This may be due to the fact that it is more questionable to classify such provisions as non-self-executing since in some cases national courts have applied treaty provisions couched in very general terms or scholars have contended that such provisions may be directly applied. It will be recalled that Ramírez Gronda contended that the very general provisions of the Equal Renumeration Convention could be considered as self-executing in Argentine law.[6]

2. U.S. Inquiry to ILO

While the case of *Warren* v. *United States*[7] was pending before the United States Supreme Court, the Solicitor General of the United States asked the International Labour Office, in writing, whether it considered paragraphs 1 and 2 of Article 2 of the Shipowners' Liability Convention[8] "to be self-executing or whether implementing legislation is required to give them effect ..."[9] The question is interesting since it implies that it might be possible to determine *at the international level* whether, as a general rule, a particular treaty provision was or was not "self-executing", without consideration of its self-executing nature within a specific constitutional system. The U.S. Solicitor General was not asking the ILO to determine whether the paragraph would be considered self-executing by an American court; he was seeking an international definition of "self-executing"—a determination as to whether the drafters of the Convention intended Article 2 to result in direct rights and obligations for individuals in states with automatic incorporation, without the necessity for implementing legislation.[10]

Thus, the question as to whether there is an international law meaning of "self-executing" was directly put to an international organization responsible for the drafting of the treaty in question. The answer of the Office implies that there is no international meaning of self-executing; the term has meaning only within a particular constitutional system. The reply states:

> As the extent to which the provisions of an international convention are self-executory differs considerably under the constitutional law of different countries, no uniformity in the matter has been, or is likely to be practicable. The International Labour Organization has been concerned to satisfy itself that, in cases in which no legislation which

> clearly implements the provisions of a convention has been enacted, the convention is effectively self-executory under the constitution or general law of the country concerned ... Subject to their being satisfied on this point, the competent bodies of the International Labour Organization have regarded the question of whether or not legislation is, in fact, necessary to make effective the provisions of such a convention as being a matter for decision by each Member of the Organization in the light of its constitutional practice and its existing law.[11]

The Office's opinion did not state that the self-executing nature of a provision was a matter to be determined *solely* by the individual country and, therefore, was not a matter of concern to the ILO. Such a reply would have negated the supervisory function of the ILO organs and have been contrary to the prior efforts of the Committee of Experts and Conference Committee to point out that it was not sufficient for a country simply to presume that automatic incorporation guaranteed the application of particular treaty provisions. The Office's reply added:

> The obligation undertaken by a Member of the International Labour Organization when ratifying a convention is defined by the Constitution of the Organization in the following language: "... the Member ... will take such action as may be necessary to make effective the provisions of the convention." The nature of the action required in the particular country to make effective the provisions of the convention is left to be determined *in the first instance* by that country, subject to the procedure for international examination of annual reports made by ratifying Members provided for in the Constitution of the Organization ...[12] [italics added]

The reply states that the type of action necessary to make effective the provisions of a convention are to be left to the country concerned "in the first instance," but subject to the supervisory procedures of the ILO. It also states, without referring to specific provisions, that in most cases, the provisions of ILO conventions require some national legislation to make them effective—thus they are not self-executing.[13]

The reply thus emphasizes practical implementation but avoids comment on the legal aspects. At a later date, when the Committee of Experts dealt in some detail with the self-executing nature of conventions in its 1963 report, it did so under the rubric of "practical application." This preference for a practical approach is understandable given the "confused legal situation" regarding self-executing referred to by the Conference Committee on another occasion. It also perhaps signifies the natural reluctance of the ILO to trespass on the domain of the constitutional law of particular states. Little guidance is given, however, as to what the Office means by the "criterion is solely whether or not the provisions of a convention can be made fully effective on a self-executory basis." Governments attempting to arrive at a determination of whether a particular treaty provision is or is not self-executing have been given little assistance by this reply.

In a separate paragraph of the reply the ILO expressed an opinion regarding the meaning of "national laws or regulations."[14] It does not, however, link its interpretation of that expression to a determination of the self-executing character of Article 1.

In any event, it refused to answer directly a question as to whether a particular provision of a treaty was or was not self-executing. Several explanations may be suggested for such refusal: (1) a conviction based on experience that it is exceedingly difficult to determine the intention of drafters of a multilateral treaty as to whether a particular treaty provision is or is not self-executing (the Office reply does not refer to the intention of the drafters in this regard); (2) hesitancy in pronouncing concerning a case then pending before the U.S. Supreme Court which would undoubtedly make its own determination of "self-executing" regardless of the opinion of the ILO; (3) confusion as to whether the treaty provision in question was or was not self-executing;[15] (4) the perception that it was practical application and not legal classification that should be the concern of the ILO and (5) that it was for the ILO supervisory Committees, and not the secretariat, to make determinations concerning the need for laws or regulations in a particular case.

The appeal by the U.S. to the ILO while a case was pending before the U.S. Supreme Court on the point in question is interesting from another point of view. It has been suggested at various times that when a case involving the interpretation of an ILO convention is pending before a national court it might be helpful to ask the ILO for an informal opinion regarding such interpretation.

The Committee of Experts referred to such a possibility in its 1937 report:

> The attention of the Committee was drawn to the question whether it would be desirable that the International Labour Organization should be given the opportunity of submitting information to national courts in proceedings before such courts where questions are raised which concern the Constitution of the Organization or the conventions adopted. The Committee wishes to draw attention to the interesting analogy of the status granted to the Office by the Statute of the Permanent Court of International Justice. While recognizing that this is not a matter upon which it would be competent to make a specific recommendation, the Committee realized its importance and decided to mention it in its Report in order that the Governing Body may have an opportunity of considering whether it is not desirable to have the whole matter fully explored.[16]

The Ministry of Foreign Affairs is consulted by judges in France when a question of the interpretation of a treaty is involved and this is a common practice also in other countries. Valticos has suggested that the Ministry might, in turn, consult the ILO when the interpretation of an ILO treaty is involved.[17]

Some of the cases concerning the interpretation of ILO conventions might relate to whether or not their provisions are self-executing. It would appear, from the 1950 reply of the ILO to the U.S. government's request, that an appeal to the ILO to elucidate the self-executing nature of a provision would not be useful. The very interesting suggestions of Valticos and the Committee of Experts, while helpful in a number of cases, would not appear to be of any aid to national organs in one substantial category of cases arising in municipal courts concerning ILO conventions.

3. The ILO and Mexico: Efforts to Clarify the Problem of Self-Executing Convention Provisions

Mexico has continually contended that Article 133 of its Constitution providing for automatic incorporation is sufficient to guarantee application of conventions in its national law. Until very recently, the Mexican government seemed to show little appreciation of the problem of non-self-executing provisions of conventions and the fact that, according to its own law, such provisions would not be directly applied by its courts.

The supervisory organs have raised the problem of non-self-executing provisions with the Mexican government both generally and with regard to specific provisions of conventions.

In 1952 the Committee of Experts addressed the following observation to Mexico:

> ... The Committee is unable to regard this statement [that, under Article 133 of the Constitution, a ratified convention is transformed into a law and is applied throughout the Federation] as fully satisfactory. It wishes to point out that a number of conventions specifically provide for intervention by the legislative authority in order to ensure their application, and contain provisions which can only be applied by means of regulations or which require either supervision by the competent authorities or the consultation of the employers' and workers' organisations concerned ...[18]

The Report of the Conference Committee for the same year stated:

> ... The Committee held a prolonged discussion on the measures taken by Mexico to apply the conventions it has ratified. The government

had been good enough to reply in writing to the general observation made by the Committee of Experts and to explain once more that, under Article 133 of the Mexican Constitution, any convention ratified was automatically converted into a national law.

Some members expressed the opinion that, while such automatic conversion of the terms of a ratified convention into national law appeared practicable in the case of negative conventions, i.e., those which prohibited certain practices, the same did not seem to apply in the case of conventions which contained provisions for the taking of positive action such as, for instance, the definition in the national legislation of the person responsible for the marking of weights on packages (Convention No. 27), or the maintenance of a system of inspection (Convention No. 62), or the definition of sanctions in the case of non-application of the provisions contained in a number of conventions ...[19]

Analysis of the direct requests, observations and Conference Committee reports shows that on a number of occasions the supervisory organs have considered certain provisions of ILO conventions to be self-executing and thus directly applicable in Mexican law by virtue of Article 133 of the Constitution. In many of the cases where the two Committees have found provisions to be self-executing, they nevertheless determined that there were other problems complicating their application such as conflicting legislation on the books or lack of publicity given to convention provisions.

Prior to 1970 the Mexican government had referred in its reports only to Article 133 of the Constitution as guaranteeing that convention provisions were directly applied in Mexico, thus evidencing no understanding of the self-executing problem. In its reports on the application of two conventions during the 1968–70 period, however, the government employed the term "autoaplicativa" (self-executing), indicating an awareness that Article 133 did not guarantee direct application of the provisions of a convention in Mexico unless the provisions were self-executing.[20]

The government stated in those reports that the following provisions were self-executing:

The employer shall keep, and make available to inspectors, records indicating, in respect of persons who are employed to work underground and who are less than two years older than the specified minimum age—(a) the date of birth, duly certified wherever possible; and (b) the date at which the person was employed or worked underground in the undertaking for the first time.
[Article 4(4) of the Minimum Age (Underground work) Convention, 1965 (No. 123)]

The employer shall make available to the workers' representatives at their request, lists of the persons who are employed or work

underground and who are less than two years older than the specified minimum age ...
[Article 4(5) of Convention No. 123]

A thorough medical examination, and periodic re-examinations at intervals of not more than one year, for fitness for employment shall be required for the employment of work underground in mines of persons under 21 years of age.
[Article 2(1) of the Medical Examination of Young Persons (Underground Work) Convention, 1965 (No. 124)]

An X-ray film of the lungs shall be required on the one occasion of the initial medical examination and, when regarded as medically necessary, on the occasion of subsequent re-examinations.
[Article 3(2) of Convention No. 124]

In reply to the government's report on Convention No. 123, the Committee of Experts simply requested specimen copies of the records and lists referred to in Articles 4(4) and (5) and did not request implementing legislation.[21] The Committee made no comment concerning the contention that the provisions of Convention No. 24 were "auto-aplicativa".[22] In the 1970s, in response to a query from the Committee of Experts, the Swiss government also contended that Article 4(5) of Convention No. 123 was directly applicable and hence, by virtue of ratification of the Convention by Switzerland, employers were obliged to furnish lists to workers' representatives on request. The Committee accepted the government's contention.[23]

On a number of other earlier occasions, Mexico simply contended that convention provisions were directly applicable by virtue of Article 133 without referring to their self-executing character. The Committee of Experts on various occasions accepted this contention. The following articles were those considered to be self-executing by the Committee of Experts:[24]

Children under the age of fifteen shall not be employed or work on fishing vessels.
[Article 2(1) of the Minimum Age (Fishermen) Convention, 1959 (No. 112)]

Young persons under the age of eighteen years shall not be employed or work on coal-burning fishing vessels as trimmers or stockers.
[Article 3 of Convention No. 112]

In the case of the application of this same Convention by Guatemala, the Committee of Experts insisted, however, despite the government's contention that duly ratified conventions had the force of law, that laws or decrees be adopted regulating the minimum age for admission to employment as seagoing fishermen. Eventually the government adopted a decree so providing.[25] This insistence on supplementary regulations may have been due more to doubts as to whether Guatemala truly had the system of automatic incorporation than to any doubts about the self-executing character of the articles of Convention No. 112 which appear to be clearly self-executing.[26] Unlike Mexico, Guatemala has no constitutional provision providing for automatic incorporation of treaties in national law. The Committee's request may also have been related to doubts as to the actual practice in Guatemala.

The Committee also implicitly accepted as self-executing the following convention provisions:

> 1. The persons to whom this Convention applies shall be employed under a system providing for at least four shifts.
> 2. The hours of work of such persons shall not exceed an average of forty-two per week.
> 3. This average shall be calculated over a period not exceeding four weeks.
> 4. The length of a spell of work shall not exceed eight hours.
>
> [Article 2 of the Sheet Glass Works Convention, 1934 (No. 43) and The Reduction of Hours (Glass-Bottle) Works Convention, 1935 (No. 49)]

This article of the two Conventions had been published in the 1965 Mexican Labour Review and the two Committees referred to the publication of "certain self-executing" provisions of Conventions Nos. 43 and 49 as well as the need for implementing legislation for provisions of other conventions.[27]

The Committee of Experts and the Mexican government both considered Article 2 of the Unemployment Indemnity (Shipwreck) Convention, 1920 (No. 8) to be self-executing, although the Argentine Supreme Court in the *Roa* case[28] had held the same article to be non-self-executing. Article 2 reads:

> 1. In every case of loss or foundering of any vessel, the owner or person with whom the seaman has contracted for service on board the vessel shall pay to each seaman employed thereon an indemnity against unemployment resulting from such loss or foundering.
> 2. This indemnity shall be paid for the days during which the seaman remains in fact unemployed at the same rate as the wages payable under the contract, but the total indemnity payable under this Convention to any one seaman may be limited to two months wages.

This article seems clearly self-executing on its face. It will be recalled, however, that the Argentine Supreme Court in the *Roa* case found that the Convention could not be directly applied so as to alter the provisions of the Argentine Commercial Code. The Committee of Experts engaged in a long series of exchanges with the Mexican government because of a conflicting provision in the Labour Code, but both the government and the Committee considered the provision to be directly applicable. The discussions with the Committee concerned confusion resulting from conflict with an existing law and not direct application.[29]

4. Language as Indicating Self-Executing Nature of Convention Provisions

The provisions referred to in the previous section seem to be easily classifiable as self-executing. They are precise and imperative, using such language as "shall pay", "shall (not) be employed", "shall be required", "shall keep", and "shall make".

Some other provisions accepted on occasion as self-executing by the supervisory Committees and by national courts are not worded in such a clear and precise manner. The use of the term "undertakes" has caused some difficulty in determining the self-executing nature of provisions. Does the language that the ratifying state "undertakes to extend (consider as) (grant) (prohibit)" indicate that the obligation is for the ratifying state to take certain measures but that the norm is not intended to be a rule directly applicable within a national legal system? Varying answers to this question have been given.

In the *Haras "Los Cardos"* case discussed in chapter 6, the Argentine Supreme Court held that Article 1 of the Workmen's Compensation (Agriculture) Convention, 1921 (No. 12) was non-self-executing. It provided that a ratifying state

> *undertakes to extend* to all agricultural wage-earners its law and regulations which provide for the compensation of workers for personal injury by accident arising out of or in the course of their employment. [italics added]

Although the Court in that case based its decision primarily on another article of the Convention and on legislative intent, it referred to the language of Article 1 as one element in determining its non-self-executing character.[30] Some Argentine jurists differed with the Court's conclusion.[31] Two U.S. jurists writing on methods for determining the self-executing nature of a treaty provision have suggested that the term "shall undertake" indicates an intention on the part of the treaty drafters that the provision is not to be considered self-executing.[32]

French courts on two occasions, however, considered the following article of the Equality of Treatment (Accident Compensation) Convention, 1925 (No. 19) as directly applicable:[33]

> Each ratifying State ... *undertakes to grant* to the nationals of any other Member which shall have ratified the Convention, who suffer personal injury due to industrial accidents happening in its territory, or to their dependents, the same treatment in respect of workmen's compensation as it grants to its own nationals. [italics added]

Prior to the 1934 decision of the French *Cour de Cassation* in the case of *Castanié* c. *Dame Veuve Hurtado*,[34] various lower courts had held that the Convention was not directly applicable. The first report of France on the application of the Convention stated that the ratification and promulgation of the Convention had modified prior French law by requiring equality of treatment for nationals of countries which had ratified the Convention.[35] In addition, the government report cited two conflicting lower court cases relating to the impact of ratification. In a comment in 1931, the Committee of Experts asked the government whether there had been an appeal against the decision holding that ratification represented only an international undertaking and that supplementary legislation would be required to make the provisions of Convention No. 19 effective in national law.[36]

Following this query a government representative at the Conference Committee stated that no appeal had been taken but that the decision of the Court considering the Convention as an international commitment only would not be regarded as an authoritative precedent.[37] Later reports from the government continued to note divergent views by the courts although the Ministry of Labour and Justice had taken the position that the Convention guaranteed reciprocity. The Committee of Experts continued to show concern over application of the Convention. The *Castanié* decision of the *Cour de Cassation* in 1934 settled the question.

Valticos has made the following comment on France's application of this provision:

> The courts of certain countries have often directly applied certain provisions which, although drafted in terms of an international commitment, have been considered as establishing, nevertheless, certain rights for individuals. This was the situation in France as regards the Equality of Treatment (Accident Compensation) Convention No. 19.[38]

Switzerland considered this same provision to be self-executing from the earliest days of the ratification of Convention No. 19 and so reported to the ILO.[39] The Committee of Experts made no objection to this contention, apparently not finding in Switzerland the confusion on the subject which existed in France prior to 1934. The Swiss report stated

> that by ratifying the Convention Switzerland is under obligation to treat insured persons of foreign nationality residing in Switzerland as well as their survivors on a basis of equality in all respects with nationals and their survivors. But this extension of the principle of equality of treatment between foreigners and nationals does not necessitate the enactment of a separate Act ... In the matter of insurance against accidents the government has power to put into force immediately the provisions laid down in the Convention. The government has for this purpose only to instruct the National Fund to act in conformity with the Convention. This has been done, and the National Fund at present gives the same treatment in all respects to foreigners and nationals.[40]

At the time that the Swiss government contemplated ratification of the Freedom of Association and Protection of the Right to Organise Convention, 1948 (No. 87), the Federal Council expressed an opinion as to the implications of the term "undertakes". Article 1 of the Convention states: "Each Member of the International Labour Organisation for which this Convention is in force *undertakes to give effect* to the following provisions" [italics added]. In a report to the Federal Assembly regarding Convention No. 87, the Federal Council wrote:

> This Article, by the terms of which the contracting parties *undertake to give effect* to the provisions of the Convention is directed especially to States whose judicial system requires the transformation of the provisions of international treaties by the adoption of national legislation in order for them to be applicable in national law. It poses no problem for our country. According to doctrine and jurisprudence, in fact, international treaties ratified by Switzerland, provided they are directly applicable, automatically have effects in national law.[41] [italics added]

In a later part of the report, the Federal Council writes that Article 4 of Convention No. 87 has manifestly the character of a provision which is automatically applicable.[42] It provides that "workers' and employers' organisations shall not be liable to be dissolved or suspended by administrative authority." The report states that Article 4

> is conceived in terms which permit the interpretation that it is addressed not only to contracting States but to the subjects of national law; it lends itself to application by national tribunals. It is generally agreed that "obligations not to do" contained in an international treaty are directly applicable in the national legal order

of contracting States and do not necessitate a legislative intervention by them.[43]

In discussions in the States-General in the Netherlands, it was also considered that Article 3 of Convention 87 was self-executing. Thus, Article 1 providing that ratifying states "undertake to give effect" to the provisions of the Convention was not considered as rendering the entire Convention non-self-executing. Article 3 provides:

> 1. Workers' and employers' organisations shall have the right to draw up their constitutions and rules, to elect their representatives in full freedom, to organise their administration and activities and to formulate their programmes.
> 2. The public authorities shall refrain from any interference which would restrict this right or impede the lawful exercise thereof.

In an article on the impact of the European Convention on Human Rights on the legal order of the Netherlands, van Emde Boas referred to a Dutch act of 1855 which required governmental authorization for the incorporation of an association and permitted governmental refusal on grounds of public interest. He writes:

> ... the abolition of this preventive control by the public authorities on the exercise of the freedom of association is in sight. The immediate cause of this progress was an opinion of the Committee of Experts of the International Labour Organisation that Dutch law was in conflict with the Convention No. 87. The Committee of Experts held that the possession of legal personality is so essential, that if Trade Unions were not incorporated, great difficulties might arise for their freedom of action in the promotion and protection of the interest they serve. To comply with the obligations of the ILO Convention on the freedom of association, the government introduced a Bill, providing that if the recognition of a Trade Union came up for decision, the provisions of the San Francisco Convention No. 87 were to be taken into account. In the States-General it was remarked that such an Act was totally unnecessary, since according to the Constitution an international treaty takes precedence over domestic legislation and *a fortiori* over administrative decisions taken by virtue of municipal law. Parliament pressed, however, for the complete abolition of any preventive control by the public authorities over the freedom of association. All associations should be incorporated subject only to definite and objective criteria laid down by law. The government has promised to bring in legislation of the kind asked for by the Chambers, when the provisions of the Dutch Civil Code concerning legal personality come up for revision in 1967.[44]

Italy has considered Article 2 of Convention No. 87 as directly applicable.[45] It provides:

> Workers and employers without distinction whatsoever, shall have the right to establish and, subject only to the rules of the organisation concerned, to join organisations of their own choosing without previous authorisation.

Thus, Italy, in addition to Switzerland and the Netherlands, did not consider the language "undertakes to give effect" in Article 1 as negating the self-executing character of other provisions of the Convention.

The Committee of Experts has also apparently regarded a provision containing the language "undertakes to consider" as self-executing. In a general observation to Mexico in 1967 the Committee referred to the publication in the Mexican Labour Review of certain "self-executing provisions" of, inter alia, Convention No. 42.[46] The following Article 2 of Workmen's Compensation (Occupational Diseases) Convention (No. 42) was the only article of that Convention published in the Review:

> Each Member of the International Labour Organisation *undertakes to consider* as occupational diseases those diseases and poisonings produced by the substances set forth in the Schedule appended hereto, when such diseases or such poisonings affect workers engaged in the trades, industries or processes placed opposite in the said Schedules, and result from occupation in an undertaking covered by the said national legislation ... [italics added]

The oblique reference by the Committee of Experts to Article 2 of Convention No. 42 as self-executing is not strong evidence that the Committee seriously considered whether the term "undertakes" renders an article non-self-executing. The classification of Article 2 of this Convention as self-executing is also problematical given the fact that the application of the Convention as a whole clearly implies the setting up or the existence of a national scheme of compensation for occupational diseases. The comments of the supervisory Committees regarding this article show more concern over a discrepancy between the provisions of the Mexican Labour Code and the Convention than over the question of the self-executing nature of Article 2.[47]

The White Lead (Painting) Convention, 1921 (No. 13) contains two provisions employing the term "undertakes" and the supervisory Committees seem to have treated the provisions inconsistently over the years. They have sometimes asked for the adoption of specific provisions implementing them and sometimes not.[48] Article 1(1) of the Convention reads:

> Each Member of the International Labour Organisation ratifying the present Convention *undertakes to prohibit*, with the exceptions provided for in Article 2, the use of white lead and sulphate of lead

> and all products containing these pigments, in the internal painting of buildings, except when the use of white lead or sulphate of lead or products containing these pigments is considered necessary for railway stations or industrial establishments by the competent authority after consultation with the employers' and workers' organisations concerned. [italics added]

At the time of the ratification of the Convention by Mexico in 1938 there were no laws or regulations prohibiting the use of white lead. Nevertheless, until 1973 the two Committees did not ask for the adoption of any legislation to implement Article 1, although from 1953 on they had asked for specific legislation to implement other articles of the same Convention which they considered to be non-self-executing.[49] In 1973, after silence on the subject since the time of ratification, the Committee of Experts observed that Article 1 was non-self-executing and asked the Mexican government for the adoption of specific provisions implementing it.[50] The exception clause in the latter part of the article referring to action by the "competent authority" may have been the decisive element in considering the article to be non-self-executing, rather than the language "undertakes to prohibit."

On the other hand, in a series of direct requests from 1953 to 1973, the two ILO Committees asked for specific provisions regulating Article 5 of Convention No. 13 which also uses the language "undertakes".[51] This article reads:

> Each Member of the International Labour Organisation ratifying the present Convention *undertakes to regulate* the use of white lead, sulphate of lead and of all products containing these pigments, in operations for which their use is not prohibited, on the following principles: (a series of practical measures concerning the use of white lead follows in this article). [italics added]

It may be that the use of the expression "undertakes to regulate" was considered as implying more specific action by the government than "undertakes to prohibit" particularly when Article 5 is read in conjunction with Article 2 of the same Convention which provides:

> 1. The provisions of Article 1 shall not apply to artistic painting or fine lining.
> 2. The governments *shall define* the limits of such forms of painting and *shall regulate* the use of white lead, sulphate of lead, and all products containing these pigments, for these purposes in conformity with the provisions of Articles 5, 6 and 7 of the present Convention. [italics added]

Article 2 of Convention No. 13 raises a further problem regarding the self-executing nature of treaty provisions. Should Article 2 be read as a whole and thus considered to be either self-executing or non-self-executing as a whole or may it be considered as containing two separate provisions thus resulting in one paragraph of the same treaty provision being self-executing and another paragraph of the same provision non-self-executing?

A similar question arises with regard to Article 3 of the same Convention which also contains two paragraphs, the second paragraph permitting exceptions from the rule contained in the first paragraph:

> 1. The employment of males under eighteen years of age and of all females shall be prohibited in any painting work of an industrial character involving the use of white lead or sulphate of lead or other products containing these pigments.
> 2. The competent authorities shall have power, after consulting the employers' and workers' organisations concerned, to permit the employment of painters' apprentices in the work prohibited by the preceding paragraph, with a view to their education in the trade.

Early comments of the Conference Committee drawing attention to other provisions of the Convention which required implementing legislation did not refer to the need for legislation implementing this article, presumably on the assumption that the entire article was self-executing.[52] A direct request of the Committee of Experts in 1971 appeared to accept that Article 3(1) was self-executing, since the Mexican government had maintained that as a provision of a validly ratified convention it prevailed over an inconsistent provision of Mexican law.[53] No reference was made to Article 3(2). In 1973, however, the Committee of Experts treated the article as a whole, considering it as non-self-executing, and asked the government to adopt provisions to give effect to Article 3.[54]

Regarded independently, paragraphs 1 of Articles 2 and 3 would clearly be considered self-executing. Nevertheless, it seems reasonable to consider Article 2 as a whole since paragraph 2 of that article is intrinsically linked to paragraph 1. The exception contained in paragraph 1 can only apply within the limits to be defined by the government as required by paragraph 2. The article as a whole is an exception to a rule laid down in Article 1. In Article 3, on the other hand, the rule and the exception are contained in the same article. Paragraph 1 of Article 3 lays down a rule and paragraph 2 permits an exception to that rule in certain particular circumstances. It seems that in this case, the paragraphs can be separated and not considered as a whole.

This problem is reminiscent of the confusion which arose in the United States over the self-executing nature of paragraphs 1 and 2 of Article 2 of the Shipowners' Liability Convention, 1936 (No. 55) culminating in the 1951 U.S. Supreme Court decision in *Warren* v. *United States*.[55] Paragraph 2 permitted specific exceptions to the rule laid down in paragraph 1 of Article 2. The problem is a recurring one since many ILO conventions lay down a rule in one article or paragraph of an article and permit exceptions by national law, regulations or competent authorities in another article or paragraph of the same article.

While the problem may appear important from the theoretical point of view of an attempt to classify articles or paragraphs of articles as self-executing or non-self-executing, the practical relevance of the problem is minimal. It is clear that if states wish to avail themselves of the permitted exceptions in many ILO conventions they must do so by law, regulations or actions of the authorities.

While there may be confusion over whether an article as a whole must be considered as either self-executing or non-self-executing, this is not true of conventions as a whole. Clearly, some provisions of conventions may be self-executing and some non-self-executing. This has been pointed out frequently by the ILO supervisory Committees. In considering the application by Mexico of the Safety Provisions (Building) Convention, 1937 (No. 62)[56] and the Plantations Convention, 1958 (No. 110)[57] the Committees referred in detail to some of the provisions as self-executing and some as non-self-executing.

5. Conclusion

The self-executing nature of treaty provisions is a question for national legal systems. The question has international aspects, however, since the interpretation of the language of a treaty provision may be relevant to whether it is considered self-executing in a particular state. The ILO supervisory organs have necessarily become involved in matters relating to the problem of self-executing treaty provisions in their work of supervising the effective national application of conventions.

One of the most common subjects of comments made by the supervisory Committees to governments of automatic incorporation states has related to the non-self-executing nature of convention provisions. Many of the provisions of ILO conventions are clearly non-self-executing since they refer expressly to the need for the adoption of legislation or regulations. Even in such clear cases, however, the supervisory organs have found it necessary, on occasion, to call the non-self-executing nature of the provisions to the attention of governments.

Other convention provisions which contain negative stipulations or imperative language (shall, shall not, etc.) are clearly self-executing. In the case of such convention provisions, the ILO Committees have accepted government contentions that they are directly applied in national law.

Many other convention provisions, however, are not clearly self-executing or non-self-executing. They may be considered as one or the other in different legal systems. One term which has occasioned some difficulty in the determination of the self-executing nature of a treaty provision is the term "undertakes". Both the ILO organs and national legal systems have had difficulty in categorizing provisions which contain this term.

NOTES

1. Such a decision, of course, may require consideration of international law since it may involve an interpretation of a treaty provision or a consideration of the intention of the treaty drafters.

2. Nicolas Valticos, *Droit international du travail et droit interne français*, Travaux du comité français de droit international privé, 1973–75 (Paris: Dalloz, 1977), p. 14.

3. 1956 R.C.E. 61.

4. Article 4(c) of the Sheet-Glass Works Convention, 1934 (No. 43) and the Reduction of Hours (Glass-Bottle) Works Convention, 1935 (No. 49); 1968 R.C.E. 66. Observation made to Mexico.

5. See observation made to Liberia regarding the Forced Labour Convention (No. 29); 1973 R.C.E. 74.

6. See chapter 6, sec. 2.2.

7. 240 U.S. 523 (1951). This case is discussed in chapter 6, sec. 1.

8. Article 2 of the Shipowners' Liability Convention reads as follows:

Article 2. 1. The shipowner shall be liable in respect of

(a) sickness and injury occurring between the date specified in the articles of agreement for reporting for duty and the termination of the engagement;

(b) death resulting from such sickness or injury.

2. Provided that national laws or regulations may make exceptions in respect of

(a) injury incurred otherwise than in the service of the ship;

(b) injury or sickness due to the wilful act, default or misbehavior of the sick, injured or deceased person;

(c) sickness or infirmity intentionally concealed when the engagement is entered into.

9. *International Labour Code 1951* (Geneva: ILO, 1952), vol. 1, p. 863, n.352.

10. Brief for the United States, In the Supreme Court of the U.S., October Term 1950, No. 87, Warren v. United States, at 43, referring to U.S. request to the ILO: "... the question whether paragraph 2 is self-executing is, analytically, a question of municipal, not international law. It is a question, however, which must in many instances be resolved by reference to international sources and standards. If a treaty prescribes a rule by which individual rights may be judicially determined, our Constitution makes that rule a rule of decision ... But whether the terms of the treaty lay down such a rule, or merely import an international obligation of the sovereign contracting parties to take such action as may be municipally necessary to effect the object to be accomplished, is a question which turns in major part on the language of the treaty and the intention of the contracting nation ... And this is particularly true where the question at issue concerns the intention of the treaty to abrogate an existing settled rule of domestic law. Accordingly, in construing the language of a treaty, it would seem at least equally relevant to inquire into the definition which may have

been given to the language as a matter of international law or usage as into the meaning which is domestically ascribed to the words."

11. *International Labour Code 1951*, vol. 1, 864.

12. Ibid.

13. "From an international point of view, what is essential is that the provisions of a convention should be fully applied; in regard to the manner of application, both the Constitution of the Organization and the terms of the individual conventions deliberately leave a wide measure of discretion to each country; it has frequently been pointed out that so many of the conventions require detailed national regulations, administrative arrangements or provisions for inspection, penalties and other means of enforcement, that some legislation will, in most cases be necessary to make the provisions of a convention effective; but the criterion is solely whether or not the provisions of a convention can be made fully effective on a self-executing basis." Ibid.

14. Ibid. See chapter 6, sec. 1, for the ILO's interpretation of the phrase "national laws or regulations."

15. The question of the self-executing nature of Article 2 of Convention No. 55 was even problematical for the ILO Legal Advisor. C. Wilfred Jenks, Legal Adviser of the ILO at the time of the Warren case, wrote, "The question of whether paragraph 2 is self-executing seems to me open to debate." Letter from C. W. Jenks to Judge Charles E. Wyzanski, Jr., 8 August 1950, ILO files.

16. 23 S.R., Appendix, R.C.E. 4–5 (1937).

17. "Il serait donc fort possible au ministère des affaires etrangères, comme celui du travail, lorsqu'ils auraient à donner a une jurisdiction leur avis sur l'interprétation d'une convention internationale du travail, de demander à leur tour l'avis du BIT pour que l'interprétation soit décidée en pleine connaissance de cause. C'est ainsi, avons-nous soutenu, que, sans qu'il s'agisse aucunement d'un recours préjudiciel, l'interprétation par voie interne, tant gouvernemental que judiciaire, pourrait s'appuyer sur l'interprétation par voie internationale." Valticos, op. cit., p. 11.

18. 1952 R.C.E. 15.

19. 35 R.P. 492 (1952).

20. Mexican Government Reports for 1969–70 on the Minimum Age (Underground Work) Convention, 1965 (No. 123) and the Medical Examination of Young Persons (Underground Work) Convention, 1965 (No. 124).

21. 1972 Committee of Experts' direct request to Mexican Government concerning Convention No. 123.

22. The 1972 Committee of Experts direct request to the Mexican Government concerning Convention No. 124 raised questions about other provisions of the Convention. While contending that Articles 2(1) and 3(2) were self-executing the government report also pointed out that they were applied by Industrial Hygiene Regulations of 1946.

23. Swiss Government Report on Convention No. 123 for 1968–70; Committee of Experts' direct request to Switzerland in 1971 regarding Convention No. 123.

24. The 1964 Committee of Experts' direct request to Mexico regarding Convention No. 112 simply asked what steps were taken to bring the Convention to the notice of tribunals and the competent services. On receiving the government's reply, the Committee raised no further questions.

25. 1974 R.C.E. 195.

26. See chapter 2, sec. 3.3.

27. 50 R.P. 582 (1966); 1967 R.C.E. 26–27.

28. See discussion of the Roa case in chapter 6, sec. 2.2.

29. 1967 R.C.E. 26–27.

30. See discussion of the Haras "Los Cardos" case in chapter 6, sec. 2.1.

31. Ibid.

32. Henry J. Steiner and Detlev F. Vagts, *Transnational Legal Problems* (Mineola, New York: The Foundation Press, Inc., 1976 2d ed.), p. 584.

33. See discussion of the Castanié case and the Compan-Vaquer case in chapter 6, secs. 3.2 and 3.3.

34. Req., 27 fevr., 1934, D.H., 1934, 203, S. 1935, I.1 et note Niboyet.

35. International Labour Conference, 15th session (1931), vol. II, pp. 371 and 381.

36. Ibid., p. 463.

37. International Labour Conference, 15th session (1931), vol. I (Third Part—Appendices), pp. 640–641. The problem in France relating to the direct application of this Convention is discussed extensively in Jean Morellet, *La notion de reciprocité dans les traités de travail et les conventions internationales du travail*, 26 Revue de droit international privé 642 (1931).

38. Valticos, op. cit., 16 [translation].

39. International Labour Conference, 15th session (1931), vol. II, pp. 374–375.

40. Ibid.; see also Alexandre Berenstein, *The Influence of International Labour Conventions on Swiss Legislation*, 77 I.L.R. 1, 6 (1958).

41. Rapport du conseil fédéral a l'assemblée fédérale sur les 57e et 58e sessions de la conférence internationale du travail et message concernant deux conventions internationales du travail (du 8 mai 1974), Feuille fédérale, 17 juin 1974, vol. I, No. 24, pp. 1592–1593 [translation].

42. Ibid., p. 1599.

43. Ibid. [translation].

44. Menno J. van Emde Boas, *The Impact of the European Convention of Human Rights and Fundamental Freedoms on the Legal Order of the Netherlands*, 13 Neth. Int'l L. Rev. 337, 369–370 (1966) [footnotes omitted]. It will be recalled that, according to the express language of the Netherlands Constitution only self-executing treaty provisions prevail over municipal law in the Netherlands. The comments of the Committee of Experts referred to in this quotation are found in 1959 R.C.E. 46, 1961 R.C.E. 73–75.

45. Valticos, op. cit., 15.

46. 1967 R.C.E. 26–27.

47. 1962 R.C.E. 61–62, 1964 R.C.E. 92, 1965 R.C.E. 70, 1970 R.C.E. 81–82.

48. Inconsistencies in such cases may, of course, be due to inadequate consideration of the problem at different periods of time rather than to a changing position of principle by the Committees.

49. 36 R.P. 378–379 (1953).

50. 1973 R.C.E. 56.

51. 36 R.P. 378 (1953), 1971 R.C.E. 53, 1973 R.C.E. 56.

52. 36 R.P. 378–379 (1953).

53. 1971 Committee of Experts' direct request to Mexican Government concerning Convention No. 13.

54. 1973 R.C.E. 57.

55. See chapter 6, sec. 1.

56. 1961 Committee of Experts' direct request to Mexican Government concerning Convention No. 62.

57. 1963 Committee of Experts' direct request to Mexican Government concerning Convention No. 110.

CHAPTER 8

Relative Rank of Labour Conventions and Conflicting National Norms

In addition to the question of determining whether a particular provision of a convention is or is not self-executing, ILO supervisory organs and national courts and administrators have been faced with a further difficult question regarding the application of these conventions in automatic incorporation states, i.e., the problem of the rank within a particular legal system of self-executing convention provisions in relation to other norms of national law. Do self-executing provisions of conventions prevail over conflicting constitutional provisions or conflicting statutes or do the national provisions prevail over the convention provision?[1] Does it make a difference if the statute is earlier or later in time than ratification of the convention? As will be pointed out below, the states examined in this case study have adopted different solutions to this problem.

The application by domestic courts or administrators of a national law which is in conflict with a ratified convention is a violation of international treaty law, but may be required by national law. It is also a violation of international law if the convention is not applied internally because it is contrary to the national constitution. States are obliged to conform their internal law with obligations they have undertaken in ratifying treaties. The ILO organs responsible for supervising the application of the convention must necessarily, therefore, be concerned with the rank of treaty norms in national law.

1. Preliminary Note: Separation of Powers Question—Efforts to Reconcile Conflicting Treaties and Laws

Two general aspects pervade problems involving the relative rank of treaties and national norms in automatic incorporation states: (1) separation of powers and (2) efforts to reconcile conflicting treaties and laws.

The attitude of the courts in a particular legal system with regard to separation of powers among the judicial, legislative and executive branches of government has an important bearing on determinations of which legal norms will prevail over others. In some countries, it may be accepted constitutional theory that treaty norms have a higher rank than either earlier or later laws but separation of powers considerations may inhibit the courts from applying a treaty provision rather than a law enacted by the legislature. In such a case the theoretical hierarchy of certain norms may remain a dead letter. The question of whether the courts in a particular legal system have the power to review statutes or treaties for unconstitutionality is also relevant in this context. This separation of powers issue will be referred to below, where relevant, in the consideration of the various legal systems, but its significance as a general problem should be kept in mind.[2]

In situations of apparent conflict between a treaty and a law, the courts in various countries generally attempt to reconcile the two and thus avoid the necessity of deciding on their relative rank. In some cases, unusual efforts are made to interpret a treaty so that it does not conflict with an earlier statute or to interpret a statute so that it does not conflict with an earlier treaty. One frequently used interpretive technique is to consider the treaty as *lex specialis* and thus to be applied in a particular case despite a conflict with a more general statute.[3] Such efforts occasionally lead to rather extraordinary interpretations but they emphasize the desire of courts in most automatic incorporation systems to avoid facing the issue of conflict and to attempt to uphold both norms. Thus, courts frequently avoid deciding which norm must prevail in cases of conflict despite clear constitutional provisions governing the matter.

2. National Legal Systems and the Relative Rank of Treaty Provisions and National Norms

In most of the countries examined herein, duly ratified treaty provisions are considered to have the same rank as national laws. This is the case in the United States, Mexico, Argentina, and Italy. Thus, in the event of a conflict, the law or treaty provision later in time would be applied. This solution, based on the maxim *lex posterior derogat priori*, is the same solution as would be applied in any case of two conflicting laws. As mentioned above, however, in the case of such a conflict an effort will be made to reconcile the two.

The situation is somewhat different in France, the Netherlands and Switzerland where a treaty may prevail over even a later law. In the Netherlands, self-executing treaty provisions, according to the Constitution, take precedence over domestic laws, including later laws, and in certain circumstances may derogate from the Constitution. As pointed out in earlier chapters, however, the restrictive definition of self-executing treaty provisions by the courts has tended to limit the importance of the rank of treaties. The French Constitution also gives, in theory, precedence to treaty provisions over earlier or later national laws but until recently problems of separation of powers have caused the courts to be reluctant to apply an earlier treaty in preference to a later law. Switzerland has no constitutional provision concerning the priority of treaties and laws. Recently, the Swiss Federal Tribunal, deviating from prior decisions, gave precedence to a later law over an earlier treaty.

In addition to the problems arising from a later law in conflict with an earlier treaty, there are occasionally problems raised in various countries concerning the conflict of treaties with the Constitution.

2.1. *Primacy Given to National Laws if Later in Time*

2.1.1. *United States*

The United States Constitution provides that treaties shall be the "supreme law of the land" and that they should prevail over conflicting *state* constitutions or laws (whether earlier or later). The language of the Constitution says nothing about conflicts between treaty provisions and *federal* laws. In chapter 4, it was pointed out that this question was not of concern to the drafters of the U.S. Constitution.[4] The question of conflicting federal laws and treaties soon surfaced, however, and the courts were faced with deciding the issue.

In 1884, in the *Head Money* cases, the opinion of the U.S. Supreme Court stated that the Constitution gave a treaty "no superiority over an act of Congress" and that lacking any "superior sanctity" the treaty was "subject to such acts as Congress may pass for its enforcement, modification or repeal."[5] In a later series of cases, the Supreme Court reaffirmed that since treaties and federal statutes have equal status, the later in time would prevail.[6] And it is now settled constitutional doctrine that the U.S. Congress may pass legislation which contravenes an internationally binding treaty commitment of the United States and the legislation will be upheld in American courts.[7]

Despite this established interpretation of the U.S. Constitution, many legal scholars have pointed out that it is by no means a necessary conclusion from the constitutional provision. Henkin has stated:

> As an original matter, the equality of treaties and federal statutes seems hardly inevitable; surely there is no basis for it in the Supremacy Clause which the Supreme Court invoked ... That clause says only that treaties and statutes are both law of the land; it does not follow that they are equal to each other ... Whatever the arguments, the equality of statutes and treaties in domestic law seems established, and acts of Congress inconsistent with earlier treaty obligations are regularly given effect by the courts.[8]

In examining the first Supreme Court decision upholding the "later in time" doctrine,[9] Pitman Potter has pointed out that the Supreme Court's reasoning was based on unsound reasoning in two lower court opinions.[10] He argues that the doctrine of the superiority of treaties over later federal statutes "must prevail all along the line, in the interests of sound jurisprudence and practical convenience as well."[11] Sohn and Partan have both argued that the "later in time" judge-made doctrine should not apply in the case of constitutional type treaties such as the United Nations Charter.[12]

Despite scholarly criticism of the "later in time" doctrine, however, it appears to be solidly entrenched in judicial thinking in the U.S. and not likely to be overturned by the courts in the near future. It is also settled American doctrine that treaties may not contravene the Constitution. Henkin writes that:

> No provision in any treaty has been held unconstitutional by the Supreme Court and few have been seriously challenged there. It is now settled, however, that treaties are subject to the constitutional limitations that apply to all exercises of federal power, principally, the prohibitions of the Bill of Rights.[13]

Judicial review of the constitutionality of statutes has been an aspect of U.S. constitutional law since the Supreme Court decision in *Marbury* v. *Madison* in 1803.[14] It has also been settled since the Supreme Court decision in *Reid* v. *Covert* in 1954[15] that judicial review of the constitutionality of treaties is available in American law.

2.1.2. *Argentina*

The Argentine Constitution, like the U.S. Constitution, does not state whether treaties prevail over federal legislation, although it does state that they prevail over provincial laws or constitutions. In 1963, the Argentine Supreme Court held in the case of *Martin & Cia, Ltda. S.A.* c. *Administración General de Puertos* that treaties and federal statutes were equal in rank in Argentina and, therefore, the later in date would prevail over the earlier.[16] The Court held that a Decree-Law inconsistent with a Treaty of Commerce and Navigation with Brazil must be applied rather than the treaty since it was later in date. The opinion of the Court mentioned that this solution had also been followed by the United States judiciary in interpreting Article VI(2) of the U.S. Constitution and cited U.S. authority for the proposition.

As in the United States, scholarly criticism has been focused on this doctrine. Bidart Campos contends that while the Constitution should always prevail over a treaty, a treaty should always prevail over a conflicting law, even if the latter is later in time. He invokes the principle of *pacta sunt servanda* to support his contention, pointing out that no state may individually alter the terms of a treaty with other states.[17]

It is also clear from decisions of the Argentine Supreme Court that treaties may not prevail over constitutional provisions.[18] One much criticized case has held, however, that treaties may prevail over the Constitution in time of war.[19]

2.1.3. *Mexico*

The situation in Mexico is once again similar to that of the United States and Argentina. The Mexican Constitution provides for the superiority of treaties over state constitutions and laws but does not refer to the relative authority of treaties and federal laws. The maxim *lex posterior derogat priori* is applied in case of a conflict between a treaty and a federal law.[20]

Mexico is unique in one regard. Unlike the Constitution of Argentina and the United States, the Mexican Constitution specifically states that only treaties "made in accordance" with the Constitution shall be the supreme law of the land.[21]

Judicial review of the constitutionality of statutes and treaties is available in both the Argentine and Mexican legal systems. In Argentina, the power of judicial review is entrusted to the entire regular judiciary. In Mexico, the federal judiciary may exercise judicial review but not the state courts.[22]

2.1.4. *Italy*

In Italy, the "order of execution," adopted at the same time as the act authorizing ratification of a treaty, accomplishes the incorporation of the treaty in national law if its provisions are self-executing. It is evident that the nature of this method of incorporation, based on the dualist conception, confers no higher status on the treaty than an ordinary law. Thus, a later treaty so incorporated would abrogate an earlier conflicting law and a later law would abrogate the provisions of a conflicting treaty ratified and incorporated earlier, in accordance with the maxim *lex posterior derogat priori.*[23]

2.2. *Primacy (In Principle) Given to Treaty Norms*

2.2.1. *France*

The principle enunciated in Article 55 of the French Constitution is more far-reaching than that contained in the U.S., Argentine and Mexican

Constitutions since it provides that "treaties ... have an authority superior to that of laws." Nevertheless, the problem of which organ of government is competent to control the priority between treaties and laws has tended to emasculate the provision. The constitutional provision does not expressly confer on judges the power to control the superiority of treaties over laws. Peter Hay has stressed the difference between the French system and other systems in this regard:

> [In France] strict notions of separation of powers did not lead to judicial supervision of legislative or executive action but rather to noninterference by the judiciary and deference to the "act of government." Article 55 of the 1958 Constitution, giving constitutional rank to treaties, thus had a different impact in the light of French legal tradition than observers with different legal traditions of their own expected. Article 55 to the French, was rather a statement of state policy, even governmental obligation, but, just as its 1946 predecessor, not designed to change the role of the judiciary vis-a-vis the executive part of the government. In fact, the establishment of a Constitutional Council for limited pre-enactment review of legislation for constitutionality rather underscores that post enactment review by the courts was not intended, Article 55 notwithstanding.[24]

Despite this traditional reluctance of the French courts, however, the *Cour de Cassation* in a 1975 decision in the case of *Administration des Douanes* c. *Société "Cafés Jacques Vabre" et société J. Weigel* upheld the priority of a treaty over a subsequent law.[25] This decision may be explained in part by the decision of the Constitutional Council on 15 January 1975 in which the Council decided that its role did not include ensuring the respect of Article 55 of the Constitution conferring on treaties an authority superior to that of laws. The Council decided that treaties did not receive constitutional status solely because Article 55 conferred a superiority on them over laws.[26] Valticos suggests that, following this decision, the conviction that respect for the constitutional provision granting superiority to treaties could only be assured by judicial authorities may have led to the 1975 decision of the *Cour de Cassation* in the *"Cafés Jacques Vabre"* case. He also points out the discrepancy between the 1975 decision of the *Cour de Cassation* and decisions of the *Conseil d'Etat*, the highest administrative tribunal. The latter, in 1968 in the case of *Syndicat général des fabricants de semoules*, had declined to apply a regulation of the Council of the EEC, duly adopted in accordance with the Treaty of Rome, and applied instead a conflicting French ordinance on the grounds that it had no competence to control a legislative act in relation to a treaty norm, despite Article 55 of the Constitution.[27] The *Cour de Cassation*, however, in contrast to the *Conseil d'Etat*, is not called upon to annul a rule of inferior rank but simply to set it aside in a particular case in favor of a rule of superior rank. After pointing out the different solutions to the treaty-later law conflict, Valticos comments:

> Will the two highest courts continue for a long period to maintain opposing positions on a point of such importance? Is the difference in positions sufficiently explained by the differing missions of the two jurisdictions or will it be resolved one day—and in which sense? The year 1975, which saw the resolution of some important questions, leaves several question marks regarding the future.[28]

The 1975 *Cour de Cassation* decision related to an EEC treaty but its import, according to Valticos, is not limited solely to treaties of the European Community.[29]

An unusual result of the *Cour de Cassation* decision is that the *Cour de Cassation* may now refuse to uphold a law in conflict with an earlier treaty whereas it would feel required to uphold the law in the event of a conflict of the law with the Constitution. Determinations of the constitutionality of laws are reserved to the Constitutional Council.

2.2.2. *Switzerland*

Conflicting decisions in Switzerland regarding the relative supremacy of treaties and laws have resulted in some confusion on the subject. Lardy has written that the jurisprudence is "changing, uncertain and opens the way to contradictory interpretations."[30] He states that the doctrinal bases for the varying decisions are lacking and that similar solutions have been reached on the basis of different reasons and different solutions on the basis of the same reasons. With the exception of two cases—one in 1933 and the other in 1973—the Swiss Federal Tribunal has consistently reiterated that treaties are superior to laws, even later laws. In extensive jurisprudence in which the Federal Tribunal has emphasized the priority of treaties, it has attempted to reconcile the treaty and the law so as to find no conflict, or has applied the treaty as *lex specialis* in relation to the law, thus avoiding a decision regarding direct conflict between the two.[31]

In the 1933 decision in *Steenworden* c. *Societé des Auteurs*, the Federal Tribunal abandoned its earlier references to the superiority of treaties over laws and held that they were equal in rank and thus the later in date must prevail.[32] The Federal Tribunal found a clear conflict between a 1908 copyright treaty and a 1922 federal law and applied the later law. The decision was criticized by a number of writers as deviating from a long line of cases upholding the supremacy of treaties over laws.[33] It has been pointed out that the *Steenworden* case was an exception and until recent date was not followed by the Federal Tribunal.[34]

In 1973 the Federal Tribunal decided in *Schubert* c. *Commission cantonale tessinois*[35] that a federal law prohibiting the ownership of property by non-resident foreigners (unless cantonal authorization was obtained) should be applied in preference to an earlier Swiss-Austrian treaty which provided for equality of treatment as regards residence and property ownership for the citizens of both countries. This decision has been considered a deviation from the trend of judicial decisions in Switzerland and has been criticized by commentators.[36] It has been suggested that it is unlikely to be followed in the future since it involved a bilateral treaty ratified many years earlier and a recent law expressing an important policy decision.[37] The *Schubert* decision illustrates (as do decisions on the self-executing nature of treaty provisions in the United States) that sensitive political issues often affect determinations of the courts regarding application of treaties.

2.2.3. *The Netherlands*

The Dutch Constitution provides that laws shall not apply if they are incompatible with self-executing treaties ("agreements the contents of which may be binding on anyone") whether ratified earlier or later than the adoption of the law. Thus, Dutch courts are specifically authorized to test national statutes as regards their conformity with self-executing treaties, and treaties have priority over even later laws. The major obstacle to the application of treaties in the Netherlands appears to be a restrictive interpretation of "the contents of which may be binding on anyone" and not the question of a later law. Decisions of Dutch courts refusing to uphold statutes because of conflict with earlier treaties have been rare,[38] perhaps because the courts have given a restrictive interpretation to the constitutional provision and thus given preference to national laws on that basis.

While courts in the Netherlands may test statutes for their conformity with treaties, they may not test statutes for their conformity with the Constitution. This has raised an interesting possibility in relation to the European Convention on Human Rights. Van Panhuys writes:

> Although the rights defined in the Convention are, in principle, also enunciated in the Netherlands Constitution, its practical value, as far as the Netherlands is concerned, lies precisely in the fact that statutes (as distinct from lower legislation) cannot be reviewed as to their conformity with the Constitution, whereas such review was made possible in 1953 in respect to their conformity with treaties. Fundamental questions can now be raised in the courts, for which the latter had no competence before 1953.[39]

3. ILO Conventions and Conflicting National Norms

3.1. *Conflict with National Constitution*

The Mexican Constitution was amended in 1934 to ensure that only treaties made in accordance with the Constitution would be the supreme law of the land.[40] In 1937 the Mexican government ratified the Night Work of Young Persons (Industry) Convention, 1919 (No. 6) and in 1956 the government denounced it because a provision of the Convention was considered to be contrary to the Constitution. Apparently, at the time of ratification, a constitutional reform was envisaged which would have meant the possibility of changing the Constitution to conform to the Convention.[41] Such a change subsequently became politically impracticable. In its first report on the Convention, the government pointed out that the Mexican Constitution only forbade night work for children under sixteen, whereas the Convention forbade it for children under eighteen. It was stated that the Ministry of Labour would see with the Congress the possibility of raising the age in the Constitution to accord with the Convention.[42] The report of the government for the period 1937–39 stated that the Convention could not come into force in national law because it was contrary to Article 123(II) of the Constitution which forbids night work only for children under sixteen. A possible interpretation of this provision would be to regard the Constitution as simply establishing a minimal age for night work for children but permitting a higher age to be established by laws or treaties. The government appeared, however, to regard it as giving a right for the employment of children over sixteen in night work. Hence, the Convention was seen as contrary to the Constitution and thus inapplicable in Mexican law. The government report again spoke of the possibility of amending the Constitution.

In an observation in 1947 the Committee of Experts pointed out that serious divergencies existed between the Constitution and the Federal Labour Law (which also established the age of sixteen as the permissive age for night work for children) and the Convention provision.[43] At the 1948 Conference Committee a government representative referred to current political difficulties in amending the Constitution. After 1952 the government did not submit reports on the Convention stating that the amendment of the Constitution was a very complicated matter. In 1955 the government reported that it was ratifying the Night Work of Young Persons (Industry) Convention (Revised), 1948 (C. No. 90) and that it considered that the ratification of this Convention meant the automatic denunciation of Convention No. 6. Unlike Convention No. 6, Convention No. 90 permitted governments to retain the age limit of sixteen for night work for young persons if this age was provided for in national law at the time of ratification. The International Labour Office pointed out that Convention No. 6 did not provide for automatic denunciation by virtue of the ratification of a later revising treaty. Hence, it was necessary to specifically denounce Convention No. 6 despite the ratification of Convention No. 90 if Mexico wished not to be bound by Convention No. 6.

The impasse was resolved by the denunciation of Convention No. 6 by Mexico in 1956.[44]

3.2. *Convention Norms in Conflict with Earlier Laws*

In the judicial systems of all of the countries examined in this case study it is clear that a later in time self-executing convention provision prevails over an earlier law. There appears to be no legal confusion over this aspect of the hierarchy of norms. The maxim *lex posterior derogat priori* is followed in most of the states and in others, self-executing treaty norms take precedence over even later laws. Thus, the ILO supervisory organs and national courts have had little difficulty in determining the legal result in questions of application of convention provisions in cases of clear conflict with an earlier law once the initial question of whether a provision is or is not self-executing has been resolved.

Nevertheless it is in precisely such cases that the ILO supervisory organs have perceived the greatest difficulty in the application of convention norms because of the lack of publicity for the convention provisions. ILO organs have considered this as a difficulty of the practical order rather than the legal order. Despite the clear legal situation considerable confusion as to the *effective* application of convention norms exists in such cases. Examples of such situations are cited in the following chapter. The primary problem is one of making the convention provisions known to the persons concerned.

It suffices to state here, under the consideration of legal problems, that the legal hierarchy of ILO convention norms over earlier laws has not resulted in many legal problems.

An interesting example of a determination that a self-executing provision of an international labour convention prevails over a conflicting earlier law arose in Italy in 1973. It concerned the Night Work (Women) Convention (Revised), 1948 (C. No. 89). Article 3 of this Convention (which had been ratified by Italy in 1952) provides that

> women without distinction of age shall not be employed during the night in any public or private industrial undertaking; ...

Article 2 provides

> that the competent authority may prescribe different intervals for different areas, industries, undertakings or branches of industries or undertakings, but shall consult the employers' and workers' organizations concerned before prescribing an interval beginning after eleven o'clock in the evening.

Article 2 also defines the term "night" as signifying

> a period of at least eleven consecutive hours, including an interval prescribed by the competent authority of at least seven consecutive hours falling between ten o'clock in the evening and seven o'clock in the morning.

Italian Act 653 (Sec. 2 and 13), adopted in 1934, prohibited night work for women but contained a different definition of "night" than in the Convention. It defined night as a period of eleven hours including the interval between ten p.m. and five a.m. This differed from the Convention definition of "night". Act 653 also differed slightly from the Convention provision contained in Articles 4, 5, 6, 7 and 8 regarding requirements to be fulfilled in permitting exceptions for night work for women.

In 1972 the Committee of Experts in a direct request pointed out that Act 653 permitted exceptions for night work for women more extensive than those permitted by the Convention in Articles 4, 5, 6, 7 and 8. It also referred to the fact that the government report for 1969–71 on Convention No. 89 stated that the labour inspectorate issued fifteen authorizations to make exceptions to night work for periods varying from five days to several months and affecting 350 women workers. The government report has also stated that in granting authorizations for exceptions the labour inspectors had based their actions on Act No. 653 (not on the Convention). The Committee of Experts expressed the hope that Italy would take the necessary steps "to amend its legislation on this point and to ensure that its practice is in conformity with the Convention."

Italy did not amend its legislation on this point. Rather the Ministry of Labour and Social Welfare submitted the question of whether the Convention prevailed over earlier law to the Council of State for its opinion.[45] In an opinion dated 20 February 1973 the Council of State held that the Convention prevailed over the earlier law because the Act which had authorized ratification of the Convention had also contained the usual implementing order giving internal execution to the provisions of the Convention.[46] The Council also refers to Article 10(1) of the Italian Constitution relating to the incorporation of general international law in the Italian legal system,[47] and to Article 19(8) of the ILO Constitution which provides that the adoption of a convention may not be interpreted to repeal any more favorable provisions of national law. The Council said that the latter provision could not cast any doubt on the direct application of the Convention provisions since the more flexible provision of the Convention defining "night" was more favorable to women workers than the rigid fixed period contained in the law.

Following the opinion of the Council of State, a ministerial decree was issued in 1973 citing the Council of State opinion and providing that in accordance therewith labour inspectors in Italy should henceforth refer to Convention No. 89 rather than to the Italian Act No. 653 of 1934 for definition of night work for women and for procedure regarding the granting of exceptions.[48] A circular containing this decree was communicated to regional and provincial labour inspectors and trade unions.[49] These decrees and circulars are of particular importance since they bring to the attention of persons concerned the legal effect of treaty provisions over earlier law.

Another example of a convention provision prevailing over an earlier conflicting provision of national law is provided by the application of Convention No. 19 in Switzerland. Berenstein has written:

> It follows that an international Convention may have a decisive influence on internal law even though its ratification has not led to any legislative changes. For example, Switzerland ratified the Equality of Treatment (Accident Compensation) Convention, 1925, which materially changed the Federal Sickness and Accident Insurance Act of 13 June 1911 although this Act (section 90 of which provides for differential treatment of insured foreigners) was not formally amended. Nevertheless, the Convention—like any bilateral agreement concluded with any country—is directly applied by the Swiss National Accident Insurance Fund.[50]

3.3. *Convention Norms in Conflict with Subsequent Laws*

Unlike the question of the relative authority of ILO convention provisions and earlier national laws, the question of the relative hierarchy of convention norms and later laws has resulted in considerable uncertainty. Governments which allege that in their constitutional system treaties are national law upon ratification often fail to consider that, also according to their constitutional system, a later conflicting law will be applied by the courts in preference to an earlier treaty. When it has become apparent to the ILO Committee of Experts that an inconsistent law has been adopted subsequently to the ratification of the convention, the Committee has questioned the government's statements that the treaty is applied because it is automatically incorporated. It has pointed out that the application of the subsequent law would be a violation of the convention.

It is rare that countries take measures in deliberate derogation of ILO conventions, although that situation may arise. As a result of a shortage of electricity following World War II, the Italian government made certain derogations regarding the prohibition of night work for women which were contrary to the ILO convention ratified by Italy. When this was called to the government's attention, the provisions of the Convention (incorporated in Italian law by the "order of execution") were once again applied.[51] The more common situation is that in which the later law has been adopted without a realization that it is in contradiction with an earlier convention or where the legal situation may not be clear as to the relative hierarchy of treaties and later laws.

The Mexican government ratified the White Lead (Painting) Convention, 1921 (No. 13) in 1938. Article 3(1) of this Convention prohibits the employment of males under eighteen and all females in any painting work of an industrial character involving the use of white lead. In 1969 a new Federal Labour Law was enacted, which, in Section 175, maintained an earlier provision providing that the minimum age for admission to dangerous or unhealthy occupations was sixteen years. The government's report for 1970–72 stated that in the opinion of the Legal Adviser of the Ministry of Labour, Article 3(1) of the Convention prevailed over section 175 of the 1969 Federal Labour Law because it was a more specific provision and, in the event of a conflict between norms, the more specific prevails over the more general. This constituted a recognition that normally in Mexico a later law prevails over an earlier treaty provision. When a conflict existed between an ILO convention provision and an earlier law, the government invariably invoked Article 133 of the Constitution as guaranteeing application of the convention provision. In this situation they did not do so, recognizing that the situation was different.[52]

The supervisory Committees did not comment on this contention of the government despite the fact that the Labour Law had been enacted after the ratification of the Convention and hence the Labour Law rather than the Convention would normally have been applied. In an observation in 1973, the Committee considered Article 3 as a whole as non-self-executing (it had previously considered only Article 3(1) as non-self-executing) and asked for the adoption of provisions implementing it. This seemed to relate, however, to the need for regulations by the "competent authorities" in order for the government to avail itself of the exceptions referred to in Article 3(2).

The problem of the date to be employed in determining whether a law is prior to or subsequent to a convention when the law is reenacted or included in a new codification arose in relation to the *Klaiss* case in France in 1962.[53] In that case a discrepancy existed between Article 289 of the French Social Security Code adopted in 1956 and the ILO Maternity Protection Convention (No. 3) ratified by France in 1950. The *Cour de Cassation* determined that the Convention provision rather than the Social Security Code should be applied. The *Cour de Cassation* did not mention the fact that the Social Security Code was later in date than the ratification of the Convention. It would thus appear that in this case the Court applied an earlier treaty in preference to a later convention. Valticos, however, has written in this regard:

> In reality, the question is not so simple. ... There is no doubt that, like numerous other analogous decrees of codification since 1948 (the date when the superior Commission was established charged with the codification and simplification of legislative texts and regulations) the decree codifying the legislative texts concerning social security was formally limited, for reasons of convenience, to the classification and systematization of pre-existing legislative texts which were not basically modified ... As a result, the legislative texts thus codified conserved their earlier legal validity. The codification decree did not add anything new to that validity. It cannot be considered, in this case, that there was truly a conflict between a treaty and a later law and that the decision was decisive in this regard. At the most it can be considered indicative to a certain extent since the *Cour de Cassation* did not even raise the question whether the later date of the decree should be taken into consideration in determining if the earlier ratified Convention should prevail.[54]

In the 1960s and 1970s a series of exchanges took place between representatives of the Guatemalan government and the ILO supervisory committees relating to the priority of ILO convention provisions over later laws. In 1962 a representative of the Guatemalan government remarked at the Conference Committee that the "administrative and judicial authorities must in all cases apply ratified conventions in precedence to national legislation".[55] Subsequently, in 1969, a statement from the Guatemalan Council of State was communicated to the ILO again referring to the priority of treaties over national legislation. Neither of these statements specifically referred to the situation where the law was later in date than the treaty.

In 1969 the government transmitted to the ILO the 1967 edition of the Labour Code which contained an introduction concerning, inter alia, the relationship of ILO conventions to the Labour Code. This introduction pointed out that provisions of the Labour Code and those contained in duly ratified ILO conventions were laws of the same hierarchy or rank.[56] This excerpt implies that a subsequent law would prevail over an earlier convention provision. In the 1971 edition of the Labour Code, the statement that ILO conventions and Labour Code provisions were laws of the same hierarchy was omitted from the corresponding paragraph.[57] In 1970 the Committee of Experts had stated in their annual report that:

> The Committee notes that in certain cases the legislation on which it has commented was adopted after the ratification of the conventions in question, thus replacing or modifying the provisions of the Convention considered as municipal law. Indeed, it appears that, according to the constitutional system of Guatemala, a convention which has been ratified and has consequently become part of the national legal system, has predominance over other laws and may therefore be amended by a later law.[58]

No authority is cited by the Committee of Experts for the assumption that later laws prevail over earlier convention provisions in Guatemala. Guatemalan courts have applied treaties in preference to later conflicting laws.[59] The Committee's opinion may have been based on the statement in the introduction to the 1967 edition of the Labour Code (and dropped from the later edition) that ILO conventions and provisions of the Labour Code are laws of the same rank.

In 1970 a government representative at the Conference Committee stated that ratified treaties prevailed even over subsequent laws. Despite a conviction on the part of the Guatemalan government that an earlier treaty prevailed over a later law in their legal system, the government subsequently agreed to adopt implementing laws in response to Committee of Experts comment.[60]

The question of the relative rank of an earlier convention provision and a later national law was dealt with extensively in a 1963 Report of a Commission of Inquiry investigating the observance of an ILO convention by Liberia. Following a complaint by Portugal that Liberia was not applying the provisions of the Forced Labour Convention, 1930 (No. 29), which it had ratified in 1931, the ILO Governing Body appointed a Commission of Inquiry, in accordance with Article 26 of the ILO Constitution, to investigate Liberia's application of the Convention.

The Commission found that "The Liberian Code of Laws of 1956 contained a substantial number of important provisions the texts of which were plainly inconsistent with the provisions of the Forced Labour Convention, 1930."[61] The government contended that, under Liberian law, the Convention prevailed over earlier conflicting legislation, and that the constitutional provision guaranteeing life, liberty and property rendered unconstitutional all laws permitting forced labour adopted subsequent to the Convention. The Commission accepted the government's contention that the ratification of the Convention resulted in the repeal of earlier conflicting provisions but concerning law enacted after the ratification of the Convention, it stated:

> The Commission does not overlook the possibility that legislation subsequent to and inconsistent with a previously ratified international Convention may be invalid in certain countries by virtue of a specific constitutional provision, but the provisions of the Liberian Constitution and the Foreign Relations Law cited to it contain no provisions of this nature ... Neither the Constitution nor the Foreign Relations Law says anything of the effect of mutually inconsistent treaties and legislation upon each other ... The Commission has had the advantage of hearing the views of the Attorney-General of Liberia on the matter and has been informed by him that the Supreme Court of Liberia would hold to be unconstitutional any legislation subsequent to and inconsistent with the Convention; the Commission naturally treats with great respect the view expressed by the Attorney-General on a matter of Liberian Law, but it must also have regard to his admission that the Supreme Court has never had occasion to decide the matter and to the fact that his view, which is in the nature of an *ex parte* statement made in the course of the present proceedings, would not be binding upon the Supreme Court if the matter were to come before it.
>
> As regards the effect of the Convention, the Commission cannot entirely disregard the fact that under the law of the United States, which has been a major historical influence upon the law of Liberia, ... it is well established that subsequent inconsistent legislation does override an earlier treaty in its operation as municipal law ...[62]

The Commission's Report then cites a number of precedents in U.S. law supporting its statement. It continues:

> The Commission neither asserts nor assumes that the position in Liberia is necessarily the same, but in all the circumstances it cannot accept as convincing the contention that Liberian legislation subsequent in date to the ratification of the Convention was *ultra vires* and invalid by reason of its inconsistency with the Convention. The Commission considers that it is not open to any government to contend in international proceedings relating to an alleged failure to give effect to its obligations under an international labour Convention that the enactment on its initiative or with its consent of legislation apparently inconsistent with the Convention did not in fact involve any such failure because the legislation in question was constitutionally invalid by reason of the inconsistency.[63]

The Commission's report then went on to discuss the problem previously mentioned which has been raised frequently in ILO supervision of the application of conventions: the reenactment of pre-convention legislation in conflict with a provision of a convention. It found that such reenactment was a "serious failure to give effect to the obligations of the convention." Finally, the Commission refuted the argument that the legislation was not legally binding since it was obsolete. The Commission thus considered that Liberian law was not in accordance with the obligations which that country had undertaken in ratifying the Forced Labour Convention.

The government officially accepted the Commission's recommendations and repealed and changed certain laws. As late as 1976, however, the Committee of Experts continued to point out certain discrepancies between Liberian law and the Forced Labour Convention.[64]

4. Conclusion

As the preceding material amply demonstrates, considerable confusion and uncertainty exists in a number of legal systems employing the system of automatic incorporation as regards the relative authority of convention provisions and conflicting legislation—subsequent legislation in particular. The problem is a serious one since the application of a law in conflict with a ratified convention constitutes an international delinquency regardless of the validity of the application of the law domestically. The ILO supervisory organs have thus been legitimately concerned over the problem.

The existence of laws on the books inconsistent with conventions presents not only a legal problem but may generate uncertainty and confusion since persons who are most closely concerned with administering or obeying the laws of the country may not be certain what those laws are.

NOTES

1. Pitman B. Potter has pointed out: "Strictly speaking, there is never a conflict of valid laws, of course, for where laws appear to conflict it will always be found that one of the laws in question is invalid as *ultra vires*, and therefore no law at all. But the presentation of the problem in terms of a supposed conflict has merits of simplicity; the correct method of presentation would demand of writer and reader alike too great a degree of dialectical and mental effort in the presentation to permit due attention to the principal questions at issue." Potter, *Relative Authority of International Law and National Law in the United States*, 19 Am. J. Int'l L. 315 (1925).

2. As earlier chapters illustrate, the issue of separation of powers can also be an important underlying consideration in determining whether a treaty provision is self-executing in a particular legal system. See Charles W. Stotter, *Self-Executing Treaties and the Human Rights Provisions of the United Nations Charter: A Separation of Powers Problem*, 25 Buffalo L. Rev. 773 (1976).

3. The ILO Constitution provides a particular method for resolving conflicts between the provisions of an ILO convention and a more favorable national law. Article 19(8) of the ILO Constitution states:
"In no case shall the adoption of any Convention or Recommendation by the Conference, or the ratification of any Convention by any Member, be deemed to affect any law, award, custom or agreement which ensures more favourable conditions to the workers concerned than those provided for in the Convention or Recommendation." Hence, although a later convention provision might normally prevail over an earlier conflicting law in a particular legal system, it will not do so if the law is more favorable to workers.

4. See chapter 4, sec. 1.1.

5. Edye v. Robertson, 112 U.S. 580, 597 (1884).

6. Whitney v. Robertson, 124 U.S. 190 (1888); Hijo v. United States, 194 U.S. 315 (1904); Pigeon River Improvement, Slide & Boom Co. v. Cox, 291 U.S. 138 (1934); Moser v. U.S., 341 U.S. 41 (1951). Numerous dicta refer to the fact that a later treaty will supersede an earlier conflicting law. The first Supreme Court case which directly so holds, however, appears to be Cook v. United States, 288 U.S. 102 (1933).

7. See Diggs v. Schultz, 470 U.S. 461, cert. denied, 411 U.S. 931 (1972).

8. See Louis Henkin, *Foreign Affairs and the Constitution* (Mineola, New York: The Foundation Press, Inc., 1972), pp. 163–164.

9. Cherokee Tobacco, 11 Wallace 616 (1870).

10. Taylor v. Morton, 23 Fed. Cas. 784, No. 13,799 (C.C. Mass. 1855), aff'd 2 Black 481 (U.S. 1862); Clinton Bridge, 1 Woolworth 150 (1867).

11. Potter, *Relative Authority*. 326.

12. Louis Sohn, *Discussion, the Nuremberg Trials and Objection to Military Service in Vietnam*, 1969 Proc., Am. Soc. Int'l L. 180; Daniel Partan, *Individual Responsibility under a Disarmament Agreement in American Law*, 49 Minn. L. Rev. 889, 952 (1965).

13. Henkin, *Foreign Affairs*, p. 137. In the case of Reid v. Covert, 345 U.S. 1, 16–17 (1957), Justice Black wrote "... no agreement with a foreign nation can confer power on Congress, or on any branch of government, which is free from the restraints of the Constitution. The prohibitions of the Constitution were designed to apply to all branches of the National Government and they cannot be nullified by the Executive or by the Executive and Senate combined."

14. 1 Cranch 137, (1803).

15. 345 U.S. 1 (1957). While the Reid v. Covert decision explicitly stated that treaties may not contravene the Constitution, this had been commonly accepted to be the case long before that decision.

16. Fallos de la Corte Suprema 257:99 (6 Nov. 1963) reproduced in Salvador Maria Lozada, *Derecho Constitucional Argentino Segun El Metodo de Casos* (Buenos Aires: Abeldo-Perrot, 1972), pp. 824–826. See also Esso, S.A. Petrolera Argentina c. Nación Argentina, Fallos de la Corte Suprema (5 June 1968) reproduced in Lozada, op. cit., pp. 818–823. See, however, Martin y Cia, Ltda c. The Government, 26 *International Law Reports* 567–568 (1958), Fallos de la Corte Suprema 241:276, where the Supreme Court applied a treaty in preference to a later conflicting decree. The case concerned a 1940 treaty with Brazil exempting certain items from ordinary customs duties. Later decrees attempted to impose duties on these items. The Court's opinion stated: "As this international agreement is part of the supreme law of the land (Article 31 of the Constitution), it need hardly be pointed out that Article 7 takes precedence over the provisions of Decrees No. 26.224/51 and No. 6093/52, which provided the bases for the warehousing charges which were levied on the merchandise imported by the complainant." 26 *International Law Reports* 568 (1958).

17. German J. Bidart Campos, *Derecho Constitucional* (Buenos Aires: Ediar, 1964–66), vol. I, pp. 285–286.

18. Chantrain, Alfonso (recurso de habeas corpus), Fallos de la Corte Suprema 208:84; Salvador Maria Lozada, *Instituciones de Derecho Publico* (Cordoba, Argentina: Editions Macchi, 1966), pp. 286–287.

19. The Argentine Supreme Court held in Merck Quimica Argentina c. Gobierno de la Nación, Fallos de la Corte Suprema 211:162 (9 June 1948) that a treaty in conflict with the Constitution may prevail over the Constitution in time of war, although not in time of peace. The Court held that the war powers of the President were anterior to, pre-existent to and superior to the Constitution. Hence, his act of ratification of a treaty in conflict with the Constitution could result in the treaty prevailing over the Constitution in time of war. See Bidart Campos, *Derecho Constitucional*, pp. 282–285 for criticism of this decision.

20. Enrique Paez Stille, *Interpretación del Artículo 133 de la Constitución* (México: Tesis, Universidad Nacional de México, 1945), pp. 29–34.

21. See sec. 3.1 of this chapter, infra.

22. See Keith Rosenn, *Judicial Review in Latin America*, 35 Ohio St. L. J. 785 (1974), for a more detailed discussion of judicial review in these countries.

23. See references cited in chapter 4, note 35. Italian courts, as the courts of other countries, go to considerable lengths in interpretation to avoid finding conflicts between treaties and laws. See Luigi Condorelli and Georgio Gaja, ed., *Relationship Between Municipal Law and International Law, Judicial Decisions*, Italian Yearbook of International Law 364–373 (1976); 16–23 (1977).

24. Peter Hay, Review of Eric Bergsten, *Community Law in the French Courts: The Law of Treaties in Modern Attire*, 69 Am. J. Int'l L. 706–707 (1975).

25. Cass. Ch. mixte, D. 1975, 497, concl. Touffait, *Clunet*, 1975, 801, note Ruzié; cf. Jeantet, J.C.P. 1975 I 2743. Also see comments by Nicolas Valticos, 65 R.C.D.I.P. 60, 71 (1976).

26. Conseil constitutionnel, 15 janvier 1975, *Clunet* 1975, pp. 249–268, D. 1975.529, note L. Hamon, 64 R.C.D.I.P. 124–128 (1975). The request for a decision by the Constitutional Council originated from members of the National Assembly who contended that France's recently liberalized abortion law was contrary to Article 2 of the European Convention on Human Rights which provided that "everyone's right to life shall be protected by law ..." The claim on unconstitutionality was based on Article 55 which provided that treaties should have an authority superior to laws. The Council decided that it did not have the competence to control the superiority of treaties over ordinary statutes. It cited the fact that the superiority of a treaty is only relative since, according to the terms of Article 55, its superiority depends on reciprocity and treaties are not part of the Constitution simply because of the Article 55 reference. The Council also held that the abortion law was not contrary to the French Constitution. See comment on this decision, Georg Ress, *The Question of Precedence of International Treaties According to French Constitutional Law*, 35/3 Z.a.ö.R.V., 499–501 (1975).

27. Conseil d'Etat, 1 mars 1968, 57 R.C.D.I.P. 516 (1968), concl. Questiaux, note Kovar, D. 1968.285, note M.L. R.G.D.I.P. 1968.1128, note Ch. Rousseau.

28. See note, Valticos, 65 R.C.D.I.P. 60, 72 (1976).

29. Ibid.

30. Pierre Lardy, *La force obligatoire du droit international en droit interne* (Paris: R. Pichon et R. Durand—Auzias, 1966), p. 208.

31. Ibid., pp. 208–221; Réponse donnée le 10 décembre 1968 à l'interpellation du Conseiller national Korner par M. Spühler, chef du Département politique fédéral, 26 A.S.D.I. 91–101 (1967–70).

32. Steenworden c. Société des Auteurs (17 juillet 1933), A.T.F. 59II 331.

33. See Lardy, *La force obligatoire*, pp. 215–216.

34. "En ce qui concerne l'arrêt Steenworden, il convient de ne pas en exagérer la portée.

Cet arrêt a en effet été rendu au cours de la courte periode durant laquelle on a considéré, à tort, sous l'influence sans doute de la doctrine allemande, que les traités internationaux étaient transformés en lois internes et que, par conséquent, ils avaient rang de loi, avec toutes les conséquences qui s'ensuivent. Le raisonnement tenu par le Tribunal fédéral dans cette affaire ne serait plus pertinent depuis que la pratique suisse est revenue à la théorie de la validité immédiate des traités internationaux." Georges Malinverni, *L'Application de la Convention européenne des droits de l'homme en Suisse*, Mémoires publiés par la Faculté de Droit de Genève, Quinzième Journée Juridique (Genève, Georg, 1977), pp. 25–26.

35. Schubert c. Commission cantonale tessinoise de recours pour l'application de l'arrêté fédéral du 23 mars 1961 concernant l'acquisition d'immeubles par des personnes domiciliées à l'étranger, ATF 99 Ib 39, c. 1, 3, 4 (42–45). Reprinted also in 30 A.S.D.I. 110–113 (1974). The Tribunal stated: "En règle générale et en cas de conflit ouvert, le principe en question reconnaît la primauté de droit international, que celui-ci soit antérieur ou postérieur à la règle de droit interne. Le legislateur, source supreme du droit interne, conserve cependant la faculté de déroger intentionnellement à ce principe; cela lui permet d'assouplir certaines conséquences trop rigoureuses du principe et de sauvegarder en pratique certains intêrets essentiels. Dans la mesure où il y a effectivement eu dérogation intentionnelle, celle-ci doit être respectée dans l'ordre juridique interne; elle lie le Tribunal federal mais ne peut pas modifier la portée des droits et obligations de l'Etat au sein de la communauté internationale." Ibid., 113.

36. See Luzius Wildhaber, *Bemerkungen zum Fall Schubert betrefend das Verhältnis von Völkerrecht und Landesrecht*, 30. A.S.D.I. 195–201 (1974); Malinverni, op. cit., 26–29.

37. Ibid.

38. Jonkheer H. F. van Panhuys, *The Netherlands Constitution and International Law*, 58 Am. J. Int'l L. 88, 103 (1964).

39. Ibid.

40. The cause of the amendment was a Supreme Court decision that an international treaty must be applied even though it may be contrary to the Constitution. 19 *Semanario Judicial de la Federación*, Raja, Jesus Gregorio, 24 de diciembre de 1926, 1162–1163.

41. 30 R.P. 547 (1947).

42. Mexican Government Report on Convention No. 6, 1937.

43. 1947 R.C.E. 14.

44. Communication to the ILO by Mexico, 30 June 1956.

45. According to the Italian Constitution (Articles 100 and 103), "The Council of State is an advisory organ on judicial-administrative matters and ensures the legality of public administration. ... The Council of State and other bodies concerned with administrative justice safeguard the legitimate interests of public administration and even those subjective rights that are foreseen by law."

46. Consiglio di Stato, seconda sezione, 20 febbraio 1973, n.228/73.

47. Article 10(1) of the Italian Constitution: "Italy's legal system conforms with the generally recognized principles of international law."

48. 5 July 1973, Gazzetta Ufficiale, n.192, 26.773, p. 5298.

49. Circular No. 208 of 19 September 1973. Notiziario della Confederazione Generale dell'Industria Italiana, 30 nov. 1973, No. 22.

50. Alexandre Berenstein, *The Influence of International Labour Conventions on Swiss Legislation*, 77 I.L.R. 1, 6 (1958).

51. 35 R.P. 518 (1952); 36 S.R. 28 (1953). See Nicolas Valticos, *Conventions internationales du travail et droit interne*, 44 R.C.D.I.P. 284 (1955).

52. It is interesting to note that Article 3 had been published in the Mexican Labour Review in 1965 together with the provisions of the Labour Code which were not in

conformity with it. Yet, on the reenactment of the new Labour Code in 1969, the conflicting provision was maintained.

53. See discussion of the Klaiss case in chapter 6, sec. 3.1.

54. Nicolas Valticos, *Les conventions internationales du travail devant le juge français*, 53 R.C.D.I.P. 66–67 (1964). A similar problem arose in 1933 in the case of Cook v. United States, 288 U.S. 102. The question in that case was whether a provision of the Tariff Act first enacted in 1922 and reenacted in 1930 was to be applied although it was in conflict with a treaty ratified in 1924. The Court refused to apply the later law in this case because "a treaty will not be deemed to have been abrogated or modified by a later statute unless such purpose on the part of Congress has been clearly expressed ... Here, the contrary appears. The committee reports and the debates upon the Act of 1930, like the reenacted section itself, make no reference to the Treaty of 1924." Ibid., 120.

55. 46 R.P. 690 (1962).

56. Indicaciones Preliminares, Código de Trabajo, 1967 edition, p. XXVII, para. 10.

57. Código de Trabajo de la Republica de Guatemala, 1971, Indicaciones Preliminares, p. XXXI, para. 10.

58. 1970 R.C.E. 23–24.

59. In a 1956 article, Dihigo stated that the Guatemala Supreme Court on 31 March 1937 upheld the validity of a treaty as against a later law in conflict with it. Ernesto Dihigo, *Treaties as Law in National Courts: Latin America*, 16 Louisiana L. Rev. 734 (1956) and authorities cited therein. In the case of Tabacalera Nacional, S.A. c. Administration of Customs (31 May 1955), the Guatemalan Supreme Court upheld the validity of a treaty provision in conflict with a subsequent decree in language which suggested that it would have arrived at the same result had a conflicting law rather than a decree been involved. 22 *International Law Reports* 617–618 (1955).

60. 1974 R.C.E. 12.

61. ILO Official Bulletin, Vol. XLVI, No. 2, Supp. II, April 1963, 157.

62. Ibid., 160–161.

63. Ibid., 161.

64. 1976 R.C.E. 70–73.

CHAPTER 9

Practical Problems in Effective Application of ILO Conventions

1. ILO Concern about Practical Application of Conventions

The concern shown by the ILO Committees over the problems of non-self-executing treaty provisions and the priority of subsequent laws over treaties was to be expected. But they have also evidenced considerable concern over the problems of the lack of publicity given to treaty provisions and the uncertainty resulting from conflicting laws and treaty provisions—even in cases where the legal system clearly provides that treaty provisions prevail over conflicting laws. The Committee of Experts has insisted on the adoption of legislation or administrative regulations implementing conventions as a means of providing more publicity for convention norms and as a means of avoiding uncertainty as to the status of a particular convention norm. It has frequently requested the adoption of national legislation or administrative directives because of its conviction that national practice was not in conformity with convention norms. The governments in question have, in a great number of cases, adopted the implementing legislation or administrative measures.

The attitude of the Committee of Experts on the need for implementing legislation in such cases was clearly expressed in its 1974 report:

> In this regard the Committee has often drawn attention to the practical difficulties which arise in ensuring the effective application of conventions in countries in which, by virtue of the constitutional system or the practice followed, the terms of ratified conventions are automatically incorporated into national law. Quite apart from the problem raised by the fact that most of the provisions of international labour conventions are not self-executing, the incorporation of the terms of ratified conventions into national law sometimes results in uncertainty as to the state of the law if it is not accompanied by appropriate measures of publicity and, as far as possible, by the express amendment or repeal of the pre-existing legislative texts. *The bringing of national legislation into formal conformity with the terms of ratified conventions, which is the solution that the Committee has considered to be the most sound, is also one of the conditions of the effective application of ratified conventions.*[1] [italics added]

The Committee made similar comments in its 1963 report:

> The Committee has emphasized in this connection, the usefulness of taking appropriate measures to draw the attention of all persons concerned (judges, labour inspectors, employers and workers) to the standards laid down in the conventions which have thus automatically been incorporated in internal law.[2]

Although the suggestions of the ILO supervisory bodies that implementing legislation or administrative measures be adopted have frequently been followed by governments, the insistence of the Committees has not gone unchallenged. In some cases, exchanges between government representatives and the Committees have continued for years before the adoption of the suggested legislation or regulations. One commentator has severely criticized the ILO supervisory bodies for their insistence on the adoption of legislation when the legal system clearly provides that treaties prevail over conflicting laws. Pierre Cornil published his criticism in a 1970 article in the *Revue belge de droit international*:

> We know that more and more numerous states are rallying to the monist thesis, and introducing in their Constitution a provision establishing the supremacy of international law over internal law by conferring on a regularly ratified treaty the status of a law, even a superior status ... One would think that this evolution would be welcomed favorably by the Committee of Experts. This is not the case; just the opposite ... [Cornil reports here that the Committee of Experts has insisted that legislation be brought formally into harmony with conventions]. It could not be more clearly stated that the automatic introduction of treaties in the internal legal order is illusory and that the thesis of the supremacy of international law over internal law is utopian. ... The result of the position taken by the Committee of Experts is that the monist theory is radically put to one side ... That an international institution ... refuses to base its action on constitutional principles expressed by states whose action it is supervizing is strange. But, at the international level it is also dangerous. It goes without saying, that if the Committee of Experts refuses to admit the good faith of states who accept in their Constitution, their jurisprudence and their diplomatic practice the supremacy of the rule of international law, it is to be feared that the governments of states—and especially new states so jealous of their national independence—will cease to believe in it themselves, and make their own once again the old thesis of absolute national sovereignty. Governments are only too ready to believe that ratified treaties do not prevail over national law and that as with many other provisions, this provision of their Constitution does not make sense. But the fate of international law depends to a substantial extent on the attitude taken by these states. This attitude is, in its main principles, outlined in their Constitution. It is essential therefore that

> the provisions of this fundamental text be scrupulously applied. ... [The position of the Committee of Experts] undermines considerably the monist theory.[3]

A careful examination, however, of the instances in which the Committee of Experts has requested implementing legislation provides considerable justification for its views on this matter. As succeeding sections of this chapter point out, the Committee has observed a number of problematic situations in automatic incorporation states which could be clarified by the adoption of implementing legislation or administrative measures.

2. Judicial Decisions and Uncertainty Concerning Status of Conventions

The ILO supervisory Committees have noted on occasion that judicial decisions in countries of automatic incorporation have not taken convention provisions into account, despite their status as national law.[4] In the 1950s the Committee of Experts noted such a situation in France. Article 4 of the Maternity Protection Convention (No. 3), ratified by France in 1950, provides that a woman should not be dismissed during a period of pregnancy or confinement for any reason. A section of the French Labour Code provided that a woman could not be dismissed from employment for reasons of pregnancy or confinement but it did not prohibit dismissal for *any reason* during pregnancy or confinement (as the Convention required). In an observation to France in 1959, the Committee of Experts pointed out that a 1958 decision of the *Cour de Cassation* had referred to the provision of the Labour Code but had failed to mention the Convention (as well as another French Act on Maternity Protection which the government had previously maintained implemented the Convention). The Committee asked the government to indicate "what measures are contemplated to amend the provisions of the existing legislation" to bring it into accordance with the Convention.[5]

In a 1959 observation to France concerning the Holidays with Pay Convention (No. 52), the Committee of Experts also referred to a French judicial decision which cited Book II, sec. 54(m), of the Labour Code permitting holidays with pay to be suspended in certain undertakings and to be replaced by compensation. The Holidays with Pay Convention, ratified by France, did not permit such a substitution. A government representative had previously indicated to the Conference Committee that the section of the Labour Code in question was never applied and furthermore would be repealed. After noting that the Supreme Court of Appeals made repeated reference to the section in a decision rendered 7

February 1958, the Committee report noted "therefore, that this provision of the Labour Code cannot be considered as obsolete." The report stated that the Committee welcomed the statement of the government representative that the section would be repealed and hoped that this would be done at an early date.[6]

In the same year, the Committee's report contained the following comments in a general observation to France:

> The Committee further notes that in certain cases which have been pointed out under the relevant conventions, judicial decisions do not appear to take the conventions ratified by France into consideration, although a government representative stated to the Conference in 1953 that "treaties had priority over internal legislation." In these circumstances the Committee would be grateful if the government would consider taking all necessary measures to bring ratified conventions, which are thus incorporated in the national legislation, to the notice of the tribunals and the competent services and to ensure that all persons concerned are informed of these conventions (for example, by means of circulars, references in future editions of the Labour Code, etc.). Such measures would certainly be within the scope of the provisions of Article 19, paragraph 5(d) of the Constitution of the International Labour Organization, which requires states ratifying a convention to take such action as may be necessary "to make effective the provisions of such convention."[7]

A judicial decision in Italy conflicting with a provision of the Holidays with Pay Convention (No. 52) was also noted by the Committee of Experts in 1962. The Committee's report observed that the Court of Appeal of Milan held on 27 July 1955 that sickness occurring during a holiday did not extend the duration of the holiday, although the government had stated in its report that such a practice was inadmissible since it was not in accordance with Convention No. 52. The report continued:

> In the circumstances, it seems unlikely that all persons interested (magistrates, workers, employers, inspectors, etc.) are fully informed of the provisions of the Convention and that the latter can be effectively applied solely through the principle of incorporation of international conventions ratified in the national legislation.
>
> Consequently, the Committee must repeat its previous observations and draw the government's attention ... to the necessity of adopting legislation ensuring the minimum requirements of the Convention ...[8]

The Italian Government had replied to previous observations on Convention No. 52 that clauses of an international convention are inserted directly into Italian internal legislation and automatically receive "full and entire application" upon ratification and the simultaneous adoption of the "order of execution." Following comments by the Committee of Experts, the government informed the Conference Committee in 1964 that it would examine what measures would have to be taken with a view to securing full conformity with the Convention.[9]

Reference has been made in chapter 6 to decisions by the highest courts of the United States, Argentina and France, all involving the application of ILO conventions. In the 1940 case of *Haras "Los Cardos"* in Argentina and the 1934 *Castanié* case in France, in particular, the decisions of the highest courts were preceded by a number of conflicting lower court decisions concerning the application of the Conventions in question. This occasioned considerable confusion among administrators and individuals and led the ILO supervisory organs to question the respective governments repeatedly with regard to the application of the Conventions. Although the highest court may ultimately decide in a country with the system of automatic incorporation that a convention provision should be directly applied, in many cases a long period of uncertainty may precede the decision of the highest court.

But even when the courts of a particular state have clarified the legal status of a convention provision, the ILO supervisory bodies have sometimes insisted that administrative decrees or circulars publicize the court's decision in order that individuals and administrators may be aware of the status of the convention provision as national law. Following the *Cour de Cassation* decision in the *Klaiss* case in France in 1962 (referred to extensively in chapter 6), the Committee of Experts requested that the decision be clearly brought to the attention of directors of the social security system.[10] The Court had held in that case that a provision of the Maternity Protection Convention was to be applied in preference to a less liberal provision of the French Social Security Code. In accordance with the suggestions of the Committee of Experts, the Ministry of Labour informed the regional social security directors of the decision of the *Cour de Cassation* and requested them to apply the provisions of the Convention in the future. The Committee of Experts noted this with approval but pointed out that the communication of the Ministry of Labour included a limitation on the amount of maternity benefits which could ultimately be paid which was not in accordance with the Convention. It requested the government to inform the Committee how it intended to see that the decision of the *Cour de Cassation* was carried out.[11]

While a decision of the highest court may decide a particular case, the administrative services in a country do not always apply the court's holding in similar cases. In 1975, the French *Conseil d'Etat* decided in the

Compan-Vaquer case[12] that the claimant (a Spaniard) was entitled to certain social security benefits as a result of the Equality of Treatment (Accident Compensation) Convention, ratified by France. Yet as late as 1979 it was pointed out that several hundred persons in identical situations to that of Compan-Vaquer had not yet received the benefits that the decision of the *Conseil d'Etat* in 1975 determined they were entitled to. The French administrative service responsible for paying the benefits systematically refused the demands made by foreigners in situations identical to that of Compan-Vaquer unless a court decision expressly required them to do so.[13]

In 1976, however, the Committee of Experts had already called France's attention to the need for widespread publicity concerning the *Compan-Vaquer* decision in order to ensure that the Convention was effectively applied in similar cases.[14]

It is evident from this example that the ILO Committees are correct in insisting on legislation or administrative measures to implement conventions even in cases where the law is clear.

3. Need for Express Repeal of Earlier Conflicting Legislation

The essential aspect of the technique of automatic incorporation is that self-executing provisions of ratified treaties automatically become national law and are to be applied by courts and administrators without the need for implementing legislation. Furthermore, such provisions repeal earlier conflicting legislation. Nevertheless, the ILO Committees have frequently insisted on the adoption of implementing legislation in such cases, as they would if the country had the system of legislative incorporation. In the previous section it was demonstrated that they did so because they noted that national courts were not applying convention provisions. In this section a number of cases will be cited where the Committee of Experts insisted on the express repeal of conflicting earlier legislation or the adoption of new legislation if conflicting legislation was on the books.

One such case involved the Netherlands' ratification of the Maintenance of Migrants' Pension Rights Convention (No. 48). In 1951 (before the 1953 and 1956 amendments to the Dutch Constitution) the Committee of Experts began a series of comments to the government to the effect that Section 168 of the Netherlands Invalidity Insurance Act was in conflict with Article 10 of the Convention relating to the payment of insurance benefits. The government replied that it intended to repeal Section 168 of the Act but that it wished to point out that Article 10 of the Convention, as a self-executing provision, automatically superseded national legislation under the Constitution.[15] The Committee of Experts acknowledged this statement but continued to inquire about progress in the repeal of Section 168. Government reports continued to state that Section 168 was not applied since it was superseded and would eventually be repealed. The conflicting portion of Section 168 was repealed in 1957 and the fact was duly noted with satisfaction by the Committee of Experts in 1959. Thus, even in a case where there was no suggestion that the conflicting earlier law was being applied in preference to a convention, the Committee nevertheless suggested express repeal of the conflicting law. It is conjectural whether the Committee would have required such repeal if the government itself had not stated its intention to do so.

In connection with Article 18 of the same Convention, the Netherlands report had noted that the benefits, in principle granted only to Dutch nationals by the General Old-Age Act and the General Widows and Orphans Act, were also granted to nationals of other ratifying states by virtue of the ratification of Convention No. 48. The Committee of Experts nevertheless asked in 1964 whether administrative regulations would be adopted clearly extending the benefits of those two Acts to non-nationals in accordance with the Convention.[16] The government replied that no such regulations had been issued but that Article 18 of the Convention was directly applied, when appropriate, to nationals of states which had ratified the Convention. It stated, however, that it was considering the possibility of adopting the suggested regulations.[17] Three royal decrees were later adopted placing nationals of ratifying states on the same footing as Dutch nationals under the two Acts. The Committee of Experts noted the adoption of the decrees "with satisfaction" in 1970.

A similar situation but with an additional complication arose in Mexico regarding the application of the Unemployment Indemnity (Shipwreck) Convention (No. 8). In its first report on this Convention in 1938 the government stated that Mexican legislation was not in exact conformity with the Convention and that it would "be necessary to bring the legislation into harmony with the latter ... but that under Article 133 of the Constitution the promulgation of the Convention by the President of the Republic has the effect of transforming it into a federal law."[18] Article 2 of this Convention provides that in cases of shipwreck the owner shall pay each seaman employed on the ship an indemnity for a given period. The Mexican legislation essentially subjected the payment of this indemnity to the existence of insurance covering the contingency. Article 2 appears on its face to be self-executing and appears to have been so considered by both the Mexican government and the Committee of Experts.[19] Over a long period of time, the Committee of Experts requested that the Mexican legislation be brought into harmony with the Convention as the government had stated that it would be. This was not done until 1969, however—a period of 30 years elapsing between the first report and the amendment of the legislation. In the interim the government had contended that the legislation need not be repealed because it was more favorable to the worker than the Convention, or, in the alternative, that the Convention provision had automatically repealed the law.[20]

In 1965 the government printed Article 2 of Convention No. 8 and the corresponding provisions of the Mexican legislation in the *Revista Mexicana del Trabajo* pointing out that by virtue of Article 133 of the Constitution, provisions of ILO conventions were part of national law.[21] At the 1966 Conference Committee a representative of the government stated that the purpose of this publication was to establish clearly that the provisions of the conventions had the force of law in Mexico. In 1967 the Committee of Experts recognized the value of this publicity but stated that it trusted that the government would use the opportunity of "expressly amending the legislation in question when the occasion arises."[22] The government did so when it adopted a new Labour Law in 1969 and in 1971 the Committee of Experts noted this fact "with satisfaction."[23]

The Migration for Employment Convention (No. 97) provides that: "A migrant for employment who has been admitted on a permanent basis ... shall not be returned to [his] territory of origin ... because the migrant is unable to follow his occupation by reason of illness contracted or injury sustained subsequent to entry." Guatemala had ratified the Convention in 1952 but the Aliens Act of 1936 provided, contrary to the Convention, that "the Executive has exclusive power to expel from national territory, on any grounds and without giving reasons, any alien whatever whose stay it considers undesirable for the country." The government had indicated in its reports that provisions of national law contrary to the Convention were automatically abrogated by reason of the ratification of the Convention. In an observation in 1975, the Committee of Experts, nevertheless, requested the government "in order to avoid any uncertainty as to the law and in default of legislative action to bring the Aliens Act expressly and formally into conformity with the Convention on this point."[24] The Committee's observation went on to emphasize the need for bringing the Convention provisions to the attention of interested parties. It requested the government "to take appropriate practical steps to draw the attention of all concerned (in particular, workers, the police and the courts) to the provisions of Article 8 of the Convention which modify the earlier conflicting provisions of national law."[25]

Similarly, as regards another convention ratified by Guatemala, the Committee of Experts emphasized the need for publicity of convention provisions for those most concerned with its administration. Article 6 of the Seafarers Identity Documents Convention (No. 108) provides that each ratifying state "shall permit the entry into the territory ... of a seafarer holding a valid seafarer's identity document, when entry is requested for temporary shore leave while the ship is in port." In a direct request in 1973 the Committee of Experts asked what measures had been taken to bring this Article of the Convention to the attention of "the competent port and immigration authorities." The government replied that ratified conventions were published in the *Diario Official* and in special publications periodically communicated to the competent services. The Committee again asked what instructions had specifically been given to immigration authorities and even to holders of seafarer's documents concerning their right to enter the country. In a 1975 direct request, the Committee noted that its comments had been communicated to the General Migration Authority and hoped that "the government will indicate what measures it has taken or intends to take to ensure that every seafarer who carries a valid seafarer's identity document will be permitted into the country for the purposes listed in the Article." The Committee appeared to be going to unusual lengths to ensure practical application of the Convention where there was no conflicting legislation and the provision appears self-executing.

A number of similar cases could be cited where the ILO has insisted on implementing legislation and special publicity for convention provisions. One situation which has been of obvious concern is that in which earlier legislation contrary to a convention (considered by the country concerned as having been superseded by the convention) has been reenacted as it was prior to the ratification of the convention. Such a situation was brought to the attention of the Commission of Inquiry investigating the application by Liberia of the Forced Labour Convention (No. 29).[26] The report of the Commission in 1963 stated:

> The legal nature and effect of the 1956 Code calls for special examination. The Liberian contention is that it was a codification of all previous legislation not explicitly repealed, undertaken as a first stage in a comprehensive programme of legislative reform and designed to facilitate subsequent consideration of the desirability of substantive changes. The Commission fully accepts that this was the intention of the Liberian Government at the time, but it cannot overlook the fact that the Code was not simply a republication of existing, unrepealed legislation in a comprehensive and orderly manner but was reenacted by the Congress and proclaimed by the President in the same manner as all other legislation and issued as an authoritative compilation of the laws of Liberia. The Code contained the texts of the laws which it is now alleged had been implicitly repealed or were unconstitutional, with no indication that they had been implicitly repealed or were unconstitutional, and it did not contain the text of the Convention which is alleged to have operated as an implied repeal of legislation prior to 1931 or any indication that

> the subsequent legislation was unconstitutional or any reference to the existence of the Convention or to its having been ratified by Liberia. There was therefore a clear inconsistency between the failure to reflect in the 1956 Code the obligations assumed by Liberia by the ratification of the Convention and the explicit obligations stated in Articles 23 and 24 of the Convention to "issue complete and precise regulations governing the use of forced or compulsory labour" and "to ensure that the regulations are brought to the knowledge of persons from whom such labour is exacted."[27]

The Mexican Labour Act of 1970 included a section of a previous Labour Act which the government had contended was superseded by the ratification in 1948 of the Night Work of Young Persons (Industry) (Revised) Convention (No. 90). The Committee of Experts had commented for a number of years on the discrepancy between the national legislation (which fixed a night period different from that of the Convention) and the Convention. The government had stated that when the Mexican Labour Act was being amended it would refer the comments of the Committee to the drafters. When the new Labour Act was adopted, however, it contained the earlier inconsistent provision. The Committee of Experts asked the government what measures would be taken to do away with the inconsistency in the new Act.[28] In 1976 it was able to note "with interest the Bill to supplement the Federal Labour Act of 1970 so as to give full effect to the provisions of the Convention by fixing at 12 hours the night period during which the work of persons under 18 years of age is prohibited."[29] The Committee expressed the hope that the Bill would be adopted in the near future.

4. Special Publication of ILO Conventions

In view of the repeated concern of the Committee of Experts that the provisions of ILO conventions were not sufficiently well known to concerned individuals or administrators, governments have taken various measures to ensure widespread publicity for convention provisions. These measures have been welcomed by ILO supervisory bodies but they have usually also insisted on the express repeal of conflicting legislation.

The December 1965 issue of *Revista Mexicana del Trabajo* (published by the Department of Labour and Social Welfare of Mexico) contained a section on "Important Provisions of Some Conventions Ratified by Mexico." It published not only Convention No. 8, mentioned above, but other conventions which had acquired force of law by virtue of their ratification. The provisions were followed by the relevant provisions of the Federal Labour Act which, although not yet expressly repealed or amended, had been superseded by the Conventions. The Committee of Experts' 1967 report stated:

> While recognising the undeniable value of such measures publicising the provisions of conventions, in order to dissipate any doubt regarding the effective application of conventions in Mexico—as the government had previously stated—the Committee trusts that the government will use all other opportunities available to give such publicity, particularly when the Federal Labour Act is published in any official document or review, and of expressly amending the legislation in question when occasion arises.[30]

Several countries have appended relevant provisions of ILO conventions to their Labour Codes—an action welcomed by the ILO supervisory Committees. In 1975 the Committee of Experts stated in an observation to France that they had "recently learned with interest from a government communication that an edition of the Labour Code is presently being printed by the Administration of the Official Gazettes and that it will include the texts of the Conventions in question as an appendix to the legislative section."[31] In the same observation the Committee also "noted with interest that the principle of appending to the Social Security Code the international Labour Conventions dealing with social security questions, ratified by France, has been adopted and will soon be put into practice."[32] The Committee had suggested in 1958 that France include a reference to the ILO conventions on social security ratified by France in the Annex of the Social Security Code, since treaties had priority over internal legislation in France.[33]

The Committee of Experts also noted "with satisfaction" in 1975 that "the official edition of 'Leyes Sociales de Venezuela' (Social Laws of Venezuela), ordered and authorised by the Labour Ministry, contains the complete texts of all the International Labour Conventions ratified by Venezuela."[34]

The Committee of Experts expressed its strong approval of the action of appending the texts of ILO conventions to relevant national codes in an observation to France in 1974. It stated that

> the publication in this way of the provisions incorporated in domestic law by the act of ratification would enable the institutions and individuals concerned—courts of law, administrative authorities, social security institutions and socially insured persons—to be fully aware of any amendments of the national legislation resulting from the ratification of certain Conventions, and would avoid any uncertainty which might exist as to the state of the law applicable.[35]

5. Conclusion

The ILO Committees have gone to unusual lengths to be assured that, whatever the legal situation, the provisions of ILO conventions are known to individuals most likely to benefit from them. This concern has not always met with understanding from government representatives who have felt that if their legal system incorporated self-executing provisions into national law there was no need for further measures to be taken.

Nevertheless, experience has shown that courts do not always take conventions into account even when they have been incorporated into national law; that administrators are not always aware of the implications of court decisions; that a law on the books conflicting with a convention provision which, in theory, supersedes the law, may be more accessible and known to administrators and individuals than the convention provision.

Thus, the insistence of the ILO Committees on repeal of conflicting legislation, on the taking of administrative measures and on adequate publicity for convention provisions appears amply justified.

NOTES

1. 1974 R.C.E. 21.
2. 1963 R.C.E. 11.
3. Pierre Cornil, *Le rôle de la commission d'experts de l'OIT dans le contrôle de l'application des conventions internationales du travail*, 6 R.B.D.I. 265, 270–273 (1970–71) [translation].
4. Governments are requested to include in their reports information on judicial decisions in their country relevant to the application of conventions. In addition, the Committee also takes notice of information on judicial decisions obtained from other sources.
5. 1959 R.C.E. 19–20.
6. 1959 R.C.E. 37.
7. 1959 R.C.E. 15.
8. 1962 R.C.E. 67. See also 1964 R.C.E. 102.
9. 48 R.P. 668 (1964).
10. See Nicolas Valticos, *Les conventions internationales du travail devant le juge français*, 53 R.C.D.I.P. 69 (1964).
11. 1965 R.C.E. 32.
12. See chapter 6, sec. 3.3., for a discussion of this case.
13. Accueillir, Bulletin mensuel du service sociale d'aide aux emigrants, fevrier 1979, No. 57, 3: "Cependant les cas identiques [au cas de Compan-Vaquer] des autres étrangers (4000 à l'epoque, quelques centaines seulement aujourd'hui) restent en instance de paiement à la Caisse des Dépôts. Pour ce qui est, de même, des prestations de vieillesse, la Caisse National refuse toujours systèmatiquement les demandes émanent des étrangers et ne verse les sommes qui leur sont dues que sur condamnation expresse prononcées par un tribunal, comme s'il était indispensable chaque fois de redire le droit."
14. 1976 R.C.E. 50.

15. 39 S.R. 92 (1956).

16. Direct request to the Netherlands concerning Convention No. 48, 1964.

17. 50 S.R. 128 (1966).

18. 24 S.R. 70–71 (1938).

19. It should be recalled, however, that the Argentine Supreme Court held in the Roa case in 1961 that this provision was non-self-executing. See chapter 6, sec. 2.2.

20. See 48 R.P. 660 (1964).

21. Revista Mexicana del Trabajo, diciembre 1965, No. 3–4, 99–100.

22. 1967 R.C.E. 26–27.

23. 1971 R.C.E. 49.

24. 1975 R.C.E. 128.

25. Ibid.

26. The Commission was set up by the ILO Governing Body, in accordance with Article 26 of the ILO Constitution, to investigate a complaint by Portugal that Liberia was not applying the provisions of the Forced Labour Convention which it had ratified in 1931.

27. Report of the Commission of Inquiry Appointed under Article 26 of the Constitution of the International Labour Organization to Examine the Complaint Filed by the Government of Portugal concerning the Observance by the Government of Liberia of the Forced Labour Convention, 1930 (No. 29), ILO Official Bulletin, vol. XLVI, No. 2, Supp. II, April 1963, p. 162. The Commission of Inquiry made a specific recommendation that all ratified conventions should be published in a new edition of the Liberian Code of Laws, or pending a new edition of the Code, that a supplement be published containing the text of the ratified conventions.Liberia did not carry out the Commission's recommendation. It subsequently became clear that the texts of the ratified conventions had never been published by the Liberian government although, according to section 80 of the Liberian Foreign Relations Law, conventions became national law only from the date of their *publication*.

28. 1974 R.C.E. 155.

29. 1976 R.C.E. 134.

30. 1967 R.C.E. 26–27.

31. 1975 R.C.E. 26.

32. Ibid. France has also included the text of the ILO maritime conventions in the Maritime Code.

33. 1958 R.C.E. 9–10.

34. 1975 R.C.E. 29.

35. 1974 R.C.E. 32.

CHAPTER 10

Beyond Labour Conventions: Reflections on the Wider Relevance of the ILO Experience

1. Interaction between International Law and National Law: Significance of ILO Experience

The more narrow focus of this study is the automatic incorporation of labour conventions in national law, but the broader scope is the interaction between international law and national law in the contemporary international community. The significance of the circumscribed examination of national implementation of ILO conventions is apparent in the light of current developments in international law. A recapitulation of these developments may help to emphasize the importance of the ILO experience.

In classical international law, prior to World War I, concepts of jurisdiction and non-intervention were used to separate international law and internal law into clearly defined spheres. Even under classical international law, however, some treaties, particularly friendship, commerce and navigation treaties, were intended to have effects within national legal systems. As it became clear that national law and international law might conflict, theorists began to ponder the relationship between the two legal systems, and theories of monism and dualism were elaborated in the late 19th century and early 20th century to explain the proper relationship between the two.[1]

Progressively, the boundaries between international law and national law became less water-tight with further developments in international relations. The Permanent Court of International Justice held in 1923 in the case of the *Nationality Decrees in Tunis and Morocco*[2] that "domestic jurisdiction" was an essentially relative concept which could become more limited in scope as international law moved into areas traditionally considered to be the sole province of national states.

The adoption of labour conventions following World War I constituted one of the first inroads of international conventional law into areas formerly within the jurisdiction of national states. The domain of internal labour standards became a concern of the international community. Labour conventions were only a harbinger, however, of the increasing adoption of quasi-legislative agreements aimed at regulating the internal social and economic policies of states. Human rights treaties are perhaps the most typical current examples of such agreements. One of the basic purposes of the United Nations Organization is "promoting and encouraging respect for human rights," and the U.N. has stimulated the drafting of a number of human rights treaties, of which the most important are the International Covenant on Civil and Political Rights and the International Covenant on Economic, Social and Cultural Rights. A 1970 compilation of human rights documents lists twenty-two such agreements and more have been adopted since that date.[3] These treaties must be implemented in national law if they are to be effective. The adoption of the Treaty of Rome in 1957 establishing the European Economic Community also focused attention on the relationship between international law and national law.

Concomitant with these developments, states adopted constitutional provisions regulating the status of treaties in their national legal system. The system of legislative incorporation adopted by some states required legislation specifically enacting the norms of treaties by the usual legislative process. The system of automatic incorporation, examined extensively in this study, provided, in theory, for the immediate application in national law of treaties which had been ratified and promulgated or published. Some states apparently adopted one system or the other because of the influence of monist or dualist theory. It is said that Germany and Italy adopted the quasi-automatic system because of the influence of the two eminent proponents of dualism, Triepel and Anzilotti.[4] The emphasis on monist doctrine by Scelle was influential in the adoption of the system of automatic incorporation in France.[5]

The system of automatic incorporation had been adopted at an earlier date in the United States, not because of any influence of monism, but because of problems concerning federalism. The lack of the influence of the monist theory has had some practical effects in the United States, as will be pointed out later in this chapter. Although the influence of monism has had some effect in Argentina and Mexico, these countries adopted constitutional provisions for automatic incorporation almost identical with the relevant provision of the U.S. Constitution because of their federal structure.

Following World War II a more pronounced trend towards the adoption of automatic incorporation in national constitutions became apparent. This method was perceived as more effective than legislative incorporation in ensuring the application of international treaties in national law. The shock of the Nazi atrocities and the inability of the international community to cope with serious human rights violations led, after World War II, both to constitutional trends for improved application of international law in national law and the adoption of treaties on human rights. The Federal Republic of Germany included Article 25 in its Basic Law, providing that customary international law was part of national law. A similar provision is contained in Article 10(1) of the 1943 Italian Constitution. In the two post-World War II Constitutions adopted by France, an article was included explicitly stating that treaties were superior to other forms of law (as had previously been determined only by judicial decisions). The Netherlands adopted the most progressive of all constitutional provisions on the incorporation of international law, providing that under certain circumstances treaties may take precedence over the Constitution. A number of newly independent countries provided for the system of automatic incorporation in their new constitutions. The United Kingdom, and Commonwealth countries following British practice, remained apart from this trend.

Thus, with the increasing development of treaties intended primarily for national implementation, and provisions in national constitutions providing for automatic incorporation, the former largely theoretical problem of international and national law relationships became an eminently practical one. It is clear that international policies concerning human rights and other social and economic matters cannot be carried out unless national law implements international treaties.

Yet, despite these current developments, it is apparent from the ILO experience that the system of automatic incorporation does not in itself guarantee that treaties will be effectively applied in national law. Once again, it is evident that the law in action is different from the law on the books. The significance of the study of the automatic incorporation of ILO conventions is evident. If the international community wishes to promote social and economic policies effectively through the adoption of treaties it is important that it be aware of the problems and obstacles uncovered in the experience of the application of ILO conventions. Very few studies of the application *in practice* of international conventional law in national law exist. The experience gained in the application of ILO conventions is thus particularly important.

2. Conclusions Concerning Incorporation of ILO Conventions in National Law

2.1. *Where the Twain Meet: Importance of ILO Supervisory Organs in Harmonizing International Conventional Law and National Law*

For more than fifty years, ILO supervisory organs have played a central role in harmonizing international conventional law and national law. The development of international labour conventions has always been closely linked with the International Labour Organization. The conventions are drafted and adopted within the Organization, they are ratified only by Member States of the Organization and their application in national law is supervised by ILO organs. ILO supervisory Committees and Commissions of Inquiry necessarily have become concerned with problems involving the incorporation of conventions in national law, in their work of supervising the application of conventions. This has led to the sensitive situation of an international organization commenting on inadequacies in the constitutional systems of ratifying states.

The relationship between the ILO and national governments, although not always without tension, has not been an antagonistic one, but rather one in which the Organization has attempted to provide an opportunity for explanation and discussion concerning problems in the application of conventions. Thus, the Organization has been the place where the twain meet, i.e., the locale where international conventional law and national legal systems interact most closely. The mere fact that this has proved to be possible is a success story. It is also unusually strong evidence of the ever-increasing interaction between the two legal systems in the current development of international law. Some lessons may be drawn from the ILO experience.

The capability of an international organization to provide a forum where conflicts between treaties and national law may be worked out depends on the degree of respect accorded to the organization by national governments. In the present international system such organizations have neither the mandate nor the practical ability to impose their decisions on governments. They may only persuade, not impose. The ILO has been able to provide a forum for resolution of differences as a result of a number of factors: the recognized technical ability and independence of members of the Committee of Experts, the careful analysis of national constitutional and legislative provisions by a sufficiently numerous and competent ILO staff and, not least, the input provided to the ILO supervisory system by the composition of the Conference Committee on the Application of Conventions. One-third of the members of the Conference Committees represent governments; this provides a necessary realistic political aspect to the supervisory system. But the productive work of the Committee has resulted from the presence of the remaining two-thirds of the members who represent workers and employers.

A study of the work of the ILO Committee of Experts illustrates a conservative approach in language and action. Questions addressed to national governments are invariably courteously expressed; indeed, they are sometimes so diplomatically phrased that it is doubtful whether junior clerks in labour ministries understand easily what is being asked. This conservative approach has been coupled, however, with persistence and patience in the pursuit of the elimination of discrepancies between national law and the provisions of ratified conventions. The supervisory Committees have not always been successful in persuading governments to their point of view but their diplomatic persistence has been successful on many occasions. The effectiveness of the ILO supervisory system has been documented elsewhere[6] but it is the central role which the supervisory organs play in facilitating the resolution of conflicts between national law and international conventional law which is significant in this study.

2.2. *Is the Technique of Legislative Incorporation Preferable to Automatic Incorporation?*

The question posed in this study is whether the technique of automatic incorporation has been an effective method of incorporating labour conventions in national law. The conclusion is clearly that the technique of automatic incorporation is not per se a guarantee of effective domestic implementation of treaties. It may or may not be an effective method based on a number of factors other than the mere constitutional choice of the system.

Indeed, the findings herein illustrate that the classification, "states with the system of automatic incorporation," simplifies a problem with many complications. Each national system has its own unique aspects. All automatic incorporation states may be aware of the problem of self-executing treaty provisions, but the courts of one state may apply a liberal definition to that term and the courts of another state may define "self-executing" narrowly. The courts of a state may normally attempt to reconcile conflicting laws and treaties (with the express aim of upholding treaties), yet, when faced with a conflicting law incorporating an important political policy, feel compelled to enforce the law. The courts of a state whose constitution accords supremacy to treaties over later as well as earlier laws may be reluctant, because of strict notions of separation of powers, to uphold a treaty which conflicts with a later law.

The discretion allowed judges by the elastic concept of self-executing treaty provisions and the extensive possibilities available for ranking treaties and national laws make not only each national system sui generis but—one often has the impression—even each case. Thus, this study illustrates that the efficacy of automatic incorporation cannot be judged in general; one may judge the effectiveness of automatic incorporation in particular states only. It is important to take into account aspects of the specific national legal system under consideration—its concepts of separation of powers, of self-executing provisions, the hierarchy accorded treaty norms and the attitude of judges towards international law, as well as the complexity of incorporating a given treaty provision into the structure of the national legal system. These factors may differ in states which have all adopted the system of automatic incorporation. The only common denominator of states with the system of automatic incorporation appears to be that, unlike states with the system of legislative incorporation, it is not necessary in *every* case in such states to adopt legislation in order for a treaty to be applied directly in national law. The problem in such systems is the difficulty in discerning in a particular case whether legislation must be adopted to implement the treaty or whether the treaty will be directly applied by the courts. The system of legislative incorporation lacks such complexity; legislation implementing the treaty clearly must be adopted in every case in order for the treaty norms to be applied by national courts.

But in examining these aspects of a specific legal system a further problem emerges from the ILO experience. It is often unusually difficult for an international supervisory body to obtain the necessary information. Governments normally report that a convention is applied in their country because under their constitution treaties are automatically incorporated in national law. As is evident from the research undertaken in connection with this study, the mere invocation of automatic incorporation should not be accepted as a proof of national application of treaties. Government reports are often inadequate in this respect and government representatives at ILO Conferences rarely have seemed aware of the complications which the self-executing concept and the problems of subsequent law may create in their own legal system.

The international supervisory bodies may, of course, do their own research on national legal systems. The International Labour Office has a substantial staff assisting the Committee of Experts in examining government reports on ratified conventions. But even a competent staff, located at a distance from a particular country, may have difficulty researching the constitutional law of a given country in the absence of reference to constitutional law treatises, relevant national judicial decisions and administrative practice by the government concerned.

Furthermore, as shown in the preceding chapters, governments themselves may erroneously report their national constitutional law, or the constitutional law may change. Colombian authorities considered at one point that Colombia had the system of automatic incorporation; a few years later—presumably because of a change in the interpretation of the Constitution—it was maintained that Colombia had, on the contrary, the system of legislative incorporation.

Even if there is no confusion about which system prevails in a given country, it is not possible to know—and often very difficult to make a reasoned guess—as to whether a given provision of a convention is self-executing and thus will be applied by the courts. Lower courts differed as to whether the Workmen's Compensation (Agriculture) Convention was directly applicable in Argentina until the supreme Court decided that it was not. A similar confusion reigned among lower courts in France concerning the Equality of Treatment (Accident Compensation) Convention until the matter was settled by the *Cour de Cassation.*[7] During such periods not only do international supervisory bodies have difficulty perceiving the eventual outcome, but national observers as well. Indeed, the outcome may not even be clear following a decision of the highest court. Government representatives and legal scholars gave conflicting interpretations of the *Haras "Los Cardos"* decision in Argentina in which the Supreme Court refused to apply the Workmen's Compensation (Agriculture) Convention.[8]

Finally—perhaps for all the reasons given in the preceding paragraphs—countries which have the clearest constitutional law or judicial precedent supporting the concept of automatic incorporation of treaties have tended not to rely on the direct application of ILO conventions under their constitutional system, and have preferred to adopt legislation implementing conventions. The Netherlands, France and—until recently—Switzerland provide examples.

Given all this uncertainty concerning the legal situation, coupled with problems of obtaining sufficient publicity for the provisions of ILO conventions, it is not surprising that the ILO supervisory organs have insisted so frequently on the adoption of legislation specifically implementing ILO conventions—thus, often treating states with automatic incorporation systems in the same manner as those with the system of legislative incorporation. The supervisory organs have discovered on so many occasions that automatic incorporation does not per se guarantee effective application, that the burden has been placed on ratifying states to assure the supervisory Committees of effective application.

The conclusions of this case study suggest a paradox. On the one hand, there has been a marked tendency, since World War II, for countries to choose the system of automatic incorporation because it, presumably, guaranteed the implementation of treaties in national law more effectively than the system of legislative incorporation. Jurists who are proponents of the monist theory and the superiority of international law over national law favor the system of automatic incorporation. On the other hand, the ILO experience seems to demonstrate that the technique is no better than legislative incorporation and may indeed be less effective, since reliance on it may create more uncertainty than the adoption of implementing legislation. ILO supervisory organs who are certainly in favor of more effective national implementation of ILO conventions have been skeptical about automatic incorporation.

The paradox may be more apparent than real. The difficulty is not, perhaps, that automatic incorporation has been tried and found wanting, but that it has not been tried. By a variety of devices—ranging from giving a very narrow scope to the concept of self-executing treaty provisions, to courts upholding laws in conflict with treaties because of separation of powers concerns, to failure to give sufficient publicity to treaty provisions—states have failed to employ automatic incorporation. The ILO experience includes numerous examples of such situations. Where the ILO Committees have been assured in a particular case that a convention is automatically applied— such as Switzerland's assurance that the Swiss National Accident Insurance Fund was applying the Equality of Treatment (Accident Compensation) Convention or that the concerned French administrative services were applying the provisions of the Maternity Protection Convention (No. 3)—they have accepted that automatic incorporation may be effective. It would be erroneous, therefore, to conclude that the ILO experience proves that automatic incorporation is never effective. Rather, this experience shows that the technique of automatic incorporation has been often adopted in theory, but not in practice.

The value of a study of ILO experience, then, may be that it illustrates that the mere constitutional choice of automatic incorporation does not necessarily accomplish what its proponents are seeking to achieve. Persons seriously concerned with the effective application of treaties in national law must seek to limit the many exceptions and inadequate applications of the technique which presently exist in many countries. It is unrealistic, in view of the ample documentation to the contrary, to believe that automatic incorporation alone provides for effective internal application of treaties.

Does the ILO experience prove that the technique of legislative incorporation is, therefore, preferable to that of automatic incorporation? Not necessarily, although that is an arguable conclusion. The argument can be made that an important element of the law is certainty, that administrators and individuals must be able to know what the law is with some degree of security, and that the technique of automatic incorporation results in an unacceptable degree of uncertainty in the law. For the author, however, the system of automatic incorporation remains the preferable system, and it is contended that such a view is compatible with the ILO experience. One of the reasons has been given previously, i.e., the system of automatic incorporation has not truly been tried. There is another important aspect, however, which should not be overlooked. The application of conventions has been examined here primarily from the point of view of international supervisory bodies. The ILO supervising Committees have the mandate to assure themselves, to the fullest reasonable extent, that conventions are effectively applied. It is obviously much more simple to be so assured—at least to the extent of the law if not the practice—if a specific implementing law has been adopted. Thus, in view of their mandate, the attitude of the ILO supervisory bodies is eminently reasonable.

But the technique of automatic incorporation should also be considered from the point of view of individuals within states who may wish to invoke the provisions of a convention which their country has ratified. Chapter 6 contains an extensive discussion of occasions on which individuals in automatic incorporation states have invoked the provisions of ILO conventions in the courts when there was no implementing legislation or even where there was contrary legislation on the books. In some cases they were successful and in some cases they were not. In legislative incorporation states, an individual who wishes to avail himself of the provisions of an ILO convention—and such conventions, as we have seen, are ultimately intended for the benefit of individuals—is relegated to seeking a legislative remedy (the enactment of implementing legislation) rather than a remedy in the courts.

Imposing upon an individual who wishes to invoke a validly ratified treaty the necessity of seeking legislative implementation is to effectively deprive him of any individual capacity to pressure for the application of international law internally. In another context—but one which can be analogized to the present subject—it has been asserted that "relegating a challenger to a legislative remedy is itself a decision on the merits."[9] A single individual may file a lawsuit but a single individual has almost no leverage to pressure the legislature to adopt legislation implementing a treaty. At the time of the ratification of the Workmen's Compensation (Agriculture) Convention in Argentina a number of legislators expressed the opinion that implementing legislation should be adopted and yet the legislation was not adopted. Individuals then brought suits claiming compensation on the grounds that the Convention should be directly applied. Eventually the Supreme Court decided otherwise and implementing legislation was adopted. A Supreme Court decision, instigated by an individual, drew attention to the fact that Argentina was not fulfilling its international obligations (to see that the Convention was applied—either directly or by implementing legislation). It is unlikely that the individual who brought the suit could have exercised sufficient pressure on the legislature to have the implementing legislation adopted in the absence of the suit which he filed.

An eminent American professor of international law, the late Quincy Wright, has said, "I think it [the 'Supremacy Clause' of the U.S.

Constitution] is a good principle because I would rather trust the honor of the United States to the courts than to partisan debate in the Congress or the State legislatures and I think that is what the 'Supremacy Clause' means."[10] On another occasion, Wright wrote:

> National courts may not always give a sound interpretation to treaty obligations in respect of human rights, but they are more likely to be guided by general principles than are local legislatures. On the whole, the principle accepted in the United States, that courts apply international law and treaties, has led to a sounder general appreciation of international obligations and to their more regular application than has the principle, applied in varying degrees in other sections of the world, that it belongs essentially to the legislature to give domestic effect to international obligations. There is no fundamental reason why the function of incorporating international law into municipal law should be regarded as a legislative rather than a judicial function. ... Whatever may be the causes, the hesitancy of courts to refer directly to international law tends to emphasize national sovereignty, and the political, as distinct from the legal aspects of international relations. On the other hand, recognition of wide judicial authority to apply treaties and international law tends to emphasize the authority of the international community and the objectivity of international law. It provides a basis in public sentiment for a system whereby appeal from national to international courts might in time be acceptable and thus, eventually international law and human rights might receive a common interpretation and application throughout the world.[11]

Similar preferences for the system of automatic incorporation have been expressed in other contexts. Pescatore has pointed out that there is no doubt about the greater efficacy of a system in which treaties intended for internal application are directly applied than one in which they are not.[12] The head of the Swiss *Département politique fédéral* praised the Swiss automatic incorporation system in 1968:

> In my opinion, the present Swiss system assures much better the application of international law [than a system of legislative incorporation]. Ratified treaties become directly applicable in national law and create rights and obligations for individuals. If it were necessary to wait for an adaptation of our legislation to treaties, Switzerland would be in danger of not correctly fulfilling its international obligations and thus engaging its international responsibility under international law. This would be in flagrant contradiction with our traditional conception of a strict observance of commitments contracted under international law.[13]

Arguments to the contrary, however, have been made by other jurists. In an article examining how the United States has enforced its obligations under multipartite treaties, Reiff arrives at a different conclusion. After explaining the system of legislative incorporation in the United Kingdom, Reiff states, with regard to U.S. domestic enforcement, "Article VI of the Constitution, by conferring upon treaties when made status as 'supreme law of the land', regrettably complicates the process."[14] The complication, according to Reiff, results from the difficulty of determining whether treaty provisions are self-executing or not under U.S. law. He points out that awaiting a final decision by the U.S. Supreme Court places an unfair burden on litigants, and may unduly delay enforcement. He cites the example of the 1883 Convention for the Protection of Industrial Property where the question whether certain of the provisions were self-executing has given rise to considerable litigation. He points out that the story is "long and complicated." According to Reiff, terms, nature of the provisions, practice of other states, opinions of other members of the Union set up under the Convention and of several lower federal courts were all to the effect that the provisions were self-executing. Others (the Secretary of State, the Attorney General, the Patent Office, Congress and other lower courts) regarded the Convention as non-self-executing. At the time he wrote (1940) the Supreme Court had not yet made a decision on the subject. "The net results have been this recurring private litigation and charges intimating that the United States has not fulfilled its obligations."[15] Reiff concludes:

> It is evident from the foregoing that improvement of the enforcing process is necessary and desirable. The simplest and most direct reform would consist in an amendment to Article VI of the Constitution preserving the supremacy of a treaty over acts of the States, but eliminating automatic status of a treaty as 'law of the land' and requiring Congress to adopt a comprehensive enforcing statute before the agreement becomes operative infraterritorially. Such an amendment, however, is probably not feasible at present.[16] [footnotes omitted]

He goes on to suggest:

> Some improvement may nevertheless be achieved by the enumeration of self-executing stipulations of a treaty in a final act or protocol and by resorting regularly to such practices as preparation of implementing legislation by the administrative services affected by the treaty ...[17] [footnotes omitted]

The system of legislative incorporation may be preferred by some jurists because it provides certainty as to whether treaty norms are incorporated in national law. Others may consider automatic incorporation as a more progressive system since it brings the application of international law directly into national courts and permits individuals to invoke the provisions of international treaties. The system of automatic incorporation presently exists in many countries and this situation is unlikely to change. Efforts should be directed, therefore, to the improvement of the system in the various countries which have adopted it, rather than to any possible change in the constitutional system.

3. Relevance of the ILO Experience for the Future Application of Human Rights Treaties

What is the practical relevance of the ILO experience for the application of other treaties? It would seem to be particularly relevant to the application in national law of the growing number of treaties concerned with human rights. It has already been pointed out that these treaties are similar in many respects to ILO conventions. Human rights treaties are multilateral treaties which lay down general norms intended to regulate the relations of a state with persons within its jurisdiction. In addition, some of these treaties set up supervisory systems, for the same reason which occasioned the setting up of the ILO supervisory systems—the relative weakness of reciprocity as an effective enforcement mechanism for this type of treaty.

The catalogue of human rights treaties includes, inter alia, treaties on genocide, racial discrimination, slavery, the status of refugees and political rights of women. In addition to treaties dealing with specific subjects two international conventions cover a broad range of human rights: the International Covenant on Civil and Political Rights and the International Covenant on Economic, Social and Cultural Rights. Two regional conventions, the European Convention on Human Rights and the American Convention on Human Rights, also cover a broad range of rights.

The Convention on the Elimination of All Forms of Racial Discrimination and the Covenant on Civil and Political Rights provide for a reporting system by governments and for supervisory committees to review government reports. Both of these Conventions are in force and the supervisory systems are functioning. The ILO experience should be useful to these committees. The supervisory systems set up under these two treaties differ in many respects from the supervisory system of ILO conventions. It is unnecessary here to enter into the details of those differences. The important similarity is that these committees, like the ILO Committees, must necessarily be concerned with the problems and complexities involved in automatic incorporation.

The Human Rights Committee set up under the Covenant on Civil and

Political Rights has, in its short period of existence, shown a particular concern about the incorporation of treaties in national law. A comment on the work of the Committee points out:

> There is an evident pattern emerging in the questionings of States Parties. For example, Committee members consistently have expressed concern with the status of the Covenant in domestic law: i.e., does it have the force of law; if not, has legislation been adopted to give it practical effect, and may a defendant or plaintiff invoke its provisions in a judicial or administrative proceeding.[18]

It appeared, however, that most of the states which had ratified the Covenant as of 1979 were states with the system of legislative incorporation, not automatic incorporation.[19]

An embryonic reporting system is also developing in connection with the application of the European Convention on Human Rights. The Convention has been enforced at the international level to date through individual and inter-state complaints of violations, and consideration of those complaints by the European Commission on Human Rights and the European Court on Human Rights. Under Article 57 of the Convention, however, the Secretary-General of the Council of Europe may request any High Contracting Party to "furnish an explanation of the manner in which its internal law ensures the effective implementation of any of the provisions" of the Convention. Such reports have now been requested on several occasions and it is to be expected that a reporting system will increasingly become important in connection with the European Convention on Human Rights.[20] A number of studies have been made on the domestic application of the European Convention on Human Rights which illustrate the importance of the incorporation of the Convention in national law, even though the international enforcement machinery set up under the European Convention is much more effective than the system set up in most of the other human rights treaties.[21]

The ILO Committees constituted a pioneering system in the supervision of treaties and a number of years of experience were necessary before they clearly articulated, for the benefit of reporting governments, the problems involved in the domestic application of conventions in automatic incorporation states.

In view of the ILO experience, it is likely that governments of automatic incorporation states will report to other supervisory bodies that treaties are adequately implemented in their national law, and that individuals may invoke the treaty provisions before national courts, precisely because they have the constitutional system of automatic incorporation in their country. Profiting from the long experience of ILO supervision of conventions, the supervisory bodies of other treaties should inquire of states making such assertions whether a particular treaty provision would be considered self-executing in their country, whether there have been, in fact, court decisions applying the treaty, whether there are laws on the books, either earlier or later than the ratification of the treaty, which conflict with the treaty and whether such laws prevail over treaty provisions. Finally, the supervisory bodies should be aware of the serious problems raised by the lack of publicity given to treaties even in states where treaties are the "law of the land".

4. Improving the National Application of Treaties

4.1. *Why National Judges are Reluctant to Directly Apply Treaties*

Even in states with the system of automatic incorporation, judges may use various devices to apply national law rather than treaties where there is a conflict between the two, or may give a restrictive definition to self-executing treaty provisions and easily find that implementing legislation is required before a provision may be applied by the court. What accounts for this relative conservatism frequently demonstrated by national judges, even where the national constitution provides for the automatic incorporation of treaties?

One may conjecture concerning the reasons. Although the underlying assumption of this study has been that treaty provisions may and should be applied in appropriate cases by national courts, there are some intrinsic reasons for difficulty in doing so. Legal scholars have pointed out the complications of introducing foreign legal concepts and techniques into a national legal system. The problem is particularly acute in the application of human rights treaties where the language used in the treaties may differ from the language employed in national constitutional provisions concerning human rights. This problem has been much discussed in Austria in relation to the incorporation of the European Convention on Human Rights into national law.[22]

Unfortunately, it does not seem possible to remedy this problem by more careful drafting of conventions. This problem has led one commentator to a negative conclusion regarding the possibility of direct application of treaty provisions by national courts. In a book concerned with European Community Law in French courts, Bergsten asserted:

> The enforcement by the national courts of a general doctrine of the supremacy of treaties is not viable in the current world. There are both technical and political difficulties in the drafting of those treaties intended to create positive law within a state which are not generally experienced in domestic law making. These difficulties include such

> matters as divergent legal systems into which the new treaty must fit; different languages with the effect this has on the precision of translations and on the use of words of art, the greater diversity of interests which must be considered; and the fact that the negotiation and ratification of treaties involves more persons and institutions than does the enactment of a statute. The result is too often a text which can be inserted into the domestic legal system only with difficulty.[23]

Thus, the reluctance of national judges to apply treaty provisions is, to a degree, understandable. National judges, facing a source of law with which they are generally unfamiliar, tend to limit the direct application of treaties by considering their provisions as non-self-executing, or by applying conflicting national law in preference to the treaty. The situation may be exacerbated if the language used in the treaty is taken from another legal system than that to which the judge is accustomed. Although the provisions of the treaty may be no more vague or imprecise than national constitutional or statutory provisions, judges are more familiar with the language used in their own legal system and may hesitate to apply vague and imprecise terms contained in treaties.

In states with a strong tradition of separation of powers, such as France, judges may feel that they are required by virtue of the separation of powers to apply national law even if it conflicts with a ratified treaty. A constitutional provision in such systems giving priority to treaties over laws is taken to be directed to the legislature (directing them not to adopt laws contrary to a ratified treaty) rather than permitting the judiciary to refuse to apply an enacted law.

In some cases, the national application of a treaty may raise sensitive political issues. It has been pointed out on several occasions in previous chapters that when important political issues are involved which weigh against the application of a treaty, judges tend to find a technical reason for not applying the treaty even in automatic incorporation states.[24]

It will not be possible to improve the national application of treaties unless the genuine obstacles to such application are known and appreciated.

4.2. *Is Theory Important?*

In undertaking this study the author attempted to avoid a priori theories concerning the relationship between international law and national law and to carry out a pragmatic investigation of the interaction between the two legal systems in a particular context. Importance has not been given in this study to the long-standing disputes regarding the monist and dualist theories. Such controversies have essentially seemed sterile. Nevertheless, in considering how the national implementation of treaties may be improved, one is forced to consider whether theory may have an influence on practice.

4.2.1. *The Monist-Dualist Controversy Revisited*

It is unnecessary here to enter into a detailed explanation of the two theories[25] but a brief account of them may be useful. According to the dualist theory, the international legal system and the national legal system are separate and distinct systems with different subjects and sources. They are concerned with different subject-matter and both are supreme within their own sphere. According to this doctrine, there should be no conflict between the two systems since they are totally separate.

The proponents of the monist system argue, on the other hand, that all law essentially regulates human conduct, that the two systems are not totally separate, and that priority must be given to one legal system over the other in order to avoid conflict. Most proponents of monism contend that international law must be given priority over national law in the national legal order as well as in the international legal order.

On the basis of the research undertaken in this study it appears evident that neither theory adequately explains the type of interaction presently occurring between the two systems. The dualists underestimate the degree to which the two legal systems interact and even conflict. To a considerable degree, the two legal systems regulate the same activities today. On the other hand, the monists exaggerate the degree of unity which exists between the two systems. International law is not supra-national law; it does not reach directly into national legal systems. It is obvious from this study of the automatic incorporation of labour conventions in national law that the application of international law in internal law is a matter regulated by national legal systems.

While the theories may not explain the realities of present day interaction between the two systems they may, nevertheless, be important. It is possible that monist theory may have a positive influence on the application of treaties in national law. Monist theorists were influential in the ultimate inclusion of the progressive article in the French Constitution providing that treaties are superior to laws.

It has earlier been remarked that monist theory has had no noticeable influence on legal thought in the United States. There is a tendency for United States courts to construe the concept of self-executing treaty provisions more narrowly than in some other countries. And in the United States it has long been established judicial practice to apply a later law in preference to an earlier treaty despite the fact that no hierarchy between the two is established in the national Constitution.

It is difficult to verify that theoretical considerations or their lack have had an influence on practice in France or the United States. Nevertheless, it is rare that practice is not influenced to some degree by theory. Focus should perhaps be placed today not on the two theories as adequate explanations of the reality of the current situation but rather as a means of refocusing discussion on what the nature of that interaction should be. Viewed from this point of view, the monist theory appears to have the best of the argument. The two legal systems clearly interact and even conflict on occasion at the present time. But proponents of monism who urge the superiority of international law even within the national legal system should be aware of the complexities made evident by empirical studies of the interaction of the two legal systems. As more such studies are undertaken, the time may arrive for reconsideration of theories concerning the relationship between international and national law.

4.2.2. *The McDougal Approach*

Such a theoretical approach has been undertaken by Professor Myres McDougal. In a lengthy and perceptive article—but one couched in the special language of the McDougal-Laswell policy oriented school—Professor McDougal points out that the traditional monist-dualist theories based on conceptions of a "body of rules" do not explain the real situation of the relationship between international and national law which

> is most realistically viewed, not in terms of the relative supremacy ... but rather in terms of the interpenetration of multiple processes of authoritative decision of varying territorial compass.[26]

McDougal points out that national actors and decision making processes increasingly interact with international actors and processes in the creation of norms.

The ILO experience bears out McDougal's analysis. The ILO Committees are not international organs intervening in national legal affairs but one step in a process of achieving a viable international legal order on labour matters. Not only states, but employers and workers, have participated in the drafting of conventions. States ratify conventions and submit reports on them. Occupational organizations may comment on their states' reports. The Conference Committee permits government representatives—and again employers and workers—to comment on government performance. And, finally, whatever recommendations are made by the ILO supervisory organs, the ultimate decision whether to conform to their international obligations is taken by states and specifically by national judges and administrators. Thus, the ILO system, demonstrating a remarkable interplay between national and international legal systems, provides an illuminating example of what is undoubtedly an important future trend in international law and one which Professor McDougal has adequately described on the basis of other empirical studies.

4.3. *Need for Improved Understanding of the Problem at the International Level*

The ILO experience demonstrates that international treaties are often inadequately incorporated in national law even in states with the system of automatic incorporation. In view of the increasing adoption of human rights treaties and similar treaties which are intended to regulate national social and economic policies this deficiency should be of concern to the international community. Can anything be accomplished at the international level to more adequately ensure the effective incorporation of treaty norms in national law? It is clear that solutions must primarily be found at the national level. The international community, however, might well address itself to two issues which are of critical importance to the incorporation of treaties in national law: (1) the problem of the self-executing nature of treaty provisions and (2) the problem of providing adequate publicity in national legal systems for treaties.

Pescatore has pointed out that the question of the self-executing nature of treaty provisions is currently of considerable international interest. This is largely the result of problems perceived in the direct application of the Treaty of Rome in European countries.[27] It seems clear from the ILO experience that it is exceedingly difficult to determine at the international level whether a particular treaty provision will or will not be considered self-executing by a particular country. The evidence demonstrates that one country may consider a particular provision to be self-executing and another country may consider it to be non-self-executing. Different countries use different criteria to determine the self-executing nature of treaty provisions. Pescatore has pointed out that this creates a judicial distortion.[28]

Two possible international means could be suggested for improving this situation, which is essentially a national problem. The first would be to undertake a comparative study at the international level of the criteria for determining the self-executing nature of treaty provisions in various countries. Pescatore has emphasized the importance of the international aspects of the problem—the interpretation of the language of the treaty and the aim and purpose of the treaty.[29] He emphasizes that although national law must ultimately determine when a treaty provision is self-executing the international aspects mentioned above are of great importance. Although his remarks were made in the context of European Community law they have a wider relevance.

A second possible international solution would be to pay more attention in the drafting of treaties to language which would indicate more clearly whether a treaty was or was not self-executing. With the exception of occasions where treaty provisions specifically refer to the need for adoption of legislation little emphasis appears to be given at the present time—at the drafting stage—to whether language indicates that a treaty is or is not to be self-executing. This is partly due, of course, to the fact that in countries of legislative incorporation no treaty is self-executing. National courts and legal scholars differ, for example, on whether the words "undertake" or "shall secure" imply that a treaty provision is non-self-executing. More careful consideration given at the international level to the use of language which could be more clearly interpreted in this regard might be useful. Bergsten correctly points out the complexities in attempting to draft treaties more precisely. Nevertheless, the problem of the use of language to clarify the self-executing nature of provisions seems to call for more serious examination by legal scholars who might be able to provide some guidance on the matter to the drafters of treaties.

The ILO experience emphasizes that the provisions of duly ratified conventions which have the force of law in a national system often remain unknown to judges and administrators who must apply the law, as well as to individuals, the intended recipients of the benefit of treaties. Numerous examples are cited in chapter 9. Obviously, it is national legal systems which must remedy this situation. But it is clear that comments on the lack of publicity given convention provisions by the ILO has resulted in improved knowledge of the provisions. It thus seems that calling additional attention at the international level to the problem would help national legal systems to improve in this regard.

In many countries treaties are difficult to locate in collections of laws and thus remain hidden away from most legal practitioners. Salo Engel has called attention to this important point in so far as U.S. law is concerned in a note in the *American Journal of International Law*:

> In marked contrast to the data concerning two sources of the "supreme law of the land" (Article 6(2) of the Constitution), the Federal Constitution and Federal legislation, information about the third source, Federal treaties, is very incomplete, and up-to-date information thereon is completely missing. In view of the present position of the United States in the world and the tremendous increase in the number and importance of treaties concluded by her, the lack of information is all the more remarkable and regrettable.[30]

This situation is not unique to the United States. International organizations, especially those with treaty supervisory systems, and international legal scholars should be concerned about this problem which inhibits the national application of treaties.

International legal studies, conferences and international organizations might be able to draw the attention of governments and national practitioners to this problem.

It seems evident that the incorporation of treaties in national law will become an increasingly important problem in the future. The extensive experience in the application of ILO conventions has provided valuable insights into the difficulties in this regard both for national governments and for supervisory bodies. The experience also provides an example of how harmonization of international law and municipal law may be accomplished within the present international legal system. Further reflection on the ILO experience and the experience of the application of similar conventions will, it is hoped, lead to a more satisfactory implementation of international conventional norms.

NOTES

1. These theories are discussed in the last section of this chapter.

2. Nationality Decrees in Tunis and Morocco (Great Britain v. France), P.C.I.J., Ser. B, No. 4 (1923).

3. Ian Brownlie, ed., *Basic Documents on Human Rights* (Oxford: Clarendon Press, 1971). The expression "human rights treaties" is somewhat ambiguous. In a certain sense, all ILO conventions are human rights treaties since they are concerned with economic and social rights. Only the following ten out of more than 150 ILO conventions are generally classified, however, as basic human rights treaties: Right of Association (Agriculture) Convention, 1921 (No. 11); Right of Association (Non-Metropolitan Territories) Convention, 1947 (No. 84); Freedom of Association and Protection of the Right to Organise Convention, 1948 (No. 87); Right to Organise and Collective Bargaining Convention, 1949 (No. 98); Workers' Representatives Convention, 1971 (No. 135); Rural Workers' Organisation Convention, 1975 (No. 141); Forced Labour Convention, 1930 (No. 29); Abolition of Forced Labour Convention, 1957 (No. 105); Discrimination (Employment and Occupation) Convention, 1958 (No. 111); Equal Remuneration Convention, 1951 (No. 100). Brownlie also includes the ILO Social Policy (Basic Aims and Standards) Convention, 1962 (No. 117) and the ILO Employment Policy Convention, 1964 (No. 122) in his list of human rights documents.

4. Kaye Holloway, *Modern Trends in Treaty Law* (London: Stevens and Sons, 1967), p. 238.

5. Pierre Lardy, *La force obligatoire du droit international en droit interne* (Paris: R. Pichon et R. Durand—Auzias, 1966), p. 107.

6. See E. A. Landy, *The Effectiveness of International Supervision—Thirty Years of ILO Experience* (London: Stevens and Sons; Dobbs Ferry, N.Y.: Oceana Publications, Inc., 1966).

7. See chapter 6.

8. See chapter 2, sec. 3.4 and chapter 6, sec. 2.1.

9. See Eric Stein and G. Joseph Vining, *Citizen Access to Judicial Review of Administrative Action in a Transnational and Federal Context*, 70 Am. J. Int'l L. 219, 240 (1976).

10. Quincy Wright, *Discussion, The Execution of Treaty Obligations Through Internal Law*, 1951 Proc., Am. Soc. Int'l L. 101.

11. Wright, *National Courts and Human Rights—the Fujii Case*, 45 Am. J. Int'l L. 62, 80–82 (1951).

12. Pierre Pescatore, "Rapport luxembourgeois" in *Deuxième colloque international de droit européen* (Zwolle: N.V. Uitgeversmaatschappij W. E. J. Tjeenk Willink, 1966), pp. 137, 143.

13. Réponse donnée le 10 décembre 1968 a l'interpellation du Conseiller national Korner par M. Spühler, chef du Departement politique fédéral, 26 A.S.D.I. 91–101, 100 (1969–70) [translation].

14. Henry Reiff, *The Enforcement of Multipartite Administrative Treaties in the United States*, 34 Am. J. Int'l L. 661, 669 (1940).

15. Ibid., 671–672.

16. Ibid., 678.

17. Ibid., 678–679.

18. *Human Rights Committee*, 21 Review of the International Commission of Jurists, December 1978, 17.

19. Dana Fischer, *The Practice of the Human Rights Committee: An Effective Reporting System*, in preparation (1980) for publication as an occasional paper of the American Society of International Law.

20. The Secretary-General of the Council of Europe has requested information in relation to specific articles of the Convention in 1964, 1970 and 1975. When the reports are received the secretariat prepares a comparative study of the information from the governments and brings it to the attention of the Council of Ministers. H.(76) 15, Council of Europe Implementation of Article 57 of the European Convention on Human Rights, Secretariat Memorandum Prepared by the Directorate of Human Rights, Strasbourg, 15 October 1976.

21. See references cited in Introduction, n.5.

22. See Andreas Khol, *The Influence of the Human Rights Convention on Austrian Law*, 18 Am. J. Comp. L. 237 (1970).

23. Eric E. Bergsten, *Community Law in the French Courts* (The Hague: Nijhoff, 1973), p. 48.

24. E.g., see discussion of the U.S. Sei Fujii case in chapter 5, sec. 1.3.3.; discussion of the Swiss Schubert case, chapter 8, sec. 2.2.2.; discussion of a Dutch decision concerning religious processions, chapter 5, n.51.

25. See sources cited in chapter 3, n.10.

26. Myres S. McDougal, *The Impact of International Law upon National Law: A Policy-Oriented Perspective*, 4 South Dakota L. Rev. 25 (1959), reproduced in McDougal and Associates, *Studies in World Public Order* (New Haven: Yale University Press, 1960), pp. 157–236.

27. Pierre Pescatore, "Rapport luxembourgeois" in *Deuxième colloque*, op. cit., p. 137. See other national reports in *Deuxième colloque* for extensive treatment of the problem of self-executing treaty provisions in European community law.

28. Ibid., 143.

29. Ibid., 150–156.

30. Salo Engel, *On the Status of United States Treaty Law*, 65 Am. J. Int'l L. 593 (1971).

Bibliography

I. Documents

ILO Documents

1. Constitution.
2. Official Bulletin.
3. Records of Proceedings of the International Labour Conference.
4. Reports of the Conference Committee on the Application of Conventions and Recommendations (International Labour Conference).
5. Reports of the Committee of Experts on the Application of Conventions and Recommendations (International Labour Conference).
6. Report of the Commission Appointed under Article 26 of the Constitution of the International Labour Organization to Examine the Complaint Filed by the Government of Portugal concerning the Observance by the Government of Liberia of the Forced Labour Convention, 1930 (No. 29).
7. Reports and Summaries of Reports on Ratified Conventions submitted to the International Labour Conference.

United Nations Documents

8. Human Rights, A Compilation of International Instruments of the United Nations, 1978, ST/HR/1/Rev. 1.
9. U.N. Conference on the Law of Treaties, Official Records, First Session, Vienna, 1968, A/Conf. 39/11.
10. Vienna Convention on the Law of Treaties, A/Conf. 39/27.

Council of Europe Documents

11. European Convention for the Protection of Human Rights and Fundamental Freedoms (1950), 213 U.N.T.S. 221.
12. Council of Europe Implementation of Article 57 of the European Convention on Human Rights, Secretariat Memorandum Prepared by the Directorate of Human Rights, Strasbourg, 15 October 1976, H (76) 15.

Government Documents

13. Constitutions of Argentina, France, Italy, Mexico, Netherlands, Switzerland, United States (Peaslee, *Constitutions of Nations*).
14. France: Bulletin juridique de la fédération nationale des organismes de sécurité sociale.
15. Guatemala: Código de Trabajo, 1967, 1971.
16. Switzerland: Feuille fédérale.
17. United States: Message from the President of the United States Transmitting Four Treaties Pertaining to Human Rights, Senate, 95th Cong., 2d Sess., Executives C, D, E & F, February 23, 1978.

II. Books

18. American Law Institute. *Restatement (Second) of the Foreign Relations Law of the United States.* St. Paul, Minnesota: American Law Institute Publishers, 1965, 679 p.

19. Anzilotti, Dionisio. *Cours de droit international* (trans. Gidel). Paris: Sirey, 3rd ed. 1929, 536 p.

20. Bergsten, Eric E. *Community Law in the French Courts.* The Hague: Nijhoff, 1973, 141 p.

21. Bidart Campos, German J. *Manual de Derecho ConstitucionalArgentino.* Buenos Aires: Ediar, 2d ed. 1974, 863 p.

22. Bidart Campos, German J. *Derecho Constitucional.* Buenos Aires: Ediar, 1964–66, 2 vols., 822 and 709 p.

23. Bidart Campos, German J. *El Derecho Constitucional del Poder.* Buenos Aires: Ediar, 1967, 2 vols., 478 p.

24. Briggs, Herbert Whittaker. *The Law of Nations.* New York: Appleton-Century-Crofts, Inc., 2d ed. 1952, 1108 p.

25. Brownlie, Ian, ed. *Basic Documents on Human Rights.* Oxford: Clarendon Press, 1971, 531 p.

26. Burgoa, Ignacio. *Derecho Constitucional Mexicano.* México: Porrua, 1973, 1126 p.

27. Cassese, Antonio. *Il Controllo Internazionale.* Milano: A. Giuffré, 1971, 314 p.

28. Chailley, Pierre. *La nature juridique des traités internationaux.* Paris: Sirey, 1932, 343 p.

29. Condorelli, Luigi. *Il Giudice Italiano e i Trattati Internazionali. Gli Accordi self-Executing e Non-Self-Executing nell'Ottica della Giurisprudenza.* Padua: Cedam, 1974, 155 p.

30. *Deuxième colloque international de droit européen* (La Haye 1963), "Le problème des dispositions directement applicable (self-executing) des traités internationaux et son application aux traités instituant les communautés" (organisé par l'Association Néerlandaise pour le droit européen). Zwolle: N.V. Uitgeversmaatschappij W. E. J. Tjeenk Willink, 1966, 454 p.

31. Erades, L. and Wesley L. Gould. *The Relation between International Law and Municipal Law in the Netherlands and in the United States.* Leiden: Sijthoff; New York: Oceana Publications, Inc., 1961, 510 p.

32. Guggenheim, Paul. *Traité de droit international public*, vol. I. Genève: Georg, 2d ed. 1967, 352 p.

33. Henkin, Louis. *Foreign Affairs and the Constitution.* Mineola, New York: The Foundation Press, Inc., 1972, 533 p.

34. Holloway, Kaye. *Modern Trends in Treaty Law.* London: Stevens and Sons, 1967, 737 p.

35. International Labour Office. *International Labour Code, 1951.* Geneva: ILO, 1952, 2 vols.

36. International Labour Office. *The Impact of International Labour Conventions and Recommendations*, Geneva: ILO, 1976, 104 p.

37. Jenks, C. Wilfred. *Human Rights and International Labour Standards.* London: Stevens and Sons; New York: Frederick A. Praeger, Inc., 1960, 159 p.

38. Krotoschin, Ernesto. *Tratado Práctico de Derecho del Trabajo.* Buenos Aires: Depalma, 2d ed. 1965, 2 vols.

39. Landy, E. A. *The Effectiveness of International Supervision—Thirty Years of ILO Experience.* London: Stevens and Sons; Dobbs Ferry, New York: Oceana Publications, Inc., 1966, 268 p.

40. Lapidoth, Ruth. *Les rapports entre le droit international public et le droit interne en Israel.* Paris: A. Pédone, 1959, 156 p.

41. Lardy, Pierre. *La force obligatoire du droit international en droit interne.* Paris: Bibliothèque de droit international, R. Pichon et R. Durand—Auzias, 1966, 279 p.

42. Lauwaars, R. W. *Lawfulness and Legal Force of Community Decisions*. Leiden: Sijthoff, 1973, 355 p.

43. Lozada, Salvador Maria. *Derecho Constitucional Argentino Segun El Metodo de Casos*, vol. 1. Buenos Aires: Abeldo-Perrot, 1972, 858 p.

44. Lozada, Salvador Maria. *Instituciones de Derecho Publico*. Cordoba, Argentina: Editions Macchi, 1966, 482 p.

45. McNair, Lord A. D. *The Law of Treaties*. Oxford: Clarendon Press, 1961, 789 p.

46. O'Connell, D. P. *International Law*. London: Stevens and Sons, 2d ed. 1970, 2 vols., 1390 p.

47. Offeddu, Marino. *Le Convenzioni Internazionali del Lavoro e l'Ordinamento Giuridico Italiano*. Padova: Cedam, 1973, 207 p.

48. Paez Stille, Enrique. *Interpretación del Articulo 133 de la Constitución*. México: Tesis, Universidad Nacional de México, 1945, 60 p.

49. Peaslee, Amos J. *Constitutions of Nations*. The Hague: Nijhoff, rev. 3rd ed. 1970, 4 vols. 1344 p.

50. Ramírez Gronda, Juan D. *Derecho del Trabajo en la Republica Argentina*. Buenos Aires: Editorial—Claridad, 1938, 302 p.

51. *Recueil d'études de droit international en hommage à Paul Guggenheim*. Genève: Imprimerie de la Tribune de Genève, 1968, 898 p.

52. Reuter, Paul. *Introduction au droit des traités*. Paris: Armand Colin (Collection U), 1972, 236 p.

53. Robertson, A. H., ed. *Human Rights in National and International Law*, Proceedings of the 2nd International Conference on the European Convention on Human Rights, Vienna, 1965. Manchester: Manchester University Press, 1968, 396 p.

54. Rousseau, Charles. *Droit international public*. Paris: Dalloz, 5th ed. 1970, 411 p.

55. Russotto, Jean. *L'Application des traités self-executing en droit américain*. Lausanne, Montreux: Thèse, Imprimerie Ganguin et Laubscher S.A., 1969, 199 p.

56. Scelle, Georges. *Précis de droit des gens*. Paris: Sirey, 1932–1934, 2 vols., 558 p.

57. Scelle, Georges. *L'Organisation Internationale du Travail et le BIT*. Paris: Marcel Rivière, 1930, 333 p.

58. Schwebel, Stephen M., ed. *The Effectiveness of International Decisions*. Leyden: A. W. Sijthoff; Dobbs Ferry, New York: Oceana Publications, Inc., 1971, 538 p.

59. Sereni, Angelo P. *The Italian Conception of International Law*. New York: Columbia University Press, 1943, 402 p.

60. Shotwell, James T., ed. *The Origins of the International Labour Organization*, vol. 1. New York: Columbia University Press, 1934, 497 p.

61. Sohn, Louis B. and Thomas Buergenthal. *International Protection of Human Rights*. Indianapolis: The Bobbs-Merrill Company, Inc., 1973, 1402 p.

62. Sorensen, Max, ed. *Manual of Public International Law*. London: MacMillan; New York: St. Martin's Press, 1968, 930 p.

63. Stein, Eric, Peter Hay and Michel Waelbroeck. *European Community Law and Institutions in Perspective*. Indianapolis: The Bobbs-Merrill Company, Inc., 1976, 1132 p.

64. Steiner, Henry J. and Detlev F. Vagts. *Transnational Legal Problems*. Mineola, New York: The Foundation Press, Inc., 2d ed. 1976, 1429 p.

65. Tena Ramírez, Felipe. *Derecho Constitucional Mexicano*. México: Porrua, 11th ed. 1972, 583 p.

66. Triepel, Heinrich. *Droit international et droit interne* (trans. René Brunet). Paris: A. Pedone, 1920, 448 p.

67. Valdés Villareal, Mauricio. *Relaciones entre El Derecho Interno y El Derecho Internacional*. México: Tesis, Universidad Nacional de México, Facultad de Derecho y Ciencias Sociales, 1944, 53 p.

68. Valticos, Nicolas. *Droit international du travail* (Traité de Droit du Travail). Paris: Dalloz, 1970, 638 p.

69. Valticos, Nicolas. *International Labour Law.* Deventer, Netherlands: Kluwer, 1979, 267 p.

70. Whiteman, Marjorie, ed. *Digest of International Law*, vol. 14 (Treaties and Other International Agreements). Washington, D.C.: Government Printing Office, 1970, 1203 p.

71. Wildhaber, Luzius. *Treaty-Making Power and Constitution.* Basel und Stuttgart: Helbing & Lichtenhahn, 1971, 412 p.

III. Articles

72. Berenstein, Alexandre. *The Influence of International Labour Conventions on Swiss Legislation.* 77 I.L.R. 495–518 (1958).

73. Bilder, Richard. *Rethinking International Human Rights: Some Basic Questions.* 1969 Wisconsin L. Rev. 171–217.

74. Bishop, William W., Jr. *Unconstitutional Treaties.* 42 Minn. L. Rev. 773–803 (1958).

75. Blagoev, Borislav. *Conventions internationales du travail et leur application en droit interne.* 3 Revue yougoslave de droit international 417–419 (1961).

76. Blumann, Claude. *L'Article 54 de la Constitution et le contrôle de la constitutionnalité des traités en France.* 82 R.G.D.I.P. 537–618 (1978).

77. Borchard, Edwin. *The Relation between International Law and Municipal Law.* 27 Virginia L. Rev. 137–148 (1940).

78. Brand, Ronald A. Note: *Security Council Resolutions: When Do They Give Rise to Enforceable Legal Rights? The United Nations Charter, the Byrd Amendment and a Self-Executing Treaty Analysis.* 9 Cornell International Law Journal 298–316 (1976).

79. Buergenthal, Thomas. *The Domestic Status of the European Convention on Human Rights: A Second Look.* 7 Journal of the International Commission of Jurists 55–96 (1966).

80. Buergenthal, Thomas. *The Effect of the European Convention on Human Rights on the Internal Law of the Member States* (British Institute of International and Comparative Law, International Law Series, No. 5). I.C.L.Q., Supplementary Publication No. 11, 79–106 (1965).

81. Buergenthal, Thomas. *Implementing the U.N. Racial Convention.* 12 Texas Journal of International Law 187–221 (1977).

82. Buergenthal, Thomas. *Interaction of National Law and Modern International Agreements: Some Introductory Observations.* 18 Am. J. Comp. L. 233–236 (1970).

83. Caflisch, Lucius, ed. *Les rapports entre le droit international et les ordres juridiques nationaux, Pratique Suisse.* 26 A.S.D.I. 91–92, 96–103 (1969–70); 30 A.S.D.I. 110–124 (1974).

84. Cassese, Antonio. "A New Reservations Clause (Article 20 of the UN Convention on the Elimination of All Forms of Racial Discrimination)" in *Recueil d'études de droit international en hommage à Paul Guggenheim.* Genève: Imprimerie de la Tribune de Genève, 1968, pp. 266–304.

85. Claudy, Donald E. *The Treaty Power and Human Rights.* 36 Cornell Law Quarterly 699–739 (1951).

86. Comte, Philippe. *The Application of the European Convention on Human Rights in Municipal Law.* 4 Journal of the International Commission of Jurists 95–129 (1962).

87. Condorelli, Luigi and Georgio Gaja, ed. *Relationship Between Municipal Law and International Law, Judicial Decisions.* Italian Yearbook of International Law 364–373 (1976); 16–23 (1977).

88. Condorelli, Luigi. *EEC Treaty and GATT.* Italian Yearbook of International Law 21–22 (1977).

89. Cornil, Pierre. *Le rôle de la commission d'experts de l'OIT dans le contrôle de*

l'application des conventions internationales du travail. 6 R.B.D.I. 265–277 (1970–71).

90. Cortés Funes, Gerónimo. *Regimen de Incorporación de las Convenciones Internacionales a la Legislación Positiva Nacional.* Doctrina Judicial, No. 1372, 693–694, 26 de junio de 1961.

91. Courtin, Michel. *La pratique française en matière de ratification de l'article 19 de la Constitution de l'OIT.* 1970 A.F.D.I. 596–604.

92. Dearborn, Charles H., III. *The Domestic Legal Effect of Declarations That Treaty Provisions are Not Self-Executing.* 57 Texas L. Rev. 233–251 (1979).

93. Deener, David R. *International Law Provisions in Post World-War II Constitutions.* 36 Cornell Law Quarterly 505–533 (1951).

94. Dehaussey, Jacques. "Le problème de la classification des traités et le projet de convention établi par la Commission du Droit International des Nations Unies" in *Recueil d'études de droit international en hommage à Paul Guggenheim.* Genève: Imprimerie de la Tribune de Genève, 1968, pp. 305–326.

95. Dickinson, Edwin. *Are the Liquor Treaties Self-Executing?* 20 Am. J. Int'l L. 444–452 (1926).

96. Dickinson, Edwin. *The Law of Nations as National Law: Political Questions.* 104 U. Pa. L. Rev. 451–493 (1956).

97. Dickinson, Edwin. *Changing Concepts and the Doctrine of Incorporation.* 26 Am. J. Int'l L. 239–260 (1932).

98. Dickinson, Edwin. *The Law of Nations as Part of the National Law of the United States.* 101 U. Pa. L. Rev. 792–833 (1953).

99. Dihigo, Ernesto. *Treaties as Law in National Courts: Latin America.* 16 Louisiana L. Rev. 734–754 (1956).

100. Dominicé, Christian. *La Convention européenne des droits de l'homme devant le juge national.* 28 A.S.D.I. 9–40 (1972).

101. Drzemczewski, Andrew. *The Domestic Status of the European Convention on Human Rights: New Dimensions.* Legal Issues of European Integration, No. 1, 1–85 (1977).

102. van Emde Boas, Menno J. *The Impact of the European Convention of Human Rights and Fundamental Freedoms on the Legal Order of the Netherlands.* 13 Neth. Int'l L. Rev. 337–373 (1966); 14 Neth. Int'l L. Rev. 1–32 (1967).

103. Engel, Salo. *On the Status of United States Treaty Law.* 65 Am. J. Int'l L. 593–597 (1971).

104. Erades, L. *The 1924 Brussels Convention on Bills of Lading is Non-Self-Executing.* 16 Neth. Int'l L. Rev. 97–100 (1969).

105. Evans, Alona. *Some Aspects of the Problem of Self-Executing Treaties.* 1951 Proc., Am. Soc. Int'l L. 68–75.

106. Evans, Alona. *Self-Executing Treaties in the United States of America.* 30 Brit. Y. B. Int'l L. 178–205 (1953).

107. Fatouros, A. A. *International Law in the New Greek Constitution.* 70 Am. J. Int'l L. 492–506 (1976).

108. Feo, Edwin F. *Self-Execution of United Nations Security Council Resolutions Under United States Law.* 24 U.C.L.A. L. Rev. 387–421 (1976).

109. Fischer, Dana. *The Practice of the Human Rights Committee: An Effective Reporting System,* in preparation (1980) for publication by the American Society of International Law.

110. Friederich, Blair Phillips. *Criteria for Self-Executing Treaties.* University of Illinois Law Forum 238–248 (1968).

111. Hay, Peter. Review of Bergsten, *Community Law in the French Courts.* 69 Am. J. Int'l L. 706–707 (1975).

112. Henkin, Louis. *The Treaty Makers and the Law Makers: The Niagara Reservation.* 56 Colum. L. Rev. 1151–1182 (1956).

113. Henry, Leslie. *When is a Treaty Self-Executing?* 27 Mich. L. Rev. 776–785 (1928–29).

114. Hudson, Manley O. *Charter Provisions on Human Rights in American Law.* 44 Am. J. Int'l L. 543–548 (1950).

115. Jenks, C. Wilfred. *The Conflict of Law-Making Treaties.* 30 Brit. Y. B. Int'l L. 401–453 (1953).

116. Jenks, C. Wilfred. *The Revision of International Labour Conventions.* 14 Brit. Y. B. Int'l L. 43–64 (1933).

117. Jenks, C. Wilfred. *The Present Status of the Bennett Ratifications of International Labour Conventions.* 15 The Canadian Bar Rev. 464–477 (1937).

118. Jenks, C. Wilfred. *The Significance for International Law of the Tripartite Character of the International Labour Organisation.* 32 Transactions of the Grotius Society 45–81 (1936).

119. Jenks, C. Wilfred. *The Interpretation of International Labour Conventions by the International Labour Office.* 20 Brit. Y. B. Int'l L. 132–141 (1939).

120. Jenks, C. Wilfred. *Can the Obligation to Ratify International Labour Conventions be Time-Barred?* 15 The Canadian Bar Rev. 86–92 (1937).

121. Jenks, C. Wilfred. *Are International Labour Conventions Agreements between Governments?* 15 The Canadian Bar Rev. 574–578 (1937).

122. Jenks, C. Wilfred. *Some Characteristics of International Labour Conventions.* 13 The Canadian Bar Rev. 448–462 (1935).

123. Jenks, C. Wilfred. *La compétence de l'OIT, Examen de 4 avis consultatifs rendus par la Cour Permanent de Justice International.* 28 Revue de droit international et de législation comparée 586–623 (1937).

124. Jenks, C. Wilfred. *The Application of International Labour Conventions by Means of Collective Agreements.* 19 Z.a.ö.R.V., No. 1–3, 197–224 (1958).

125. Kelsen, Hans. *Les rapports de système entre le droit interne et le droit international public.* 14 R.C.A.D.I. 231–326 (1926–IV).

126. Khol, Andreas A. *The Influence of the Human Rights Convention on Austrian Law.* 18 Am. J. Comp. L. 237–258 (1970).

127. Landy, E. A. *The Influence of International Labour Standards: Possibilities and Performance.* 101 I.L.R. 555–604 (1970).

128. Liebscher, Viktor. *Austria and the European Convention for the Protection of Human Rights and Fundamental Freedoms.* 4 Journal of the International Commission of Jurists 282–293 (1963).

129. Mahaim, Ernest. *Quelques questions de droit au sujet des conventions internationales du travail.* 20 R.I.T. 807–838 (1929).

130. Mahaim, Ernest. *Les conventions internationales du travail—à propos de débats recents.* 10 Revue de droit international et de législation comparée, 699–734 (1929); ibid. 11, 123–146 (1930).

131. Malinverni, Georges. *L'Application de la Convention européenne des droits de l'homme en Suisse.* Mémoires publiés par la Faculté de Droit de Genève, Quinzième Journée Juridique, 4–50 (1977).

132. Marek, Krystyna. *Les rapports entre le droit international et le droit interne à la lumière de la jurisprudence de la Cour Permanente de Justice International.* 66 R.G.D.I.P. 260–298 (1962).

133. McDougal, Myres. *The Impact of International Law upon National Law: A Policy-Oriented Perspective.* 4 South Dakota L. Rev. 25 (1959), pp. 25–92. Republished in McDougal and Associates, *Studies in World Public Order.* New Haven: Yale University Press, 1960, pp. 157–236.

134. McLaughlin, C. H. *The Scope of the Treaty Power in the United States.* 42 Minn. L. Rev. 709–771 (1958).

135. McMahon, J. F. *The Legislative Techniques of the International Labour Organization.* 41 Brit. Y. B. Int'l L. 1–102 (1965–66).

136. Morellet, Jean. *The Influence of International Labour Conventions on French Legislation.* 101 I.L.R. 331–358 (1970).

137. Morellet, Jean. *At What Moment do International Labour Conventions Become Applicable?* 16 I.L.R. 755–772 (1927).

138. Morellet, Jean. *La notion de réciprocité dans les traités de travail et les conventions internationales du travail.* 26 Revue de droit international privé 642–656 (1931).

139. Morellet, Jean. *Un type original de traités: les conventions internationales du travail.* 33 R.C.D.I.P. 1–21 (1938).

140. Morgenstern, Felice. *Judicial Practice and the Supremacy of International Law.* 27 Brit. Y. B. Int'l L. 42–92 (1950).

141. Mosler, Hermann. *L'Application du droit international public par les tribunaux nationaux.* 91 R.C.A.D.I. 625–705 (1957–I).

142. van Panhuys, Jonkheer H. F. *The Netherlands Constitution and International Law.* 58 Am. J. Int'l L. 88–108 (1964).

143. van Panhuys, Jonkheer H. F. *Relations and Inter-actions between International Law and National Scenes of Law.* 112 R.C.A.D.I. 7–21 (1964–II).

144. Parry, Clive. "The Law of Treaties" in Sorenson, Max, ed. *Manual of Public International Law*, 1968, p.197.

145. Perez, Benito. *Alcance de las Convenciones Internacionales de la OIT Ratificadas por el Congreso.* 21 Derecho del Trabajo 635–637 (1961).

146. Pescatore, Pierre. "Rapport luxemburgeois" in *Deuxième colloque international de droit européen* (La Haye 1963). Zwolle: N.V. Uitgeversmaatschappij W. E. J. Tjeenk Willink, 1966, pp. 137–158.

147. Plata-Castilla, Alfonso. *International Labour Standards and Colombian Legislation.* 99 I.L.R. 137–158 (1969).

148. Potter, Pitman B. *Relative Authority of International Law and National Law in the United States.* 19 Am. J. Int'l L. 315–326 (1925).

149. Preuss, Lawrence. *Article 2, Paragraph 7 of the Charter of the United Nations and Matters of Domestic Jurisdiction.* 74 R.C.A.D.I. 553–653 (1949–I).

150. Preuss, Lawrence. *The Execution of Treaty Obligations Through Internal Law—System of the United States and of Some Other Countries.* 1951 Proc., Am. Soc. Int'l L. 82–100.

151. Preuss, Lawrence. *On Amending the Treaty-Making Power: A Comparative Study of the Problem of Self-Executing Treaties.* 51 Mich. L. Rev. 1117 et seq. (1953).

152. Ramírez Gronda, Juan D. *Validez y Vigencia de los Convenios Internacionales del Trabajo Ratificados.* 17 Derecho del Trabajo 5–12 (1957).

153. Reiff, Henry. *The Enforcement of Multipartite Administrative Treaties in the United States.* 34 Am. J. Int'l L. 661–679 (1940).

154. Rice, William J. *The Position of International Treaties in Swiss Law.* 46 Am. J. Int'l L. 641–666 (1952).

155. Riesenfeld, Stefan A. *The Doctrine of Self-Executing Treaties and Community Law: A Pioneer Decision of the Court of Justice of the European Community.* 67 Am. J. Int'l L. 504–508 (1973).

156. Riesenfeld, Stefan A. *The Doctrine of Self-Executing Treaties and GATT: A Notable German Judgment.* 65 Am. J. Int'l L. 548–550 (1971).

157. Riesenfeld, Stefan A. and Richard M. Buxbaum. *N.V. Algemene Transport—en Expeditie Onderneming Van Gend and Loos c. Administration Fiscale Néerlandaise: A Pioneering Decision of the Court of Justice of the European Communities.* 58 Am. J. Int'l L. 152–159 (1964).

158. Rosenn, Keith. *Judicial Review in Latin America.* 35 Ohio St. L. J. 785–819 (1974).
159. Ruiz Moreno, Hector. *La Organización Internacional del Trabajo.* 13 Derecho del Trabajo 5–22 (1953).
160. Ruiz Moreno, Hector. *Ratificación de Convenios Internacionales de Trabajo.* 16 Derecho del Trabajo 440–443 (1956).
161. Schachter, Oscar. *The Charter and the Constitution: The Human Rights Provisions in American Law.* 4 Vand. L. Rev. 643–659 (1951).
162. Scheuner, Ulrich. "An Investigation of the European Convention on Human Rights and Fundamental Freedoms on National Legislation and Practice" in Asbjorn Eide and August Schou, ed., *International Protection of Human Rights* (Proceedings of the Seventh Nobel Symposium, 1967, Oslo). Stockholm: Almqvist and Wiksell, 1968, pp. 193–215.
163. Schlüter, Bernhard. *The Domestic Status of the Human Rights Clauses of the United Nations Charter.* 61 Calif. L. Rev. 110–164 (1973).
164. Secretan, Jacques. *Swiss Constitutional Problems and the International Labour Organisation.* 56 I.L.R. 1–20 (1947).
165. Seidl-Hohenveldern, I. *Relation of International Law to Internal Law in Austria.* 49 Am. J. Int'l L. 451–476 (1955).
166. Seidl-Hohenveldern, I. *Transformation or Adoption of International Law into Municipal Law.* 12 I.C.L.Q. 88–124 (1963).
167. Solomon, Jack. *When are Treaties Self-Executing?* 31 Neb. L. Rev. 463–474 (1952).
168. Starke, J. G. *Monism and Dualism in the Theory of International Law.* 17 Brit. Y. B. Int'l L. 66–81 (1936).
169. Stein, Eric and G. Joseph Vining. *Citizen Access to Judicial Review of Administrative Action in a Transnational and Federal Context.* 70 Am. J. Int'l L. 219–41 (1976).
170. Stotter, Charles W. *Self-Executing Treaties and the Human Rights Provisions of the United Nations Charter: A Separation of Powers Problem.* 25 Buffalo L. Rev. 773–786 (1976).
171. Triepel, Heinrich. *Les rapports entre le droit interne et le droit international.* 1 R.C.A.D.I. 77–118 (1923).
172. Unsain, Alejandro M. *Ratificación de Convenciones Internacionales del Trabajo.* 9 Derecho del Trabajo 497–501 (1949).
173. Valticos, Nicolas. *Monisme ou dualisme? Les rapports des traités et de la loi en Grèce (spécialement à propos des conventions internationales du travail).* 3–4 Revue hellénique de droit international 203–235 (1958).
174. Valticos, Nicolas. *Fifty Years of Standard-Setting Activities by the International Labour Organization.* 100 I.L.R. 201–257 (1969).
175. Valticos, Nicolas. *Un système de contrôle international: la mise en oeuvre des conventions internationales du travail.* 123 R.C.A.D.I. 315–407 (1968–I).
176. Valticos, Nicolas. *Droit international du travail et droit interne français.* Travaux du comité français de droit international privé, 1973–75 (Paris: Dalloz, 1977), p. 11 et seq.
177. Valticos, Nicolas. *Conventions internationales du travail et droit interne.* 44 R.C.D.I.P. 251–288 (1955).
178. Valticos, Nicolas. *The Influence of International Labour Conventions on Greek Legislation.* 71 I.L.R. 593–615 (1955).
179. Valticos, Nicolas. *Les conventions internationales du travail devant le juge français (à propos de l'arrêt Klaiss de la 2e section civile du 28 mars 1962).* 53 R.C.D.I.P. 41–72 (1964).
180. Valticos, Nicolas. *Les effêts des conventions internationales du travail en Suisse.* 50 Mémoires de la Faculté de Droit (Université de Genève) 327–345 (1975).
181. Virally, Michel. "Droits de l'homme et théorie générale du droit international" in *Rene Cassin amicorum discipulorumque liber*, vol. IV, *Méthodologie des droits de l'homme.* Paris: Pedone, 1972, pp. 323–330.

182. Virally, Michel. "Sur un pont aux ânes: les rapports entre droit international et droits internes" in *Mélanges offerts à Henri Rolin*. Paris: Pedone, 1964, pp. 488–505.

183. de Visscher, Paul. *Les tendances internationales des constitutions modernes*. 81 R.C.A.D.I. 516–578 (1952–I).

184. Waelbroeck, Michel. *L'effêt direct de l'accord relatif aux échanges commerciaux de 22 juillet 1972, entre la Communauté Economique Européenne et la Confédération Suisse*. 29 A.S.D.I. 113–132 (1973).

185. Weissbrodt, David. *United States Ratification of the Human Rights Covenants*. 63 Minn. L. Rev. 35–77 (1978).

186. Wengler, Wilhelm. *Réflexions sur l'application du droit international public par les tribunaux internes*. 72 R.G.D.I.P. 922–990 (1968).

187. Wildhaber, Luzius. *Bemerkungen zum Fall Schubert betrefend das Verhältnis von Völkerrecht und Landesrecht*. 30 A.S.D.I. 195–201 (1974).

188. Wright, Quincy.. *Treaties and Constitutional Separation of Powers in the United States*. 12 Am. J. Int'l L. 64–95 (1918).

189. Wright, Quincy. *Treaties as Law in National Courts: The United States*. 16 Louisiana L. Rev. 755–761 (1956).

190. Wright, Quincy. *National Courts and Human Rights—The Fujii Case*. 45 Am. J. Int'l L. 62–82 (1951).

191. Yemin, Edward. *Interpretation of Treaties Adopted Within International Organizations* (unpublished manuscript), Geneva.

Table of Cases

National Cases

Argentina

France

Guatemala

Italy

Mexico

The Netherlands

Switzerland

United Kingdom

United States

International Cases

Court of Justice of the European Communities

Permanent Court of International Justice

Table of Treaties and Conventions

ILO Conventions

(The text of these instruments is published in the *Official Bulletin* of the International Labour Office for the year of their adoption.)

Multilateral Treaties

Bilateral Treaties

Author Index

Index

ABOUT THE AUTHOR

Virginia A. Leary is at present Professor of Law at the State University of New York at Buffalo, U.S.A. Prior to this Professor Leary was with the International Labour Standards Department of the International Labour Office in Geneva.

Professor Leary has contributed to a number of other books; among these are: "U.N. Law — Fundamental Rights," edited by A. Cassese, (Sijthoff & Noordhoff International Publishers, 1979), and "International Human Rights Law and Practice," (American Bar Association, 1978).